ALIENS vs PARKER ™

SPACE-EX

BILL OF LADING

Created & Written By
**PAUL SCHEER
AND NICK GIOVANNETTI**

Colors By
VLADIMIR POPOV

Letters By
DERON BENNETT

SPACE-EX

"We know how to handle your package."

FL

BOOM! STUDIOS

ROSS RICHIE CEO & Founder • JACK CUMMINS President • MARK SMYLIE Chief Creative Officer • MATT GAGNON Editor-in-Chief • FILIP SABLIK VP of Publishing & Marketing • STEPHEN CHRISTY VP of Development
LANCE KREITER VP of Licensing & Merchandising • PHIL BARBARO VP of Finance • BRYCE CARLSON Managing Editor • MEL CAYLO Marketing Manager • SCOTT NEWMAN Production Design Manager • IRENE BRADISH Editor • SHANNON WATTERS Editor
ERIC HARBURN Editor • REBECCA TAYLOR Editor • CHRIS ROSA Assistant Editor • ALEX GALER Assistant Editor • WHITNEY LEOPARD Assistant Editor • JASMINE AMIRI Assistant Editor • MIKE LOPEZ Production Designer
HANNAH NANCE PARTLOW Production Designer • DEVIN FUNCHES E-Commerce & Inventory Coordinator • BRIANNA HART Executive Assistant • AARON FERRARA Operations Assistant • JOSE MEZA Sales Assistant

Illustrated By
MANUEL BRACCHI
with **GIANFRANCO GIARDINA**
(Chapter 4)

Cover By
JOSHUA COVEY

Editor
DAFNA PLEBAN

Designer
MIKE LOPEZ

Thanks to

GERRY DUGGAN, TUCKER VOORHEES,

JUNE DIANE RAPHAEL, OWEN BURKE, CHRISTY ALLISON

AMMABLE LI

NTSF:SD:SUV::
**SDCC 2012
EXCLUSIVE**

Written By
**PAUL SCHEER
JON STERN
CURTIS GWINN**
Illustrated By
TOM DERENICK

Colors By
BLOND
Letters By
ED DUKESHIRE
Editor
DAFNA PLEBAN

3

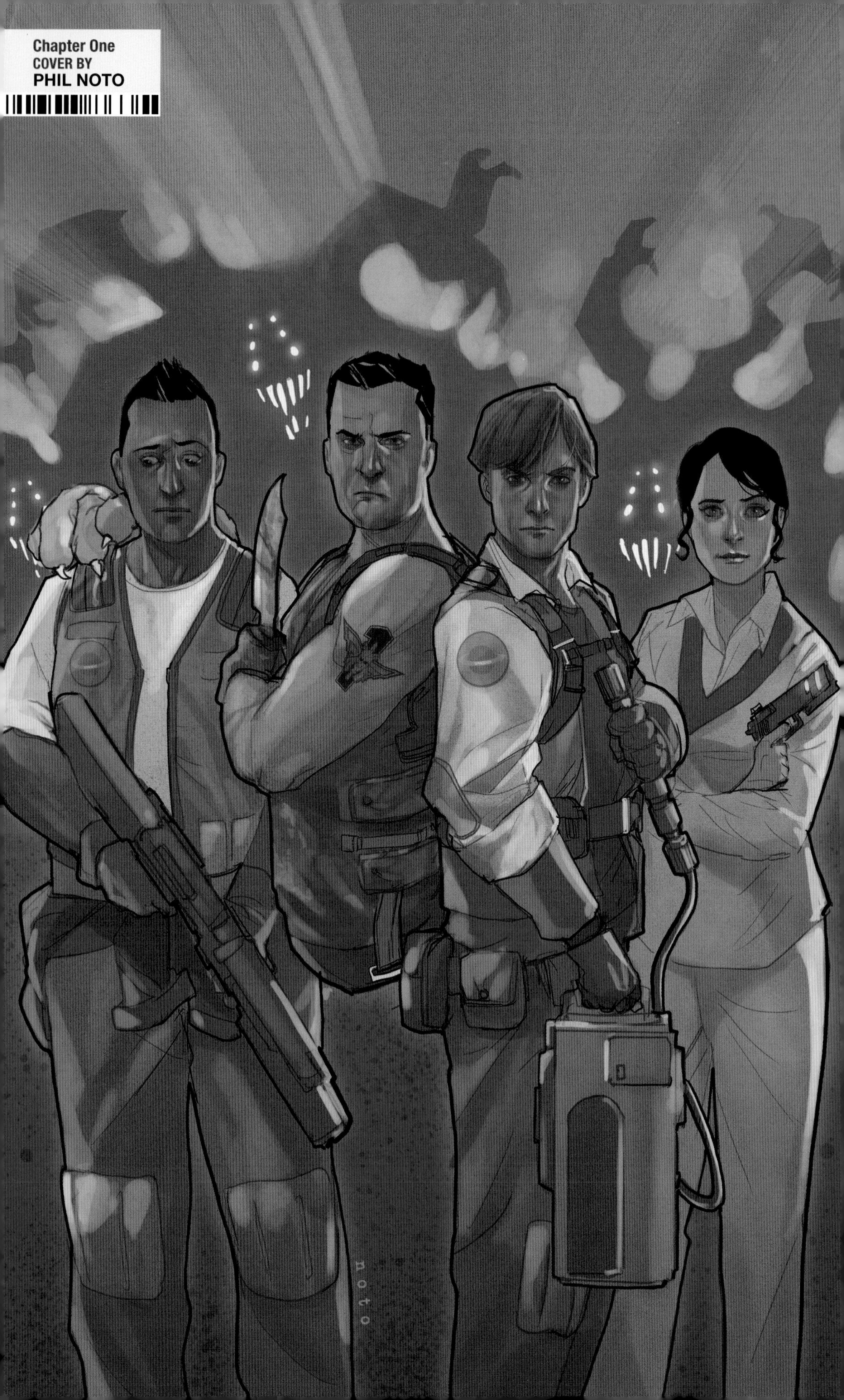
noto

Chapter One
COVER BY
PHIL NOTO

SECTOR 3, ALL CLEAR.

UGH. I'LL DIE OF BOREDOM BEFORE I EVER SEE ANY ACTION.

BATTLE MOON: EON
OUTPOST FOR THE RAKK'NAR HORDE

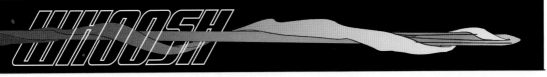

WHOOSH

SPLORC!

IN CASE YOU GUYS EVER WONDERED WHAT AN EXPLODING HEAD SOUNDS LIKE, IT'S *SPLORC!*

WHOA! IT'S LIKE HIS HEAD'S A PIÑATA THAT'S FULL OF BRAINS INSTEAD OF TASTY CANDY!

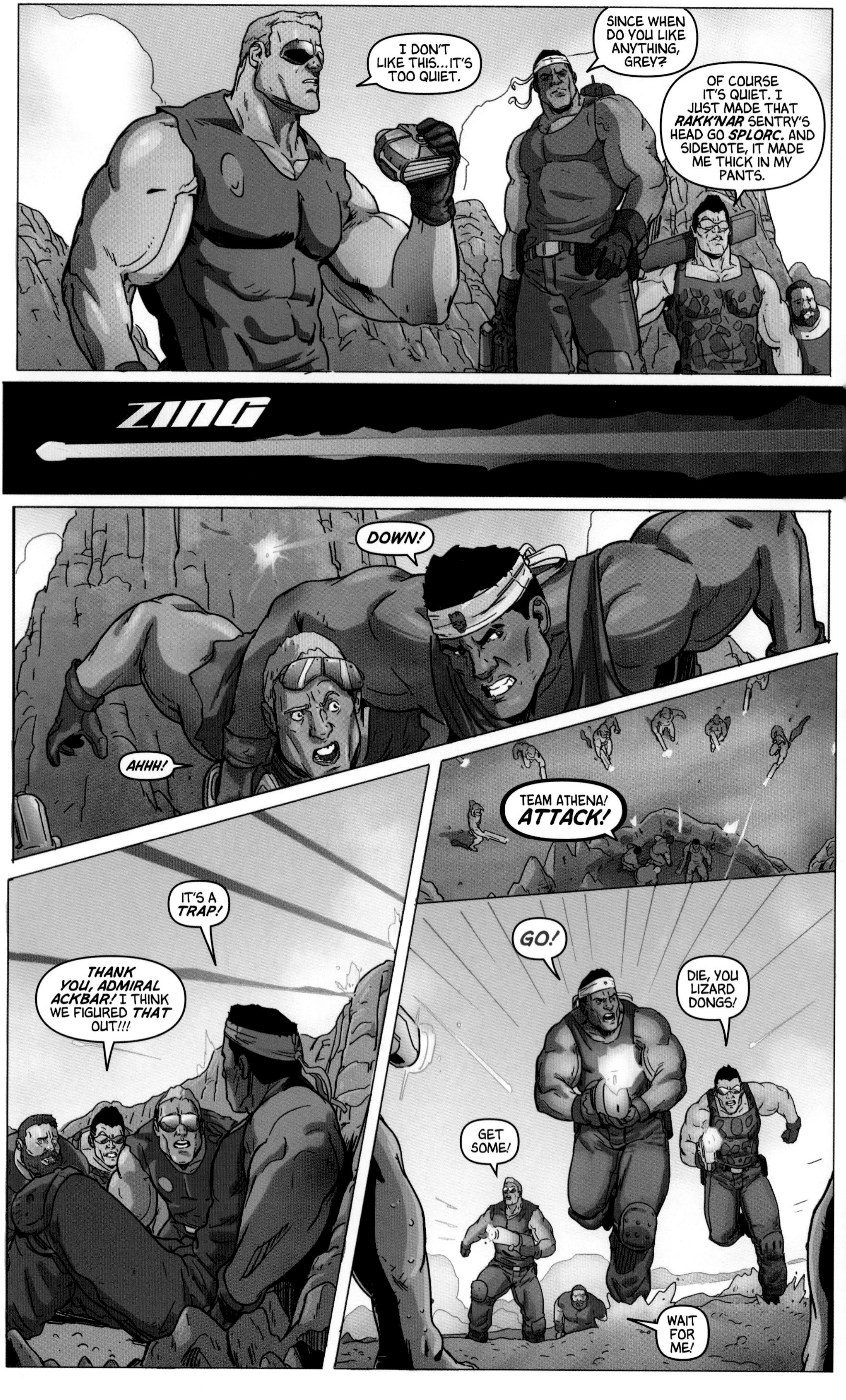
I DON'T LIKE THIS... IT'S TOO QUIET.
SINCE WHEN DO YOU LIKE ANYTHING, GREY?
OF COURSE IT'S QUIET. I JUST MADE THAT RAKK'NAR SENTRY'S HEAD GO SPLORC. AND SIDENOTE, IT MADE ME THICK IN MY PANTS.
ZING
DOWN!
AHHH!
TEAM ATHENA! ATTACK!
IT'S A TRAP!
THANK YOU, ADMIRAL ACKBAR! I THINK WE FIGURED THAT OUT!!!
GO!
DIE, YOU LIZARD DONGS!
GET SOME!
WAIT FOR ME!

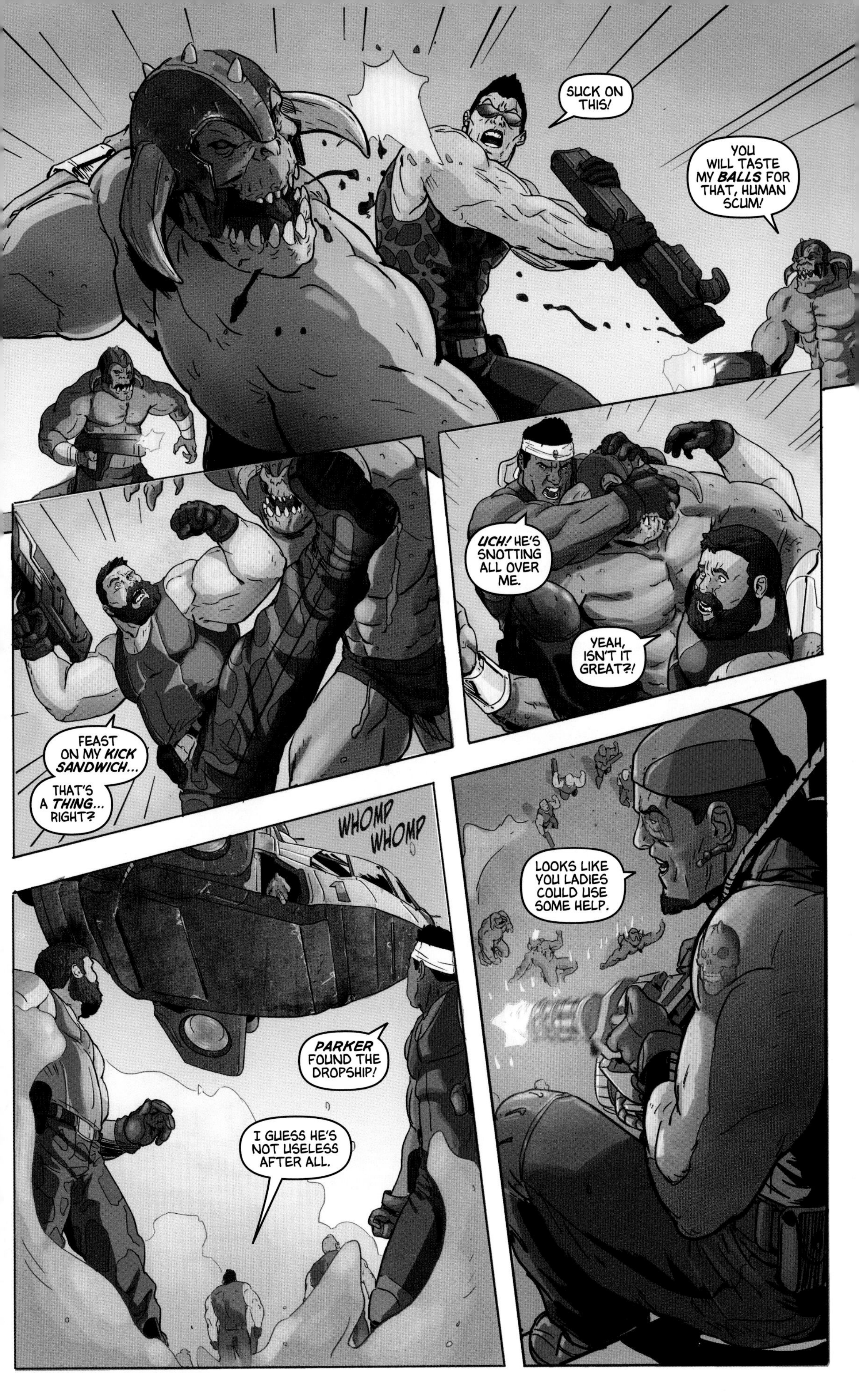
SUCK ON THIS!
YOU WILL TASTE MY BALLS FOR THAT, HUMAN SCUM!
UCH! HE'S SNOTTING ALL OVER ME.
YEAH, ISN'T IT GREAT?!
FEAST ON MY KICK SANDWICH...
THAT'S A THING... RIGHT?
WHOMP WHOMP
LOOKS LIKE YOU LADIES COULD USE SOME HELP.
PARKER FOUND THE DROPSHIP!
I GUESS HE'S NOT USELESS AFTER ALL.

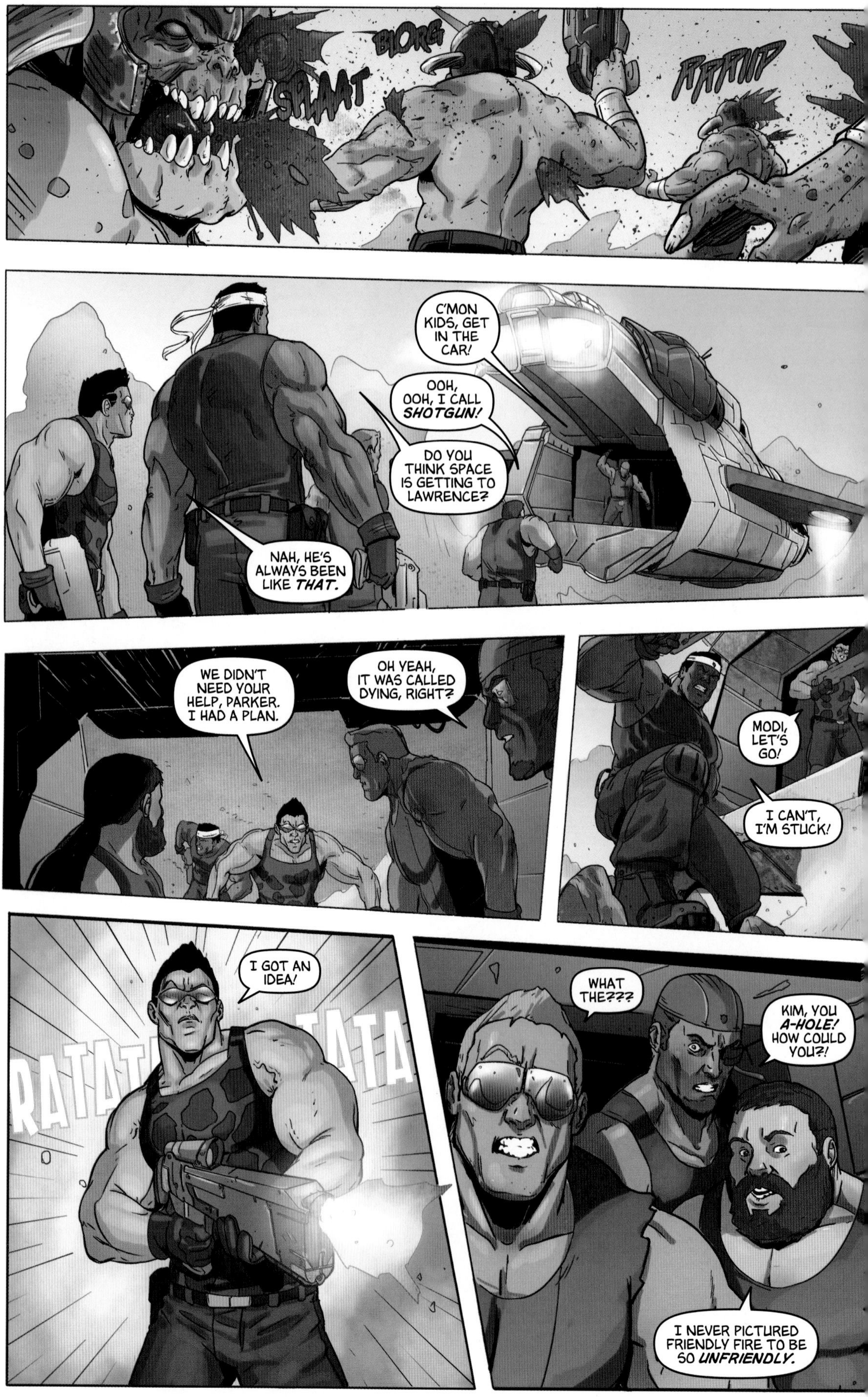
BLORG
SPLAAT
RRRIIP
C'MON KIDS, GET IN THE CAR!
OOH, OOH, I CALL *SHOTGUN!*
DO YOU THINK SPACE IS GETTING TO LAWRENCE?
NAH, HE'S ALWAYS BEEN LIKE *THAT.*
WE DIDN'T NEED YOUR HELP, PARKER. I HAD A PLAN.
OH YEAH, IT WAS CALLED DYING, RIGHT?
MODI, LET'S GO!
I CAN'T, I'M STUCK!
I GOT AN IDEA!
RATATA
TATA
WHAT THE???
KIM, YOU *A-HOLE!* HOW COULD YOU?!
I NEVER PICTURED FRIENDLY FIRE TO BE SO *UNFRIENDLY.*

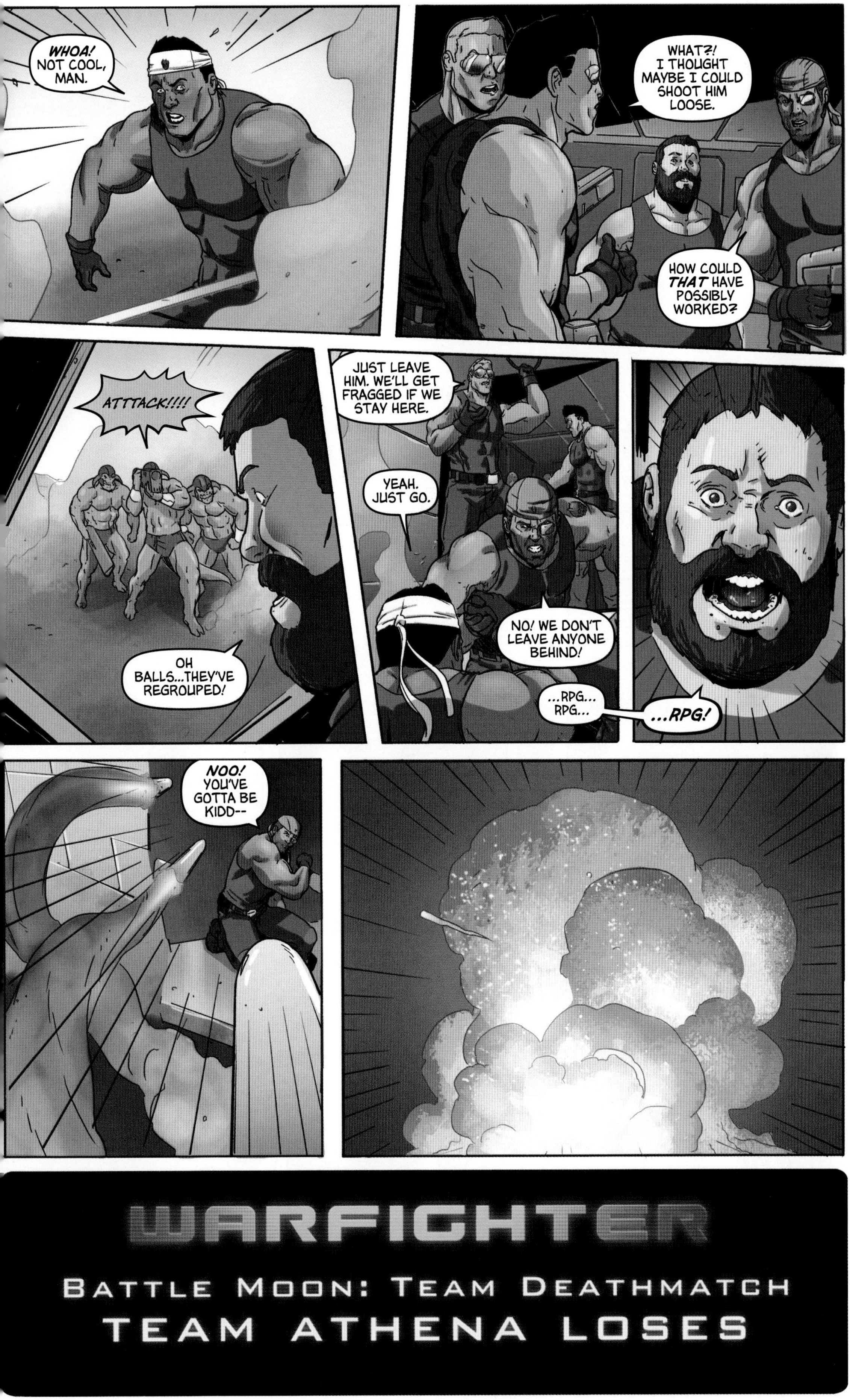
WHOA! NOT COOL, MAN.
WHAT?! I THOUGHT MAYBE I COULD SHOOT HIM LOOSE.
HOW COULD THAT HAVE POSSIBLY WORKED?
ATTTACK!!!!
OH BALLS...THEY'VE REGROUPED!
JUST LEAVE HIM. WE'LL GET FRAGGED IF WE STAY HERE.
YEAH. JUST GO.
NO! WE DON'T LEAVE ANYONE BEHIND!
...RPG... RPG...
...RPG!
NOO! YOU'VE GOTTA BE KIDD--

WARFIGHTER

BATTLE MOON: TEAM DEATHMATCH

TEAM ATHENA LOSES

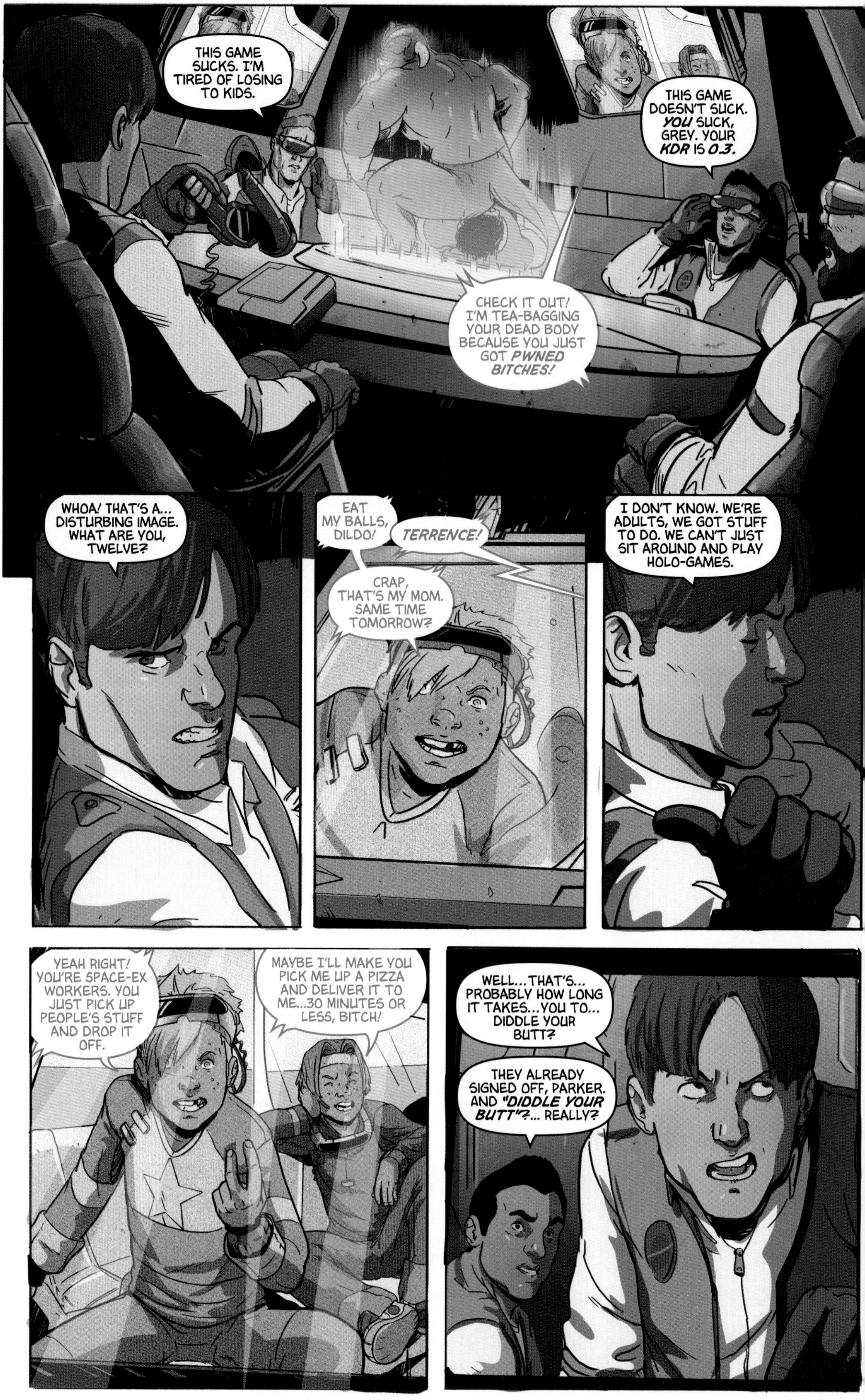
THIS GAME SUCKS. I'M TIRED OF LOSING TO KIDS.
THIS GAME DOESN'T SUCK. YOU SUCK, GREY. YOUR KDR IS 0.3.
CHECK IT OUT! I'M TEA-BAGGING YOUR DEAD BODY BECAUSE YOU JUST GOT PWNED BITCHES!
WHOA! THAT'S A... DISTURBING IMAGE. WHAT ARE YOU, TWELVE?
EAT MY BALLS, DILDO!
TERRENCE!
CRAP, THAT'S MY MOM. SAME TIME TOMORROW?
I DON'T KNOW. WE'RE ADULTS, WE GOT STUFF TO DO. WE CAN'T JUST SIT AROUND AND PLAY HOLO-GAMES.
YEAH RIGHT! YOU'RE SPACE-EX WORKERS. YOU JUST PICK UP PEOPLE'S STUFF AND DROP IT OFF.
MAYBE I'LL MAKE YOU PICK ME UP A PIZZA AND DELIVER IT TO ME...30 MINUTES OR LESS, BITCH!
WELL...THAT'S... PROBABLY HOW LONG IT TAKES...YOU TO... DIDDLE YOUR BUTT?
THEY ALREADY SIGNED OFF, PARKER. AND "DIDDLE YOUR BUTT"?... REALLY?

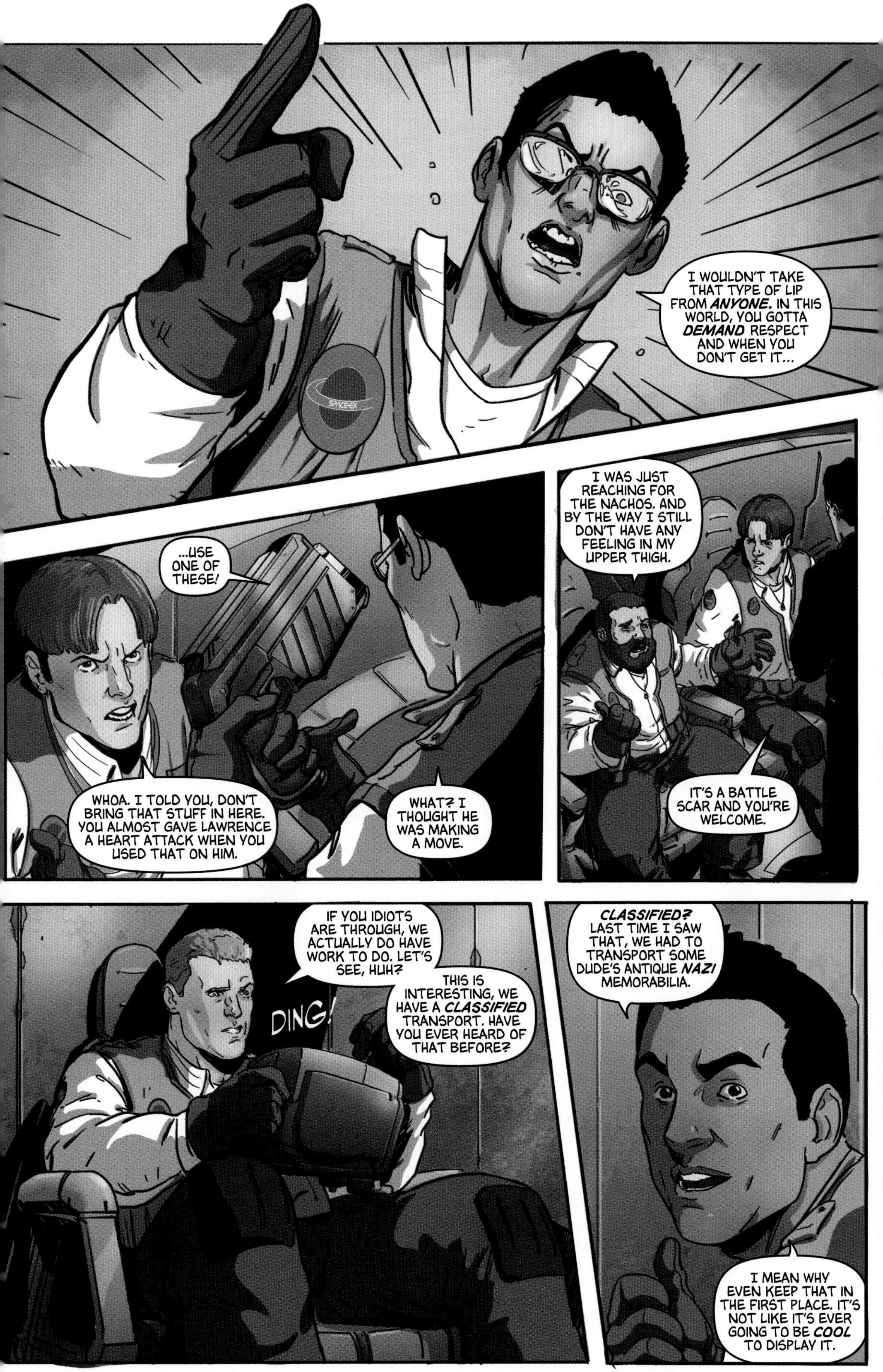
I WOULDN'T TAKE THAT TYPE OF LIP FROM *ANYONE.* IN THIS WORLD, YOU GOTTA *DEMAND* RESPECT AND WHEN YOU DON'T GET IT...
SPACE-EX
...USE ONE OF THESE!
WHOA. I TOLD YOU, DON'T BRING THAT STUFF IN HERE. YOU ALMOST GAVE LAWRENCE A HEART ATTACK WHEN YOU USED THAT ON HIM.
WHAT? I THOUGHT HE WAS MAKING A MOVE.
I WAS JUST REACHING FOR THE NACHOS. AND BY THE WAY I STILL DON'T HAVE ANY FEELING IN MY UPPER THIGH.
IT'S A BATTLE SCAR AND YOU'RE WELCOME.
IF YOU IDIOTS ARE THROUGH, WE ACTUALLY DO HAVE WORK TO DO. LET'S SEE, HUH?
DING!
THIS IS INTERESTING, WE HAVE A *CLASSIFIED* TRANSPORT. HAVE YOU EVER HEARD OF THAT BEFORE?
CLASSIFIED? LAST TIME I SAW THAT, WE HAD TO TRANSPORT SOME DUDE'S ANTIQUE *NAZI* MEMORABILIA.
I MEAN WHY EVEN KEEP THAT IN THE FIRST PLACE. IT'S NOT LIKE IT'S EVER GOING TO BE *COOL* TO DISPLAY IT.

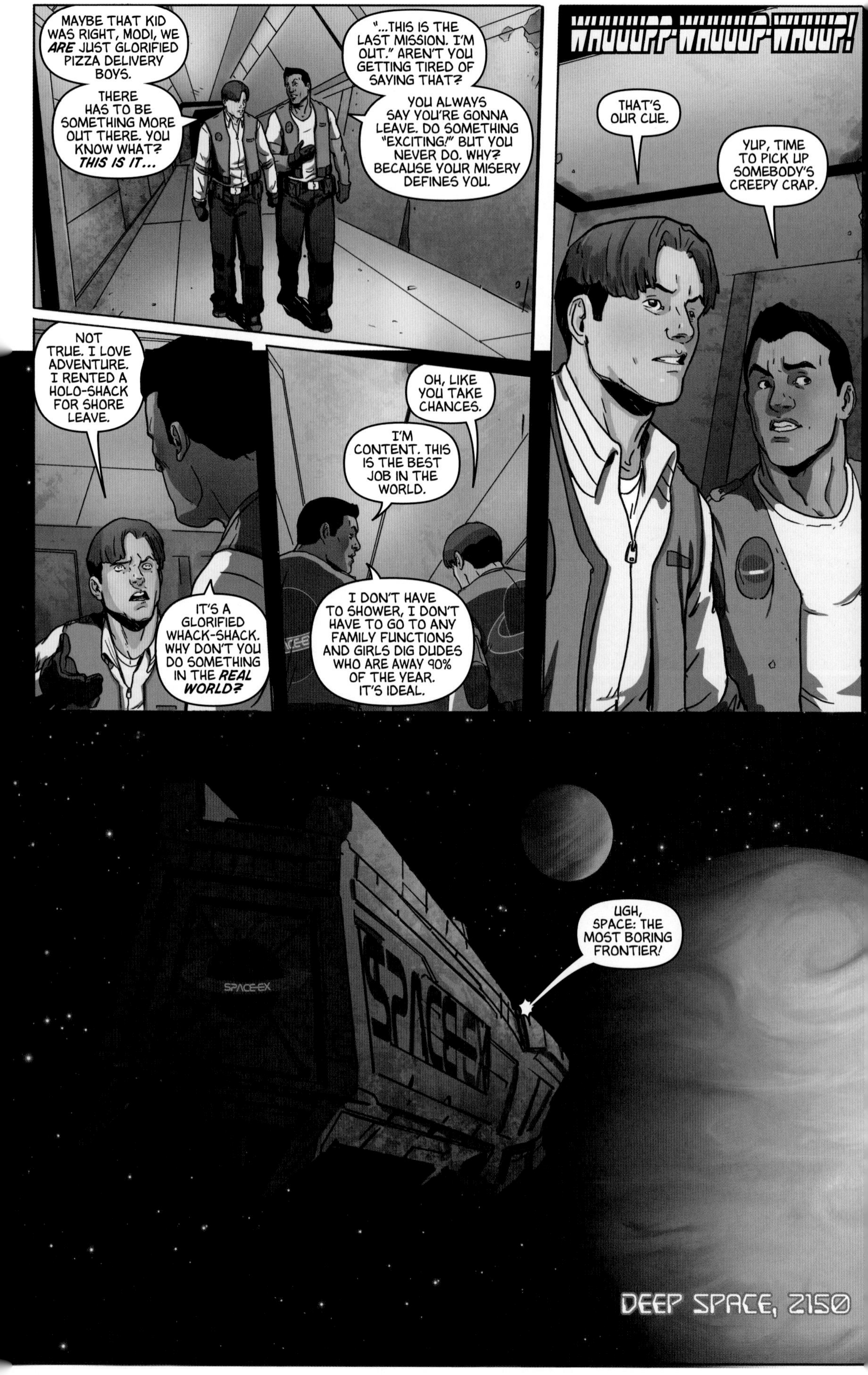
MAYBE THAT KID WAS RIGHT, MODI, WE *ARE* JUST GLORIFIED PIZZA DELIVERY BOYS.
THERE HAS TO BE SOMETHING MORE OUT THERE. YOU KNOW WHAT? *THIS IS IT...*
"...THIS IS THE LAST MISSION. I'M OUT." AREN'T YOU GETTING TIRED OF SAYING THAT?
YOU ALWAYS SAY YOU'RE GONNA LEAVE. DO SOMETHING "EXCITING!" BUT YOU NEVER DO. WHY? BECAUSE YOUR MISERY DEFINES YOU.
WHUUUPP-WHUUUP-WHUUP!
THAT'S OUR CUE.
YUP, TIME TO PICK UP SOMEBODY'S CREEPY CRAP.
NOT TRUE. I LOVE ADVENTURE. I RENTED A HOLO-SHACK FOR SHORE LEAVE.
IT'S A GLORIFIED WHACK-SHACK. WHY DON'T YOU DO SOMETHING IN THE *REAL WORLD?*
OH, LIKE YOU TAKE CHANCES.
I'M CONTENT. THIS IS THE BEST JOB IN THE WORLD.
I DON'T HAVE TO SHOWER, I DON'T HAVE TO GO TO ANY FAMILY FUNCTIONS AND GIRLS DIG DUDES WHO ARE AWAY 90% OF THE YEAR. IT'S IDEAL.
SPACE-EX
SPACE-EX
UGH, SPACE: THE MOST BORING FRONTIER!
DEEP SPACE, 2150

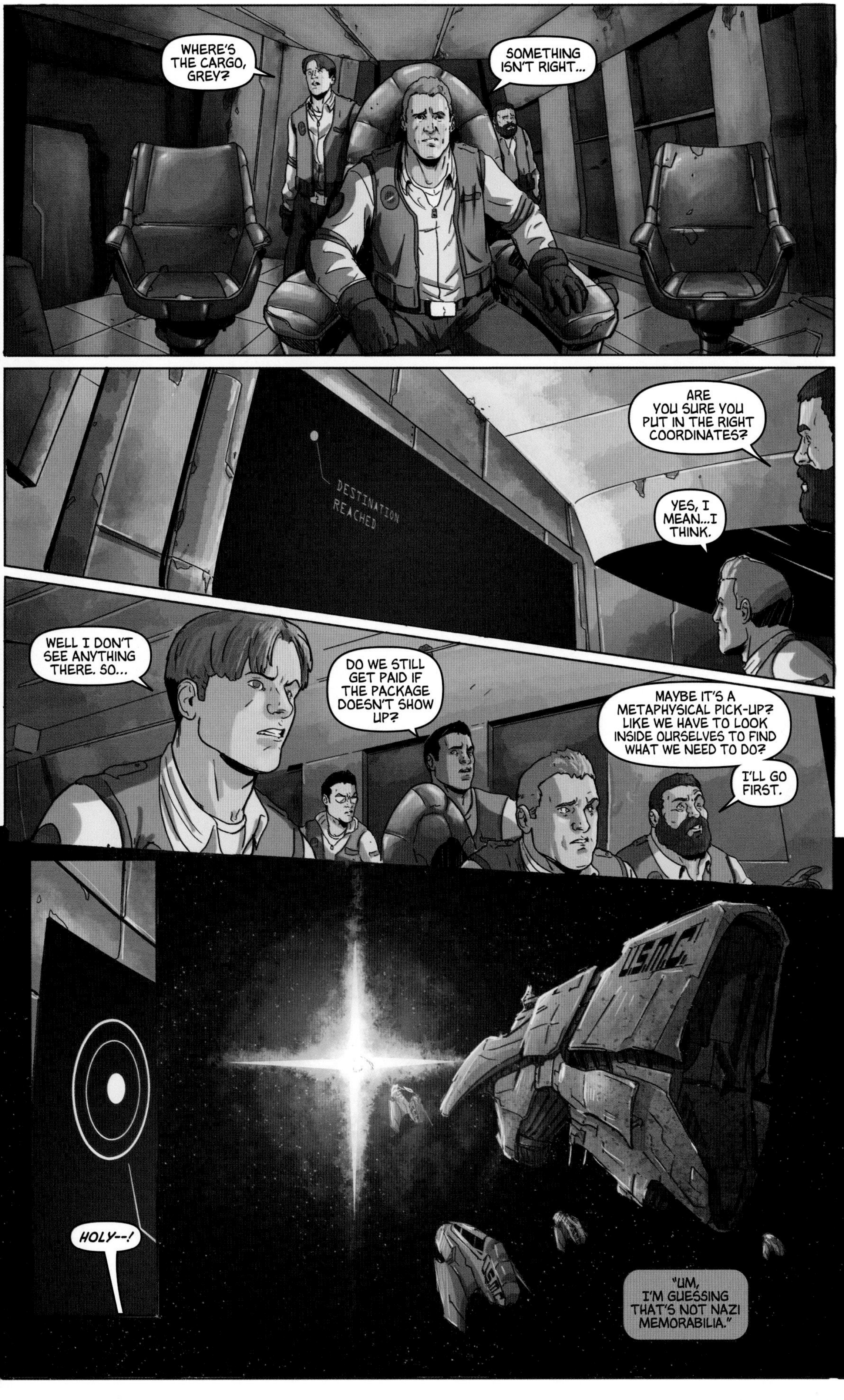
WHERE'S THE CARGO, GREY?
SOMETHING ISN'T RIGHT...
ARE YOU SURE YOU PUT IN THE RIGHT COORDINATES?
DESTINATION REACHED
YES, I MEAN...I THINK.
WELL I DON'T SEE ANYTHING THERE. SO...
DO WE STILL GET PAID IF THE PACKAGE DOESN'T SHOW UP?
MAYBE IT'S A METAPHYSICAL PICK-UP? LIKE WE HAVE TO LOOK INSIDE OURSELVES TO FIND WHAT WE NEED TO DO?
I'LL GO FIRST.
HOLY--!
U.S.M.C.
"UM, I'M GUESSING THAT'S NOT NAZI MEMORABILIA."

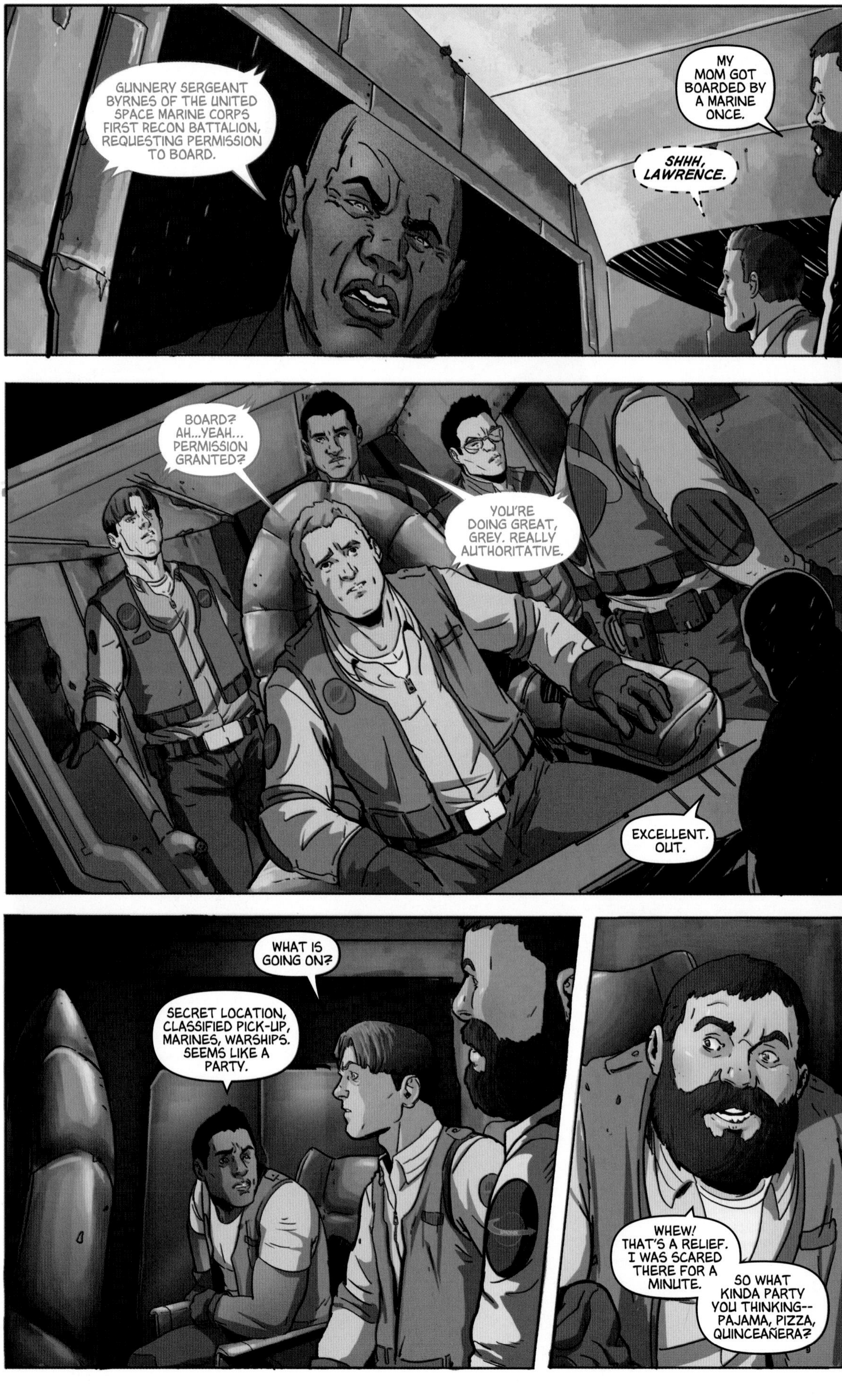
GUNNERY SERGEANT BYRNES OF THE UNITED SPACE MARINE CORPS FIRST RECON BATTALION, REQUESTING PERMISSION TO BOARD.
MY MOM GOT BOARDED BY A MARINE ONCE.
SHHH, LAWRENCE.
BOARD? AH...YEAH... PERMISSION GRANTED?
YOU'RE DOING GREAT, GREY. REALLY AUTHORITATIVE.
EXCELLENT. OUT.
WHAT IS GOING ON?
SECRET LOCATION, CLASSIFIED PICK-UP, MARINES, WARSHIPS. SEEMS LIKE A PARTY.
WHEW! THAT'S A RELIEF. I WAS SCARED THERE FOR A MINUTE.
SO WHAT KINDA PARTY YOU THINKING-- PAJAMA, PIZZA, QUINCEAÑERA?

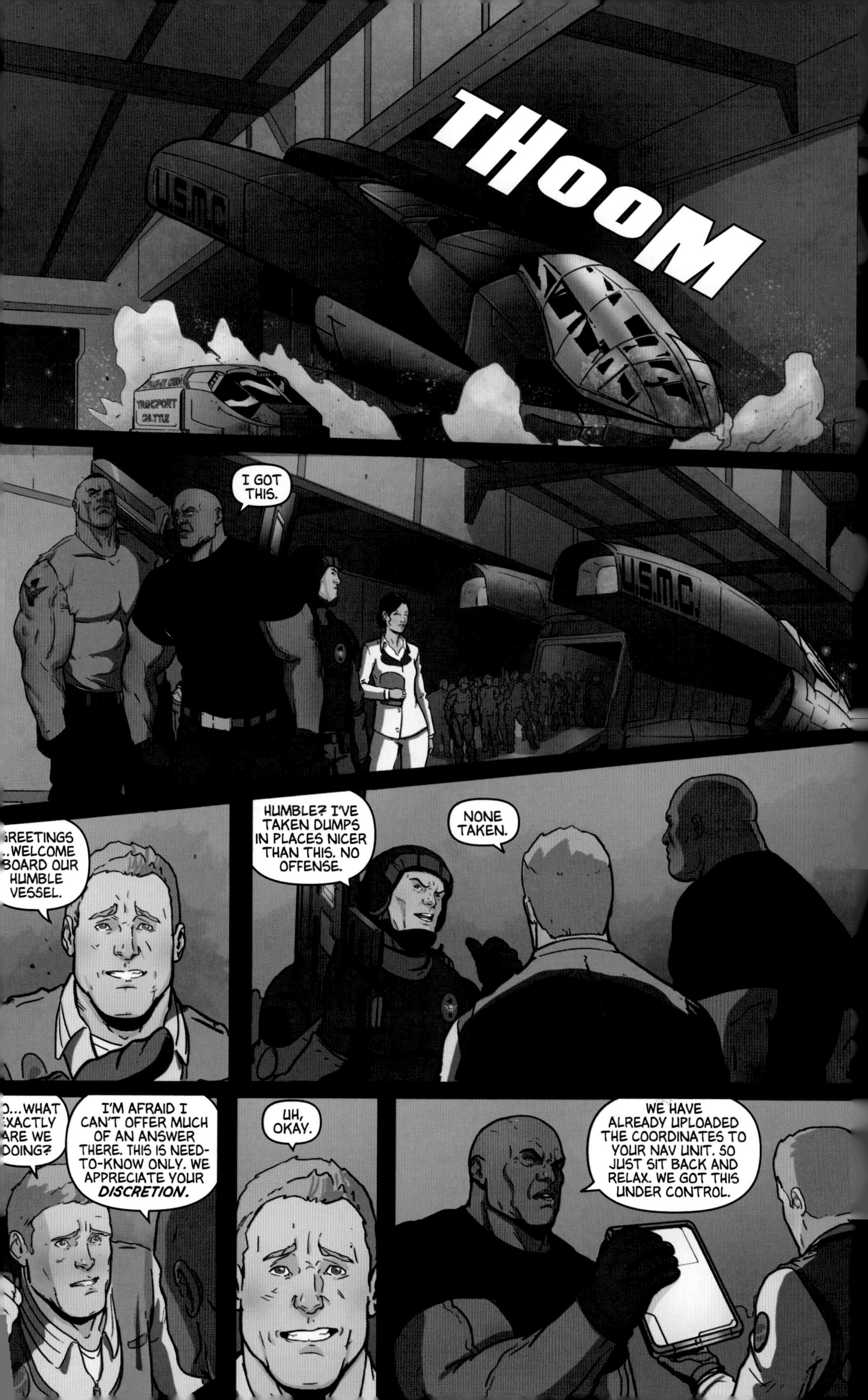

THOOM
U.S.M.C.
I GOT THIS.
GREETINGS ..WELCOME BOARD OUR HUMBLE VESSEL.
HUMBLE? I'VE TAKEN DUMPS IN PLACES NICER THAN THIS. NO OFFENSE.
NONE TAKEN.
O...WHAT EXACTLY ARE WE DOING?
I'M AFRAID I CAN'T OFFER MUCH OF AN ANSWER THERE. THIS IS NEED-TO-KNOW ONLY. WE APPRECIATE YOUR *DISCRETION*.
UH, OKAY.
WE HAVE ALREADY UPLOADED THE COORDINATES TO YOUR NAV UNIT. SO JUST SIT BACK AND RELAX. WE GOT THIS UNDER CONTROL.

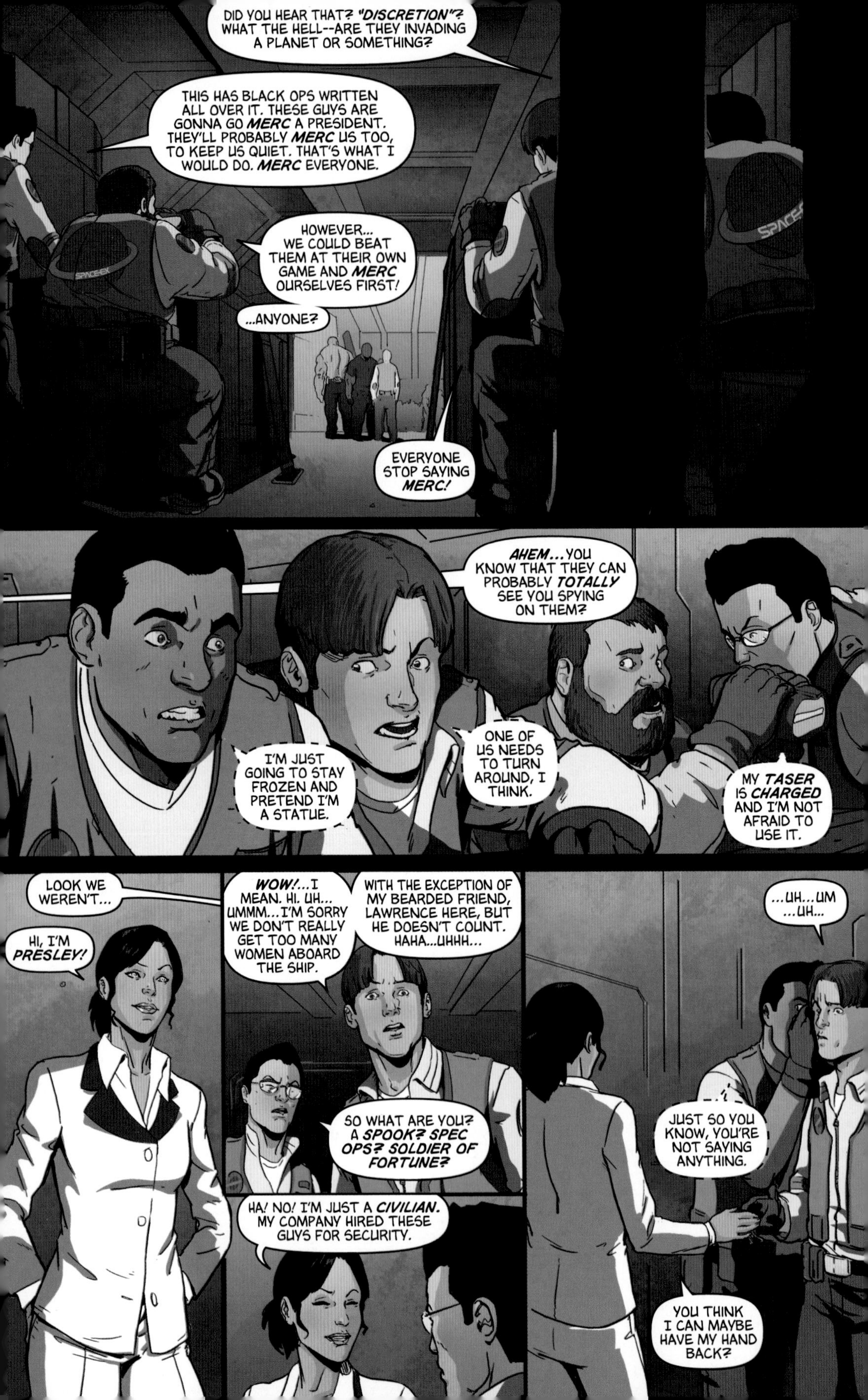
DID YOU HEAR THAT? "DISCRETION"? WHAT THE HELL--ARE THEY INVADING A PLANET OR SOMETHING?
THIS HAS BLACK OPS WRITTEN ALL OVER IT. THESE GUYS ARE GONNA GO MERC A PRESIDENT. THEY'LL PROBABLY MERC US TOO, TO KEEP US QUIET. THAT'S WHAT I WOULD DO. MERC EVERYONE.
HOWEVER... WE COULD BEAT THEM AT THEIR OWN GAME AND MERC OURSELVES FIRST!
...ANYONE?
EVERYONE STOP SAYING MERC!
AHEM...YOU KNOW THAT THEY CAN PROBABLY TOTALLY SEE YOU SPYING ON THEM?
I'M JUST GOING TO STAY FROZEN AND PRETEND I'M A STATUE.
ONE OF US NEEDS TO TURN AROUND, I THINK.
MY TASER IS CHARGED AND I'M NOT AFRAID TO USE IT.
LOOK WE WEREN'T...
HI, I'M PRESLEY!
WOW!...I MEAN. HI. UH... UMMM...I'M SORRY WE DON'T REALLY GET TOO MANY WOMEN ABOARD THE SHIP.
WITH THE EXCEPTION OF MY BEARDED FRIEND, LAWRENCE HERE, BUT HE DOESN'T COUNT. HAHA...UHHH...
SO WHAT ARE YOU? A SPOOK? SPEC OPS? SOLDIER OF FORTUNE?
HA! NO! I'M JUST A CIVILIAN. MY COMPANY HIRED THESE GUYS FOR SECURITY.
...UH...UM ...UH...
JUST SO YOU KNOW, YOU'RE NOT SAYING ANYTHING.
YOU THINK I CAN MAYBE HAVE MY HAND BACK?

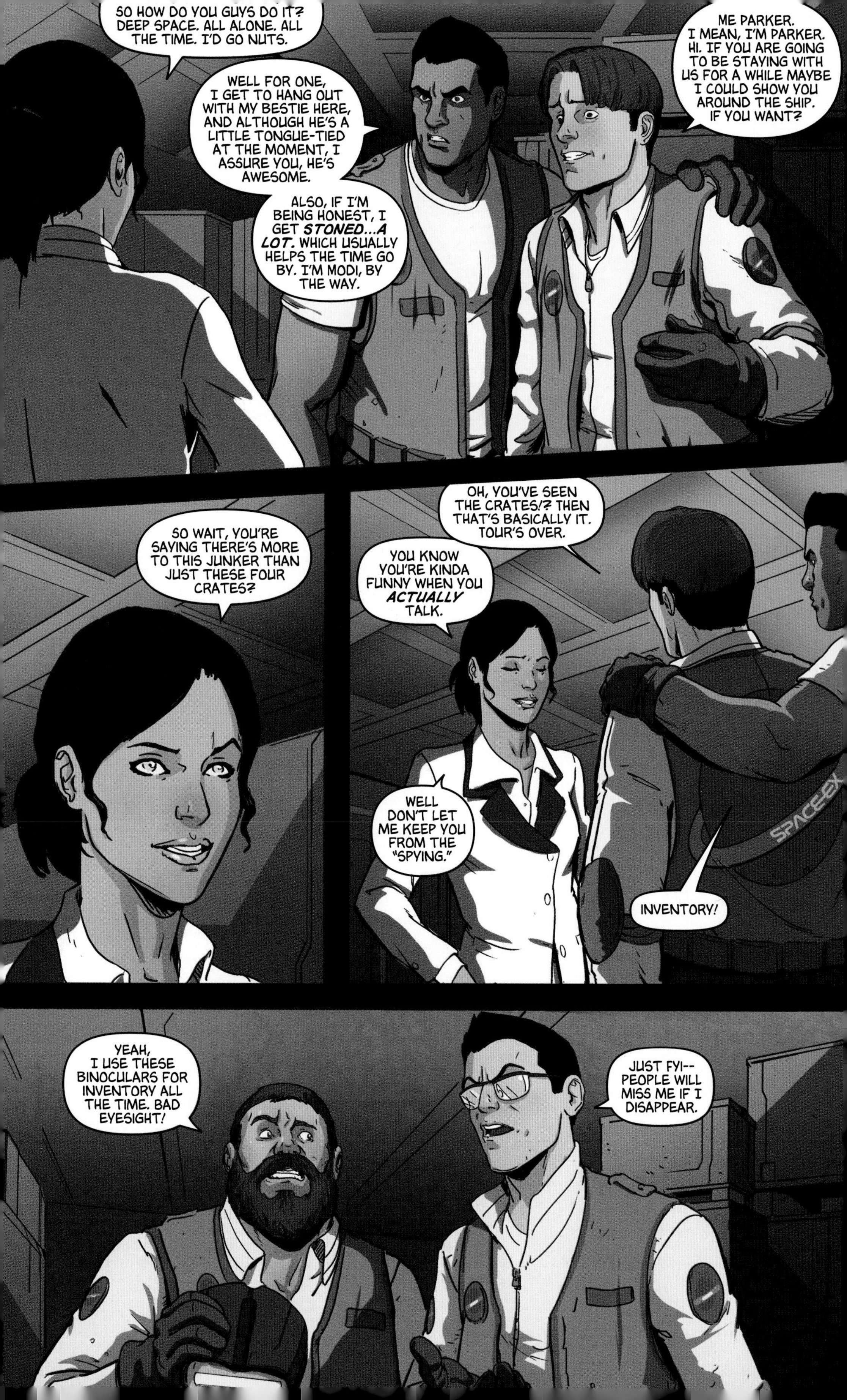
SO HOW DO YOU GUYS DO IT? DEEP SPACE. ALL ALONE. ALL THE TIME. I'D GO NUTS.
WELL FOR ONE, I GET TO HANG OUT WITH MY BESTIE HERE, AND ALTHOUGH HE'S A LITTLE TONGUE-TIED AT THE MOMENT, I ASSURE YOU, HE'S AWESOME.
ALSO, IF I'M BEING HONEST, I GET STONED...A LOT. WHICH USUALLY HELPS THE TIME GO BY. I'M MODI, BY THE WAY.
ME PARKER. I MEAN, I'M PARKER. HI. IF YOU ARE GOING TO BE STAYING WITH US FOR A WHILE MAYBE I COULD SHOW YOU AROUND THE SHIP. IF YOU WANT?
SO WAIT, YOU'RE SAYING THERE'S MORE TO THIS JUNKER THAN JUST THESE FOUR CRATES?
OH, YOU'VE SEEN THE CRATES!? THEN THAT'S BASICALLY IT. TOUR'S OVER.
YOU KNOW YOU'RE KINDA FUNNY WHEN YOU ACTUALLY TALK.
WELL DON'T LET ME KEEP YOU FROM THE "SPYING."
INVENTORY!
SPACE-EX
YEAH, I USE THESE BINOCULARS FOR INVENTORY ALL THE TIME. BAD EYESIGHT!
JUST FYI-- PEOPLE WILL MISS ME IF I DISAPPEAR.

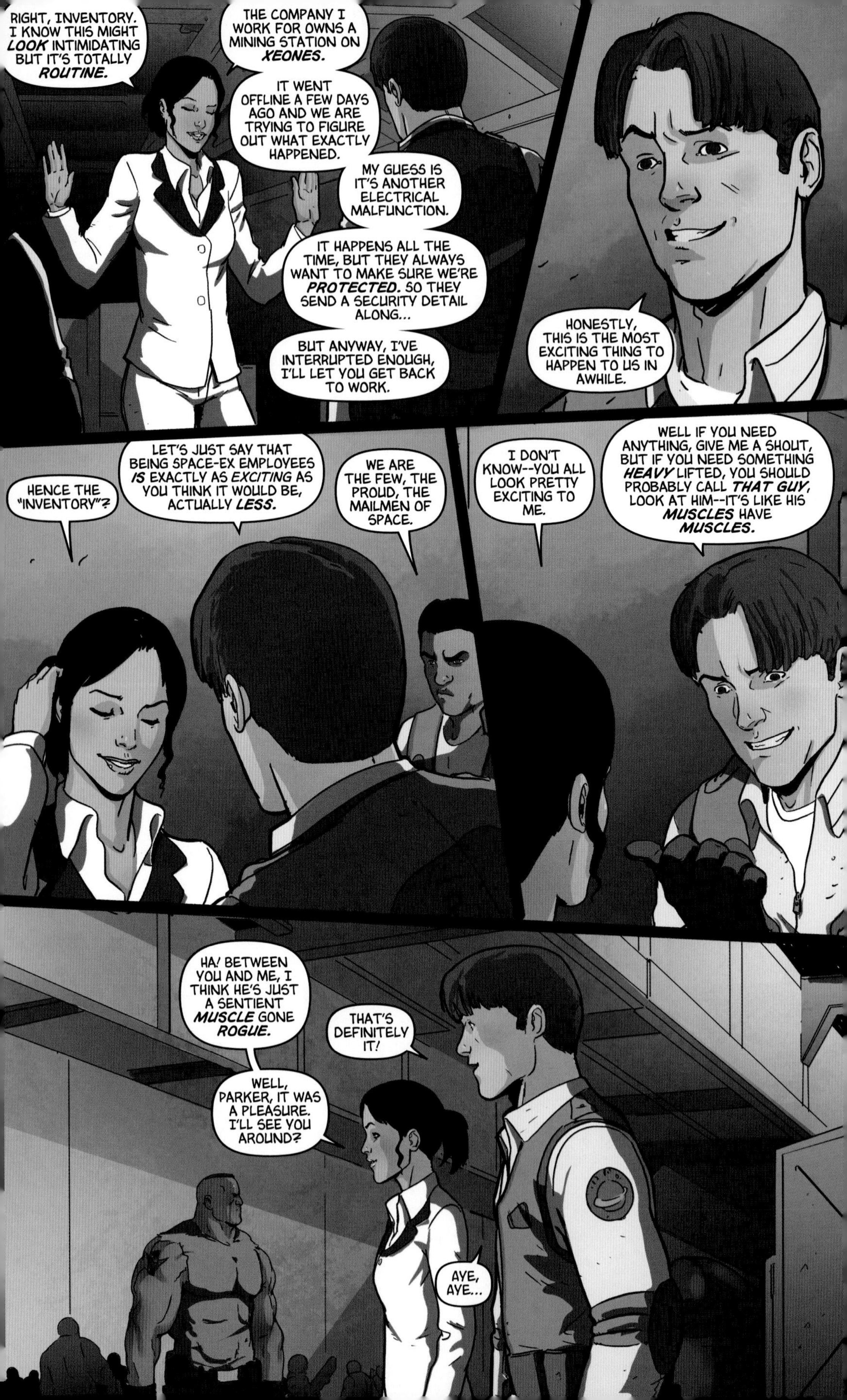
RIGHT, INVENTORY. I KNOW THIS MIGHT LOOK INTIMIDATING BUT IT'S TOTALLY ROUTINE.
THE COMPANY I WORK FOR OWNS A MINING STATION ON XEONES.
IT WENT OFFLINE A FEW DAYS AGO AND WE ARE TRYING TO FIGURE OUT WHAT EXACTLY HAPPENED.
MY GUESS IS IT'S ANOTHER ELECTRICAL MALFUNCTION.
IT HAPPENS ALL THE TIME, BUT THEY ALWAYS WANT TO MAKE SURE WE'RE PROTECTED. SO THEY SEND A SECURITY DETAIL ALONG...
BUT ANYWAY, I'VE INTERRUPTED ENOUGH, I'LL LET YOU GET BACK TO WORK.
HONESTLY, THIS IS THE MOST EXCITING THING TO HAPPEN TO US IN AWHILE.
HENCE THE "INVENTORY"?
LET'S JUST SAY THAT BEING SPACE-EX EMPLOYEES IS EXACTLY AS EXCITING AS YOU THINK IT WOULD BE, ACTUALLY LESS.
WE ARE THE FEW, THE PROUD, THE MAILMEN OF SPACE.
I DON'T KNOW--YOU ALL LOOK PRETTY EXCITING TO ME.
WELL IF YOU NEED ANYTHING, GIVE ME A SHOUT, BUT IF YOU NEED SOMETHING HEAVY LIFTED, YOU SHOULD PROBABLY CALL THAT GUY, LOOK AT HIM--IT'S LIKE HIS MUSCLES HAVE MUSCLES.
HA! BETWEEN YOU AND ME, I THINK HE'S JUST A SENTIENT MUSCLE GONE ROGUE.
THAT'S DEFINITELY IT!
WELL, PARKER, IT WAS A PLEASURE. I'LL SEE YOU AROUND?
AYE, AYE...

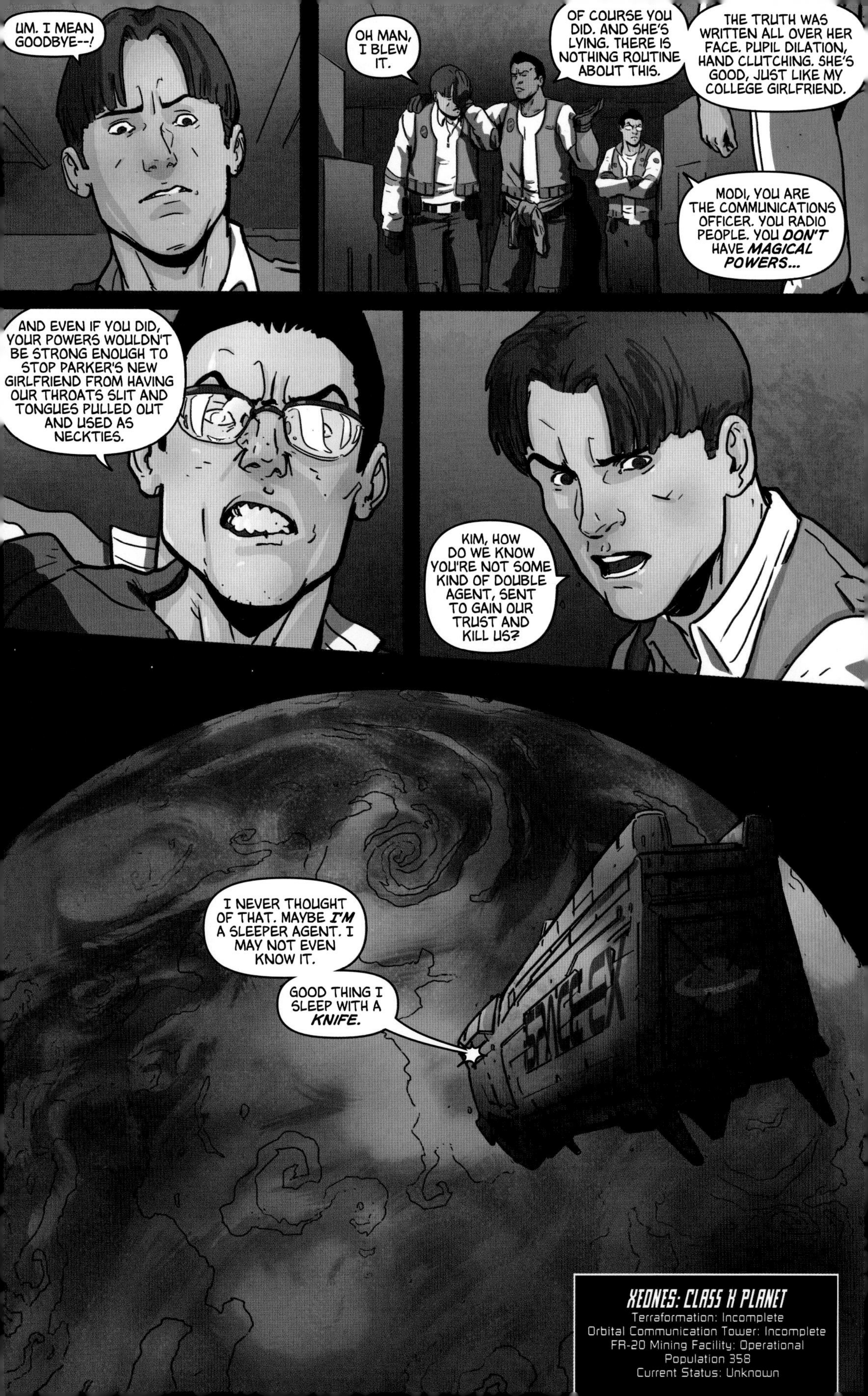
UM. I MEAN GOODBYE--!
OH MAN, I BLEW IT.
OF COURSE YOU DID. AND SHE'S LYING. THERE IS NOTHING ROUTINE ABOUT THIS.
THE TRUTH WAS WRITTEN ALL OVER HER FACE. PUPIL DILATION, HAND CLUTCHING. SHE'S GOOD, JUST LIKE MY COLLEGE GIRLFRIEND.
MODI, YOU ARE THE COMMUNICATIONS OFFICER. YOU RADIO PEOPLE. YOU DON'T HAVE MAGICAL POWERS...
AND EVEN IF YOU DID, YOUR POWERS WOULDN'T BE STRONG ENOUGH TO STOP PARKER'S NEW GIRLFRIEND FROM HAVING OUR THROATS SLIT AND TONGUES PULLED OUT AND USED AS NECKTIES.
KIM, HOW DO WE KNOW YOU'RE NOT SOME KIND OF DOUBLE AGENT, SENT TO GAIN OUR TRUST AND KILL US?
I NEVER THOUGHT OF THAT. MAYBE I'M A SLEEPER AGENT. I MAY NOT EVEN KNOW IT.
GOOD THING I SLEEP WITH A KNIFE.
SPACE-EX
XEONES: CLASS X PLANET
Terraformation: Incomplete
Orbital Communication Tower: Incomplete
FR-20 Mining Facility: Operational
Population 358
Current Status: Unknown

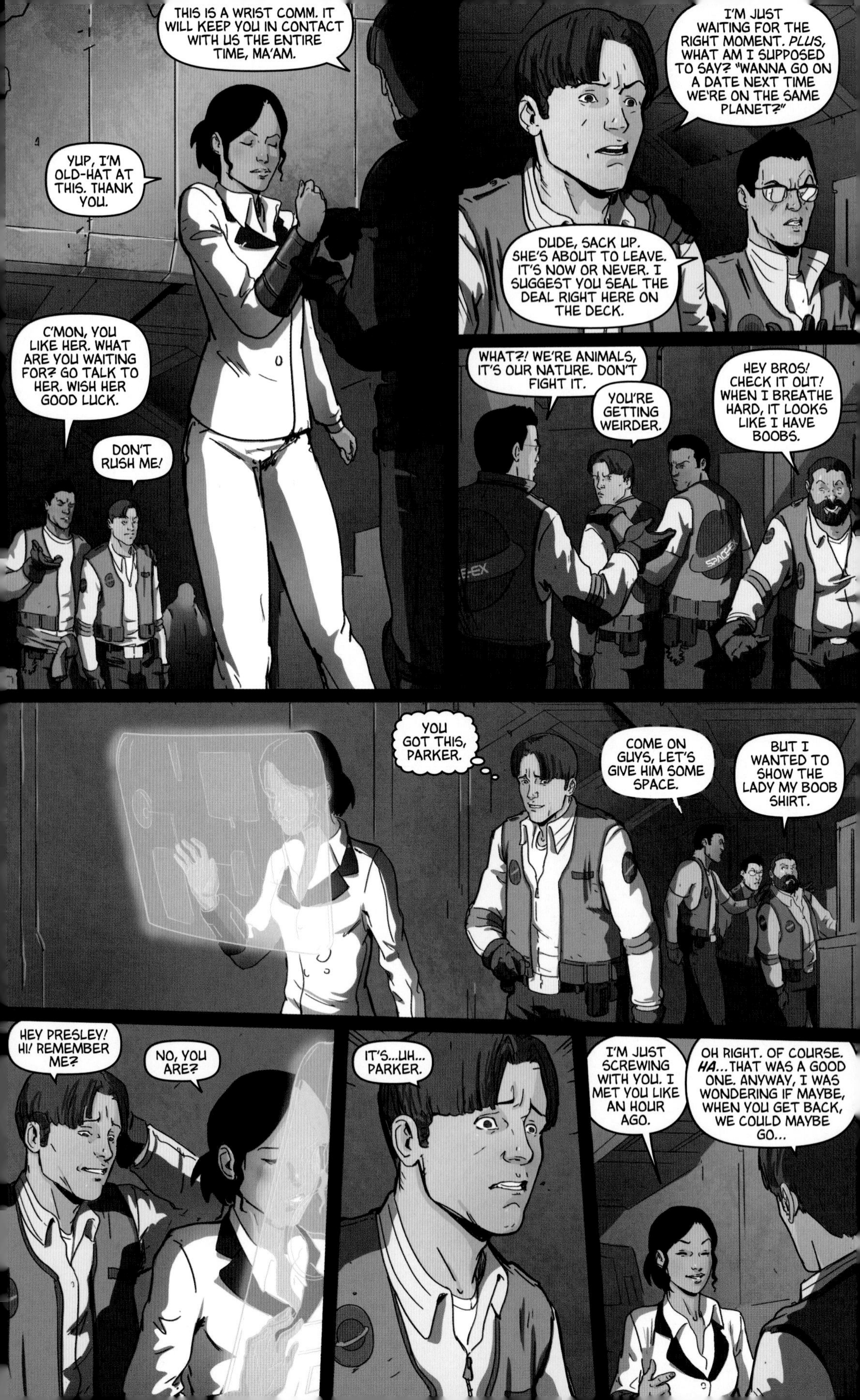
THIS IS A WRIST COMM. IT WILL KEEP YOU IN CONTACT WITH US THE ENTIRE TIME, MA'AM.
YUP, I'M OLD-HAT AT THIS. THANK YOU.
C'MON, YOU LIKE HER. WHAT ARE YOU WAITING FOR? GO TALK TO HER. WISH HER GOOD LUCK.
DON'T RUSH ME!
I'M JUST WAITING FOR THE RIGHT MOMENT. *PLUS*, WHAT AM I SUPPOSED TO SAY? "WANNA GO ON A DATE NEXT TIME WE'RE ON THE SAME PLANET?"
DUDE, SACK UP. SHE'S ABOUT TO LEAVE. IT'S NOW OR NEVER. I SUGGEST YOU SEAL THE DEAL RIGHT HERE ON THE DECK.
WHAT?! WE'RE ANIMALS, IT'S OUR NATURE. DON'T FIGHT IT.
YOU'RE GETTING WEIRDER.
HEY BROS! CHECK IT OUT! WHEN I BREATHE HARD, IT LOOKS LIKE I HAVE BOOBS.
SPACE-EX
YOU GOT THIS, PARKER.
COME ON GUYS, LET'S GIVE HIM SOME SPACE.
BUT I WANTED TO SHOW THE LADY MY BOOB SHIRT.
HEY PRESLEY! HI! REMEMBER ME?
NO, YOU ARE?
IT'S...UH... PARKER.
I'M JUST SCREWING WITH YOU. I MET YOU LIKE AN HOUR AGO.
OH RIGHT. OF COURSE. ***HA***...THAT WAS A GOOD ONE. ANYWAY, I WAS WONDERING IF MAYBE, WHEN YOU GET BACK, WE COULD MAYBE GO...

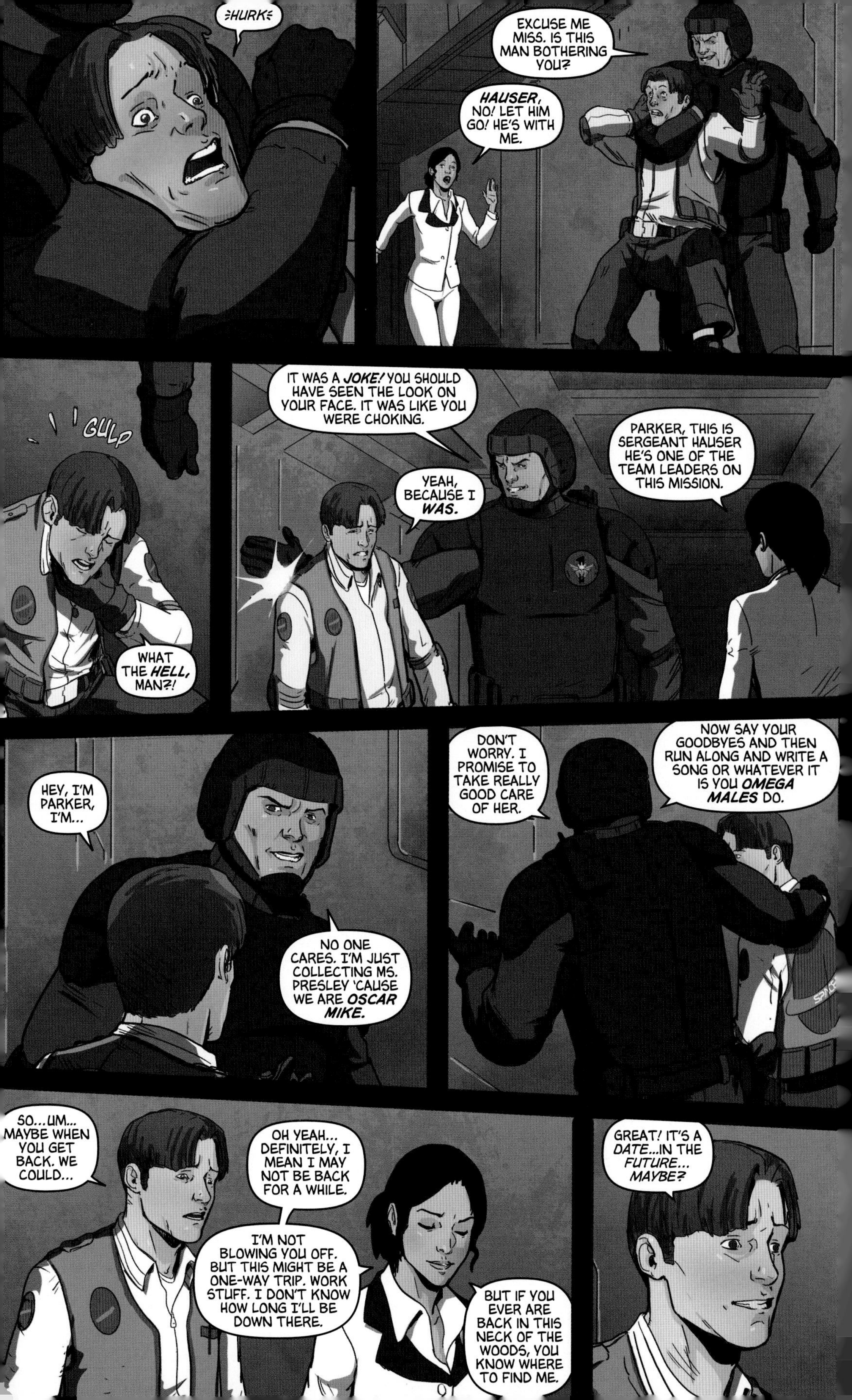

HURK
EXCUSE ME MISS. IS THIS MAN BOTHERING YOU?
HAUSER, NO! LET HIM GO! HE'S WITH ME.
GULP
WHAT THE HELL, MAN?!
IT WAS A JOKE! YOU SHOULD HAVE SEEN THE LOOK ON YOUR FACE. IT WAS LIKE YOU WERE CHOKING.
YEAH, BECAUSE I WAS.
PARKER, THIS IS SERGEANT HAUSER HE'S ONE OF THE TEAM LEADERS ON THIS MISSION.
HEY, I'M PARKER, I'M...
NO ONE CARES. I'M JUST COLLECTING MS. PRESLEY 'CAUSE WE ARE OSCAR MIKE.
DON'T WORRY. I PROMISE TO TAKE REALLY GOOD CARE OF HER.
NOW SAY YOUR GOODBYES AND THEN RUN ALONG AND WRITE A SONG OR WHATEVER IT IS YOU OMEGA MALES DO.
SO...UM... MAYBE WHEN YOU GET BACK. WE COULD...
OH YEAH... DEFINITELY, I MEAN I MAY NOT BE BACK FOR A WHILE.
I'M NOT BLOWING YOU OFF. BUT THIS MIGHT BE A ONE-WAY TRIP. WORK STUFF. I DON'T KNOW HOW LONG I'LL BE DOWN THERE.
BUT IF YOU EVER ARE BACK IN THIS NECK OF THE WOODS, YOU KNOW WHERE TO FIND ME.
GREAT! IT'S A DATE...IN THE FUTURE... MAYBE?

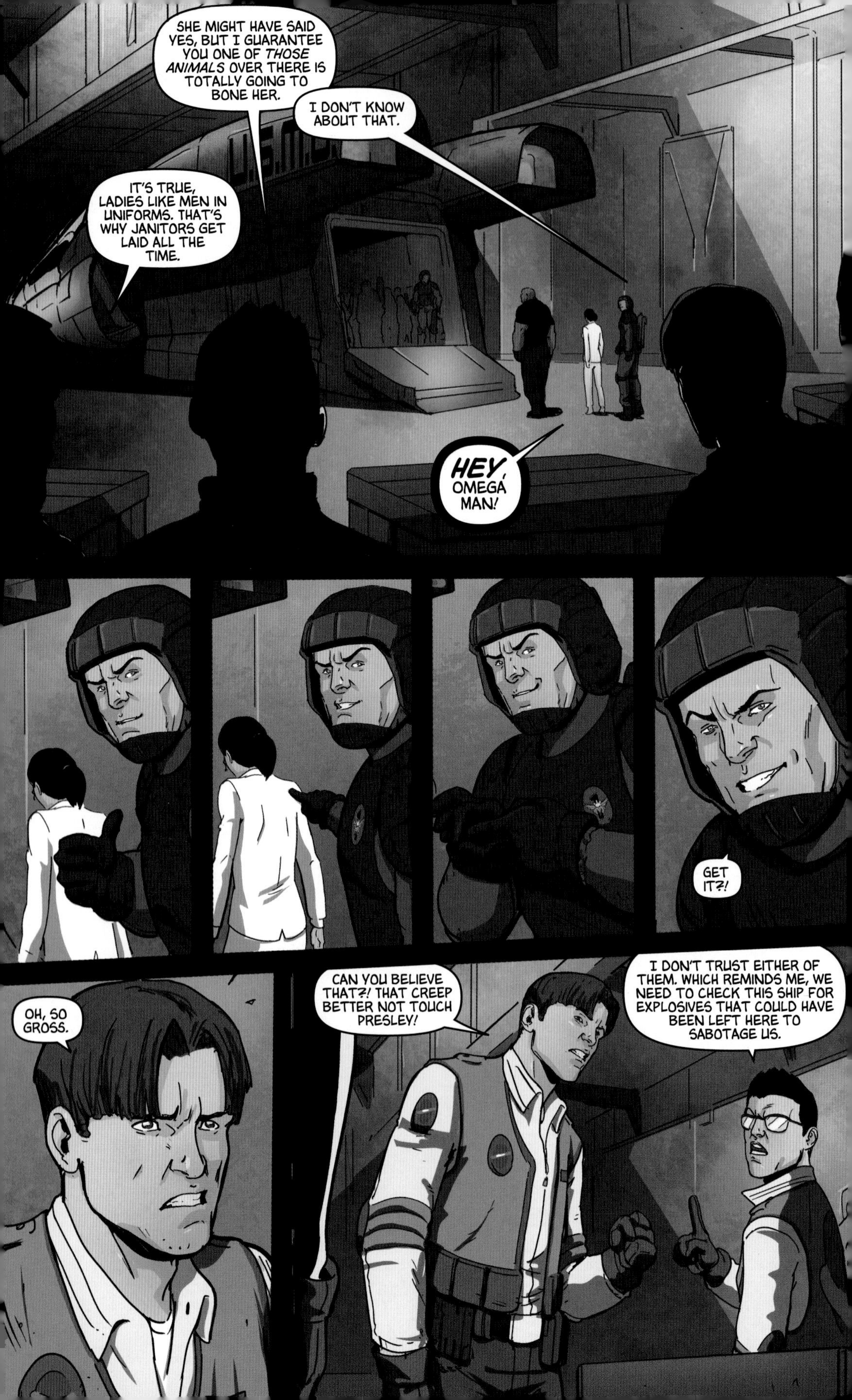
SHE MIGHT HAVE SAID YES, BUT I GUARANTEE YOU ONE OF *THOSE ANIMALS* OVER THERE IS TOTALLY GOING TO BONE HER.
I DON'T KNOW ABOUT THAT.
IT'S TRUE, LADIES LIKE MEN IN UNIFORMS. THAT'S WHY JANITORS GET LAID ALL THE TIME.
HEY, OMEGA MAN!
GET IT?!
OH, SO GROSS.
CAN YOU BELIEVE THAT?! THAT CREEP BETTER NOT TOUCH PRESLEY!
I DON'T TRUST EITHER OF THEM. WHICH REMINDS ME, WE NEED TO CHECK THIS SHIP FOR EXPLOSIVES THAT COULD HAVE BEEN LEFT HERE TO SABOTAGE US.

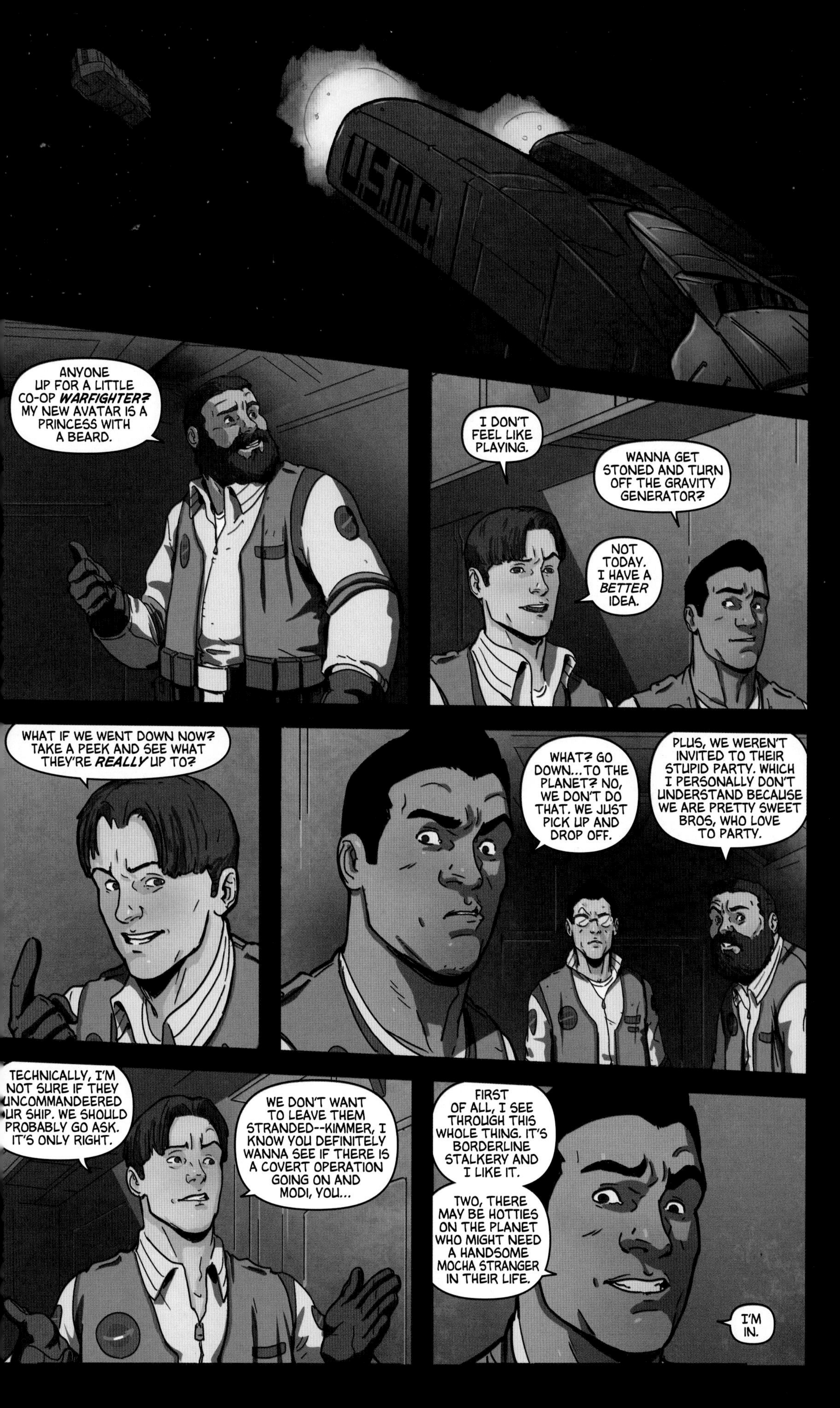
ANYONE UP FOR A LITTLE CO-OP *WARFIGHTER?* MY NEW AVATAR IS A PRINCESS WITH A BEARD.
I DON'T FEEL LIKE PLAYING.
WANNA GET STONED AND TURN OFF THE GRAVITY GENERATOR?
NOT TODAY. I HAVE A *BETTER* IDEA.
WHAT IF WE WENT DOWN NOW? TAKE A PEEK AND SEE WHAT THEY'RE *REALLY* UP TO?
WHAT? GO DOWN...TO THE PLANET? NO, WE DON'T DO THAT. WE JUST PICK UP AND DROP OFF.
PLUS, WE WEREN'T INVITED TO THEIR STUPID PARTY. WHICH I PERSONALLY DON'T UNDERSTAND BECAUSE WE ARE PRETTY SWEET BROS, WHO LOVE TO PARTY.
TECHNICALLY, I'M NOT SURE IF THEY UNCOMMANDEERED UR SHIP. WE SHOULD PROBABLY GO ASK. IT'S ONLY RIGHT.
WE DON'T WANT TO LEAVE THEM STRANDED--KIMMER, I KNOW YOU DEFINITELY WANNA SEE IF THERE IS A COVERT OPERATION GOING ON AND MODI, YOU...
FIRST OF ALL, I SEE THROUGH THIS WHOLE THING. IT'S BORDERLINE STALKERY AND I LIKE IT.
TWO, THERE MAY BE HOTTIES ON THE PLANET WHO MIGHT NEED A HANDSOME MOCHA STRANGER IN THEIR LIFE.
I'M IN.

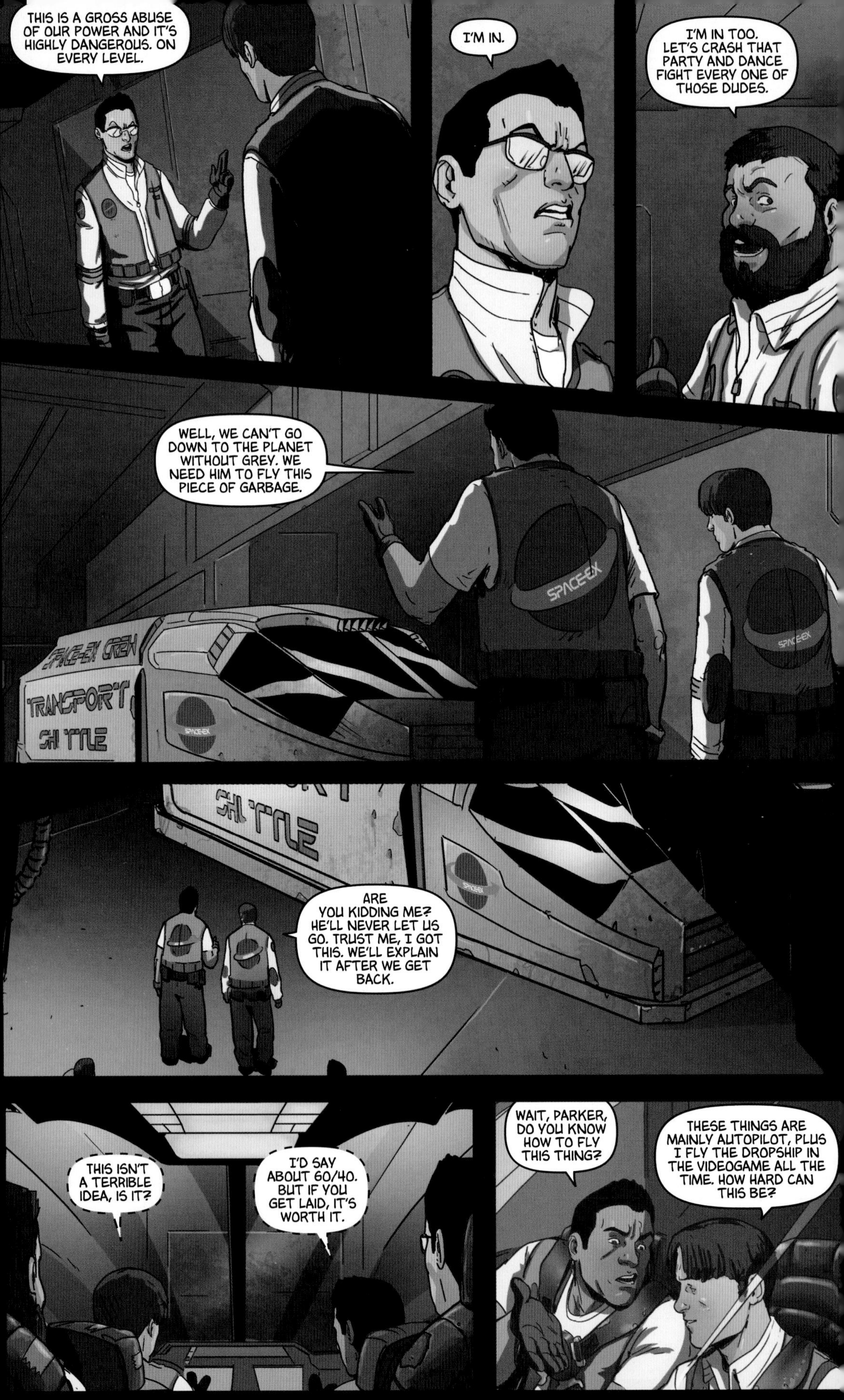
THIS IS A GROSS ABUSE OF OUR POWER AND IT'S HIGHLY DANGEROUS. ON EVERY LEVEL.
I'M IN.
I'M IN TOO. LET'S CRASH THAT PARTY AND DANCE FIGHT EVERY ONE OF THOSE DUDES.
WELL, WE CAN'T GO DOWN TO THE PLANET WITHOUT GREY. WE NEED HIM TO FLY THIS PIECE OF GARBAGE.
SPACE-EX
SPACE-EX CREW
TRANSPORT SHUTTLE
ARE YOU KIDDING ME? HE'LL NEVER LET US GO. TRUST ME, I GOT THIS. WE'LL EXPLAIN IT AFTER WE GET BACK.
THIS ISN'T A TERRIBLE IDEA, IS IT?
I'D SAY ABOUT 60/40. BUT IF YOU GET LAID, IT'S WORTH IT.
WAIT, PARKER, DO YOU KNOW HOW TO FLY THIS THING?
THESE THINGS ARE MAINLY AUTOPILOT, PLUS I FLY THE DROPSHIP IN THE VIDEOGAME ALL THE TIME. HOW HARD CAN THIS BE?

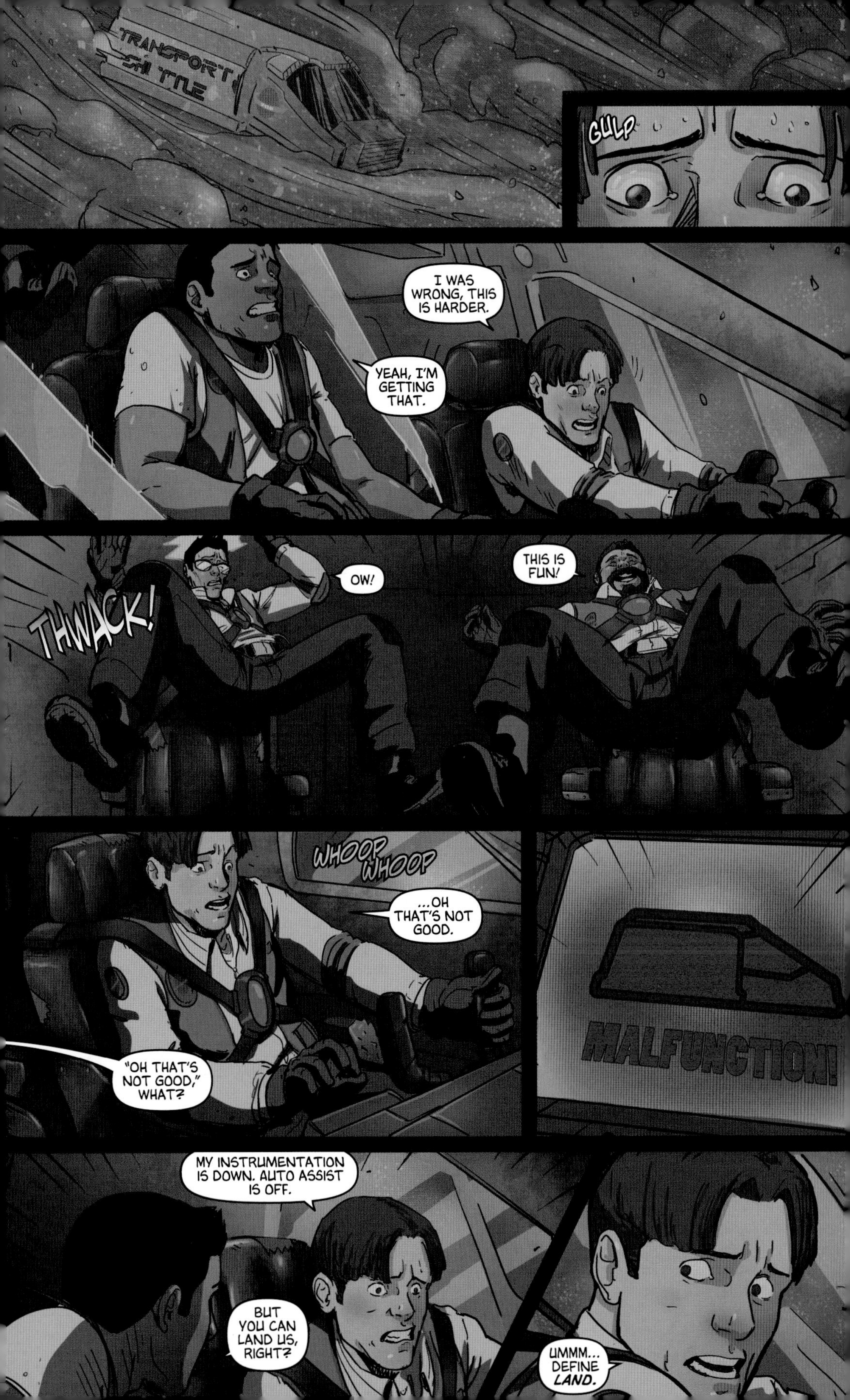
TRANSPORT SHUTTLE
GULP
I WAS WRONG, THIS IS HARDER.
YEAH, I'M GETTING THAT.
THWACK!
OW!
THIS IS FUN!
WHOOP WHOOP
...OH THAT'S NOT GOOD.
"OH THAT'S NOT GOOD," WHAT?
MALFUNCTION!
MY INSTRUMENTATION IS DOWN. AUTO ASSIST IS OFF.
BUT YOU CAN LAND US, RIGHT?
UMMM... DEFINE *LAND*.

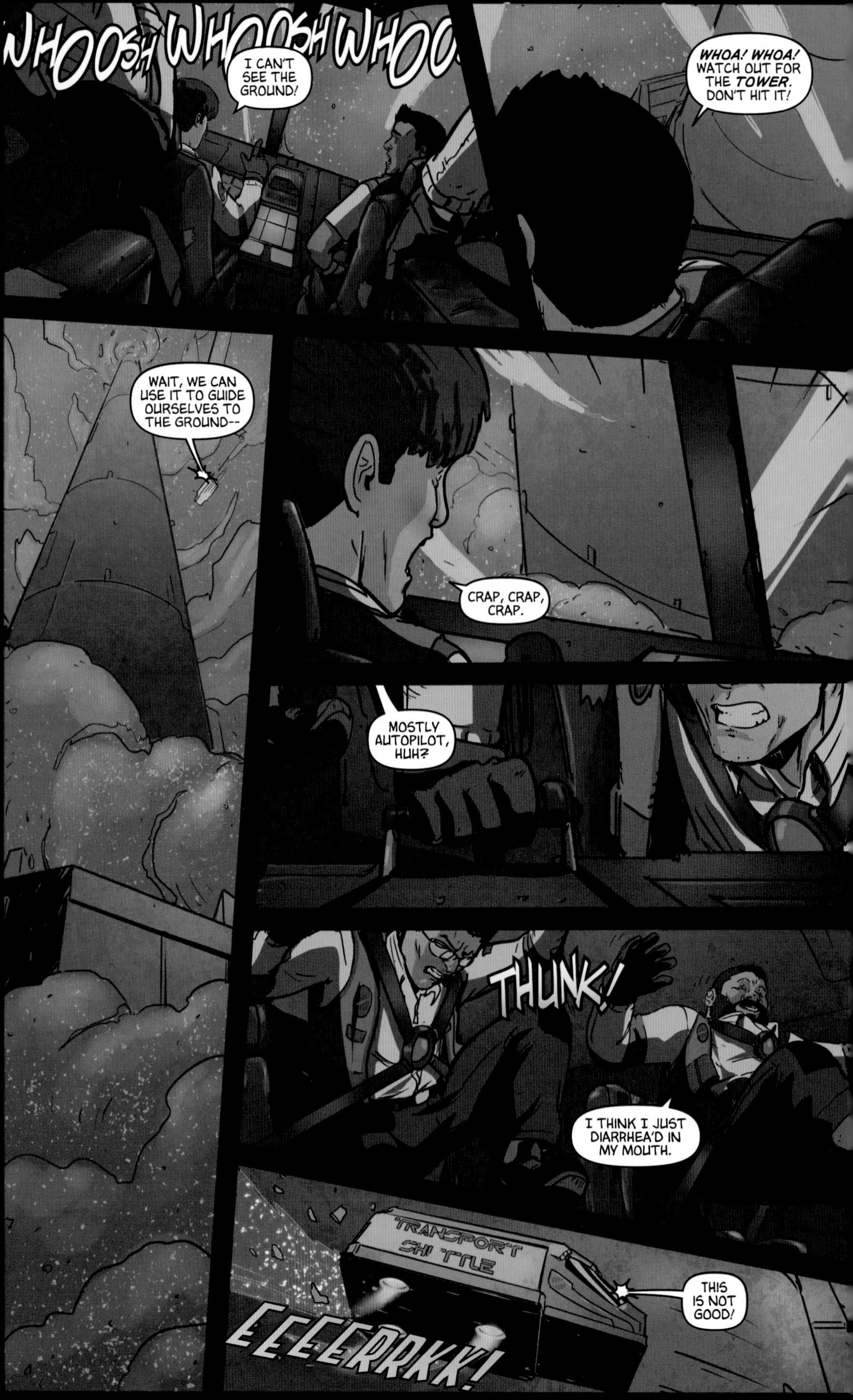

WHOOSH WHOOSH WHOOS
I CAN'T SEE THE GROUND!
WHOA! WHOA! WATCH OUT FOR THE TOWER. DON'T HIT IT!
WAIT, WE CAN USE IT TO GUIDE OURSELVES TO THE GROUND--
CRAP, CRAP, CRAP.
MOSTLY AUTOPILOT, HUH?
THUNK!
I THINK I JUST DIARRHEA'D IN MY MOUTH.
TRANSPORT SHUTTLE
THIS IS NOT GOOD!
EEEEERRRKK!

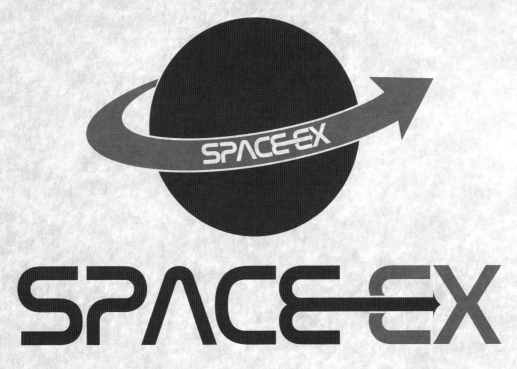

SPACE-EX

"We know how to handle your package."

Chapter Two
COVER BY
JEFF STOKELY
COLORS BY BLOND

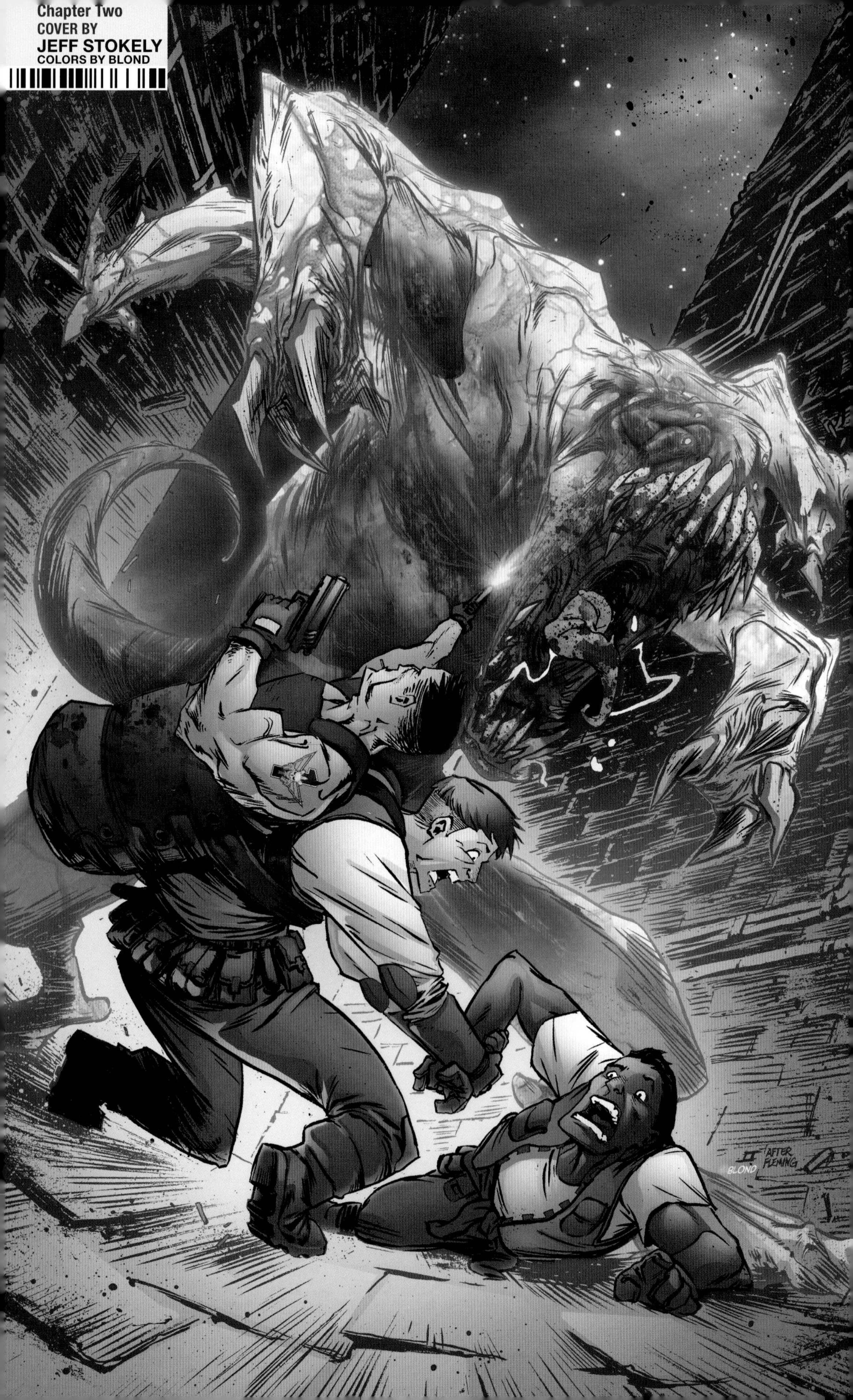
BLOND
AFTER FLEMING

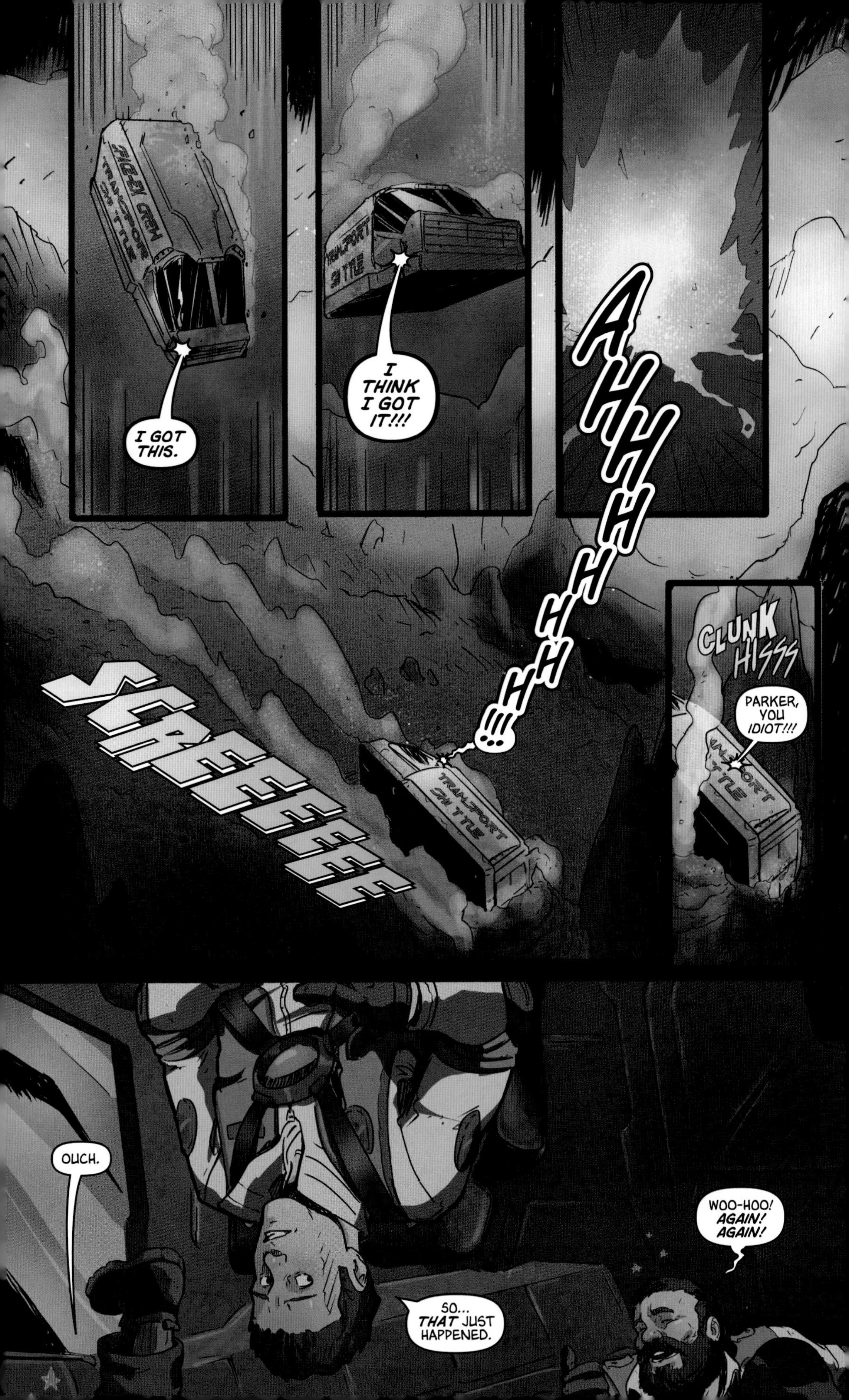
I GOT THIS.
I THINK I GOT IT!!!
AHHHHHHHH!!!
SCREEEEEE
CLUNK
HISSS
PARKER, YOU IDIOT!!!
OUCH.
SO... THAT JUST HAPPENED.
WOO-HOO! AGAIN! AGAIN!

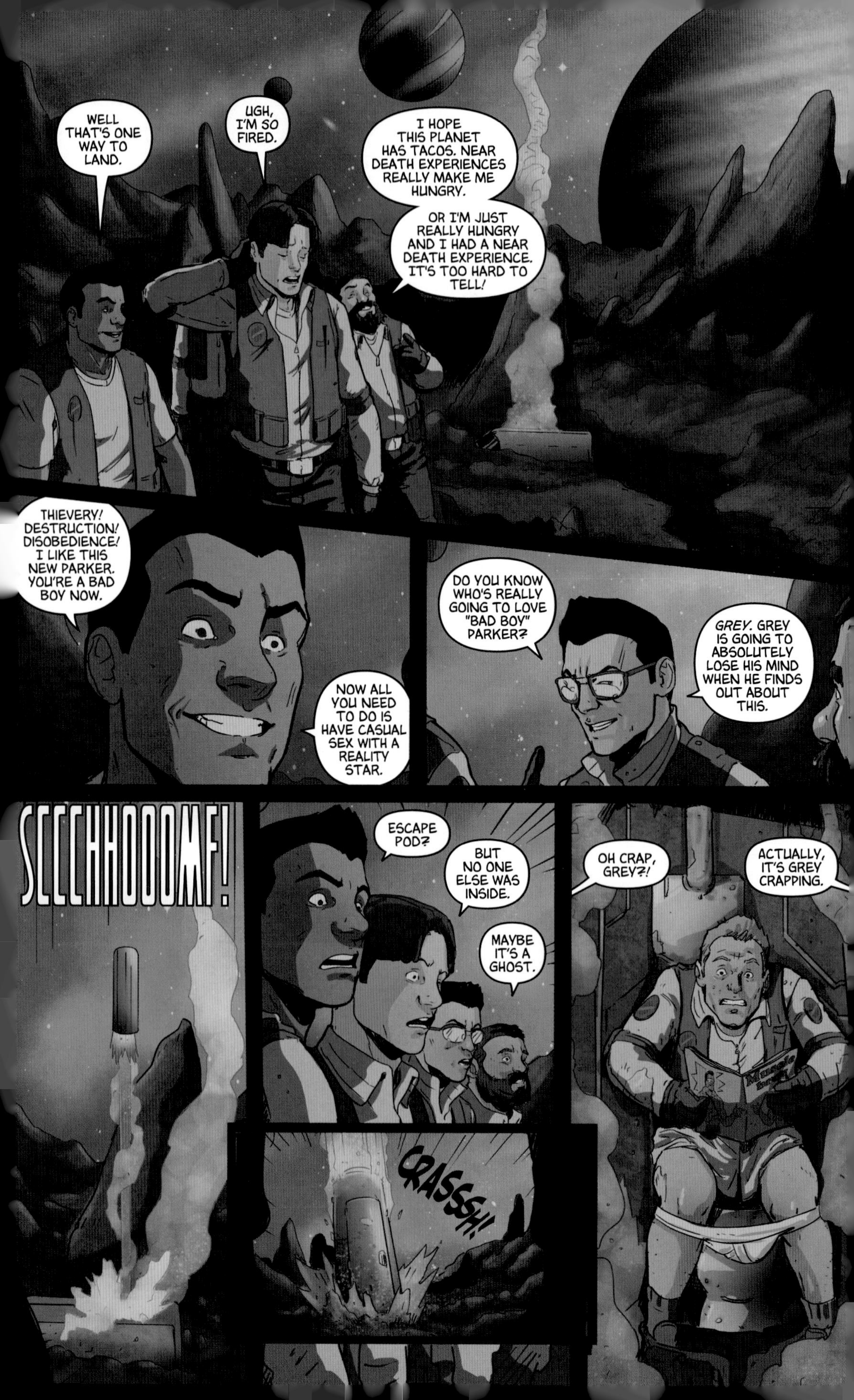
WELL THAT'S ONE WAY TO LAND.
UGH, I'M SO FIRED.
I HOPE THIS PLANET HAS TACOS. NEAR DEATH EXPERIENCES REALLY MAKE ME HUNGRY.
OR I'M JUST REALLY HUNGRY AND I HAD A NEAR DEATH EXPERIENCE. IT'S TOO HARD TO TELL!
THIEVERY! DESTRUCTION! DISOBEDIENCE! I LIKE THIS NEW PARKER. YOU'RE A BAD BOY NOW.
NOW ALL YOU NEED TO DO IS HAVE CASUAL SEX WITH A REALITY STAR.
DO YOU KNOW WHO'S REALLY GOING TO LOVE "BAD BOY" PARKER?
GREY. GREY IS GOING TO ABSOLUTELY LOSE HIS MIND WHEN HE FINDS OUT ABOUT THIS.
SCCCHHOOOMF!
ESCAPE POD?
BUT NO ONE ELSE WAS INSIDE.
MAYBE IT'S A GHOST.
CRASSSH!
OH CRAP, GREY?!
ACTUALLY, IT'S GREY CRAPPING.

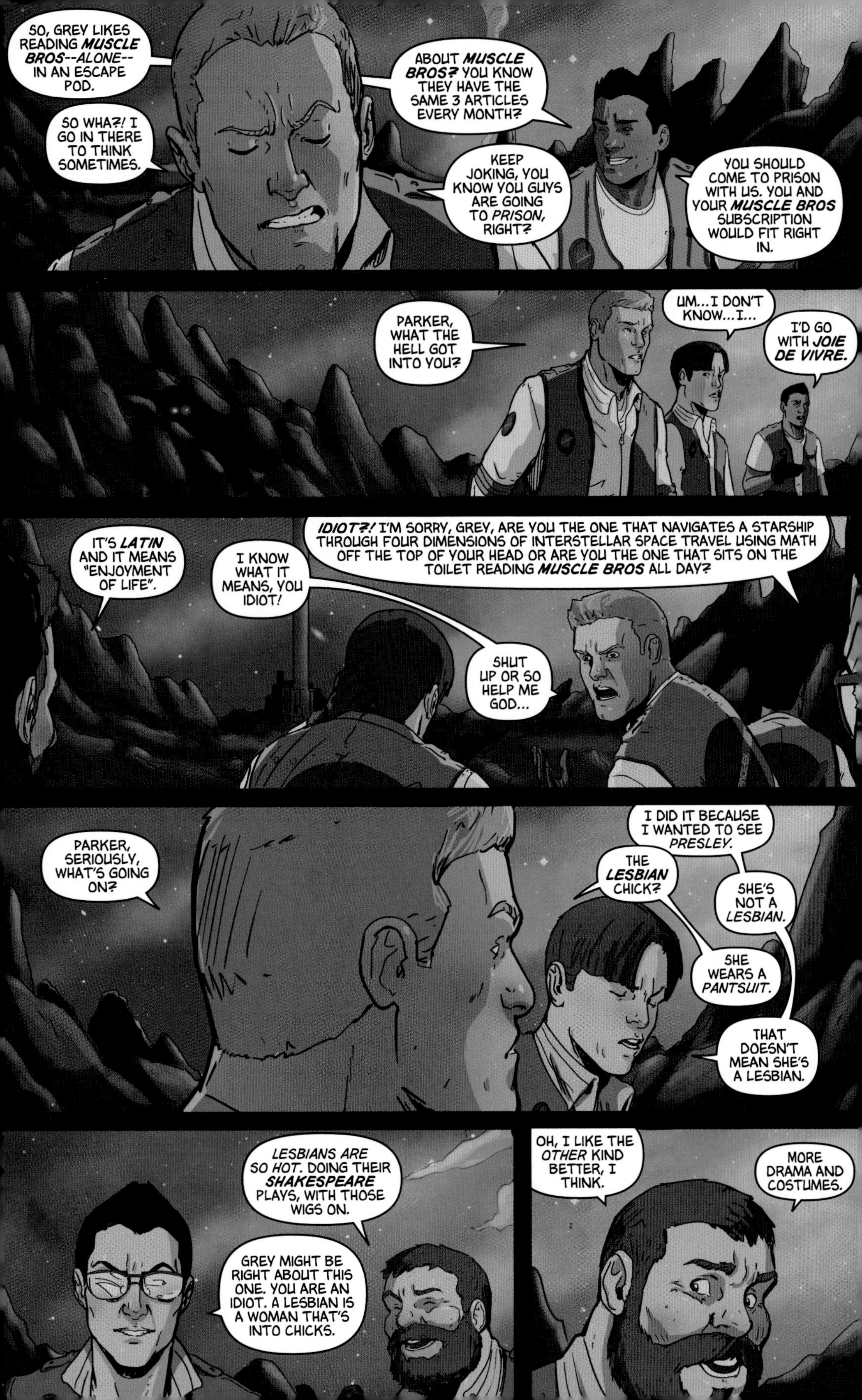
SO, GREY LIKES READING MUSCLE BROS--ALONE--IN AN ESCAPE POD.
ABOUT MUSCLE BROS? YOU KNOW THEY HAVE THE SAME 3 ARTICLES EVERY MONTH?
SO WHA?! I GO IN THERE TO THINK SOMETIMES.
KEEP JOKING, YOU KNOW YOU GUYS ARE GOING TO PRISON, RIGHT?
YOU SHOULD COME TO PRISON WITH US. YOU AND YOUR MUSCLE BROS SUBSCRIPTION WOULD FIT RIGHT IN.
PARKER, WHAT THE HELL GOT INTO YOU?
UM... I DON'T KNOW... I...
I'D GO WITH JOIE DE VIVRE.
IT'S LATIN AND IT MEANS "ENJOYMENT OF LIFE".
I KNOW WHAT IT MEANS, YOU IDIOT!
IDIOT?! I'M SORRY, GREY, ARE YOU THE ONE THAT NAVIGATES A STARSHIP THROUGH FOUR DIMENSIONS OF INTERSTELLAR SPACE TRAVEL USING MATH OFF THE TOP OF YOUR HEAD OR ARE YOU THE ONE THAT SITS ON THE TOILET READING MUSCLE BROS ALL DAY?
SHUT UP OR SO HELP ME GOD...
PARKER, SERIOUSLY, WHAT'S GOING ON?
I DID IT BECAUSE I WANTED TO SEE PRESLEY.
THE LESBIAN CHICK?
SHE'S NOT A LESBIAN.
SHE WEARS A PANTSUIT.
THAT DOESN'T MEAN SHE'S A LESBIAN.
LESBIANS ARE SO HOT. DOING THEIR SHAKESPEARE PLAYS, WITH THOSE WIGS ON.
GREY MIGHT BE RIGHT ABOUT THIS ONE. YOU ARE AN IDIOT. A LESBIAN IS A WOMAN THAT'S INTO CHICKS.
OH, I LIKE THE OTHER KIND BETTER, I THINK.
MORE DRAMA AND COSTUMES.

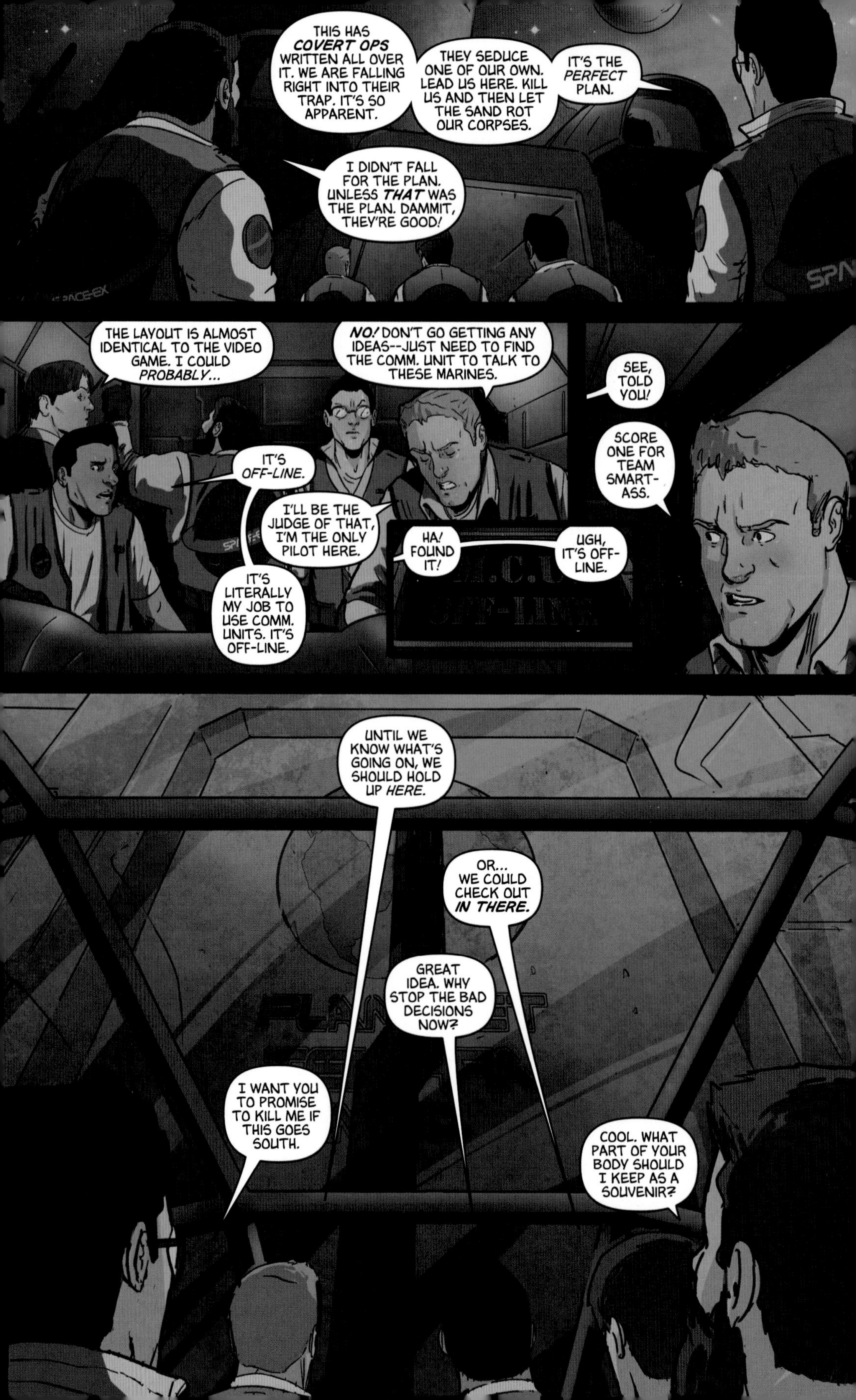

THIS HAS COVERT OPS WRITTEN ALL OVER IT. WE ARE FALLING RIGHT INTO THEIR TRAP. IT'S SO APPARENT.
THEY SEDUCE ONE OF OUR OWN. LEAD US HERE. KILL US AND THEN LET THE SAND ROT OUR CORPSES.
IT'S THE PERFECT PLAN.
I DIDN'T FALL FOR THE PLAN. UNLESS THAT WAS THE PLAN. DAMMIT, THEY'RE GOOD!
THE LAYOUT IS ALMOST IDENTICAL TO THE VIDEO GAME. I COULD PROBABLY...
NO! DON'T GO GETTING ANY IDEAS--JUST NEED TO FIND THE COMM. UNIT TO TALK TO THESE MARINES.
IT'S OFF-LINE.
I'LL BE THE JUDGE OF THAT, I'M THE ONLY PILOT HERE.
IT'S LITERALLY MY JOB TO USE COMM. UNITS. IT'S OFF-LINE.
HA! FOUND IT!
UGH, IT'S OFF-LINE.
SEE, TOLD YOU!
SCORE ONE FOR TEAM SMART-ASS.
UNTIL WE KNOW WHAT'S GOING ON, WE SHOULD HOLD UP HERE.
OR... WE COULD CHECK OUT IN THERE.
GREAT IDEA. WHY STOP THE BAD DECISIONS NOW?
I WANT YOU TO PROMISE TO KILL ME IF THIS GOES SOUTH.
COOL. WHAT PART OF YOUR BODY SHOULD I KEEP AS A SOUVENIR?

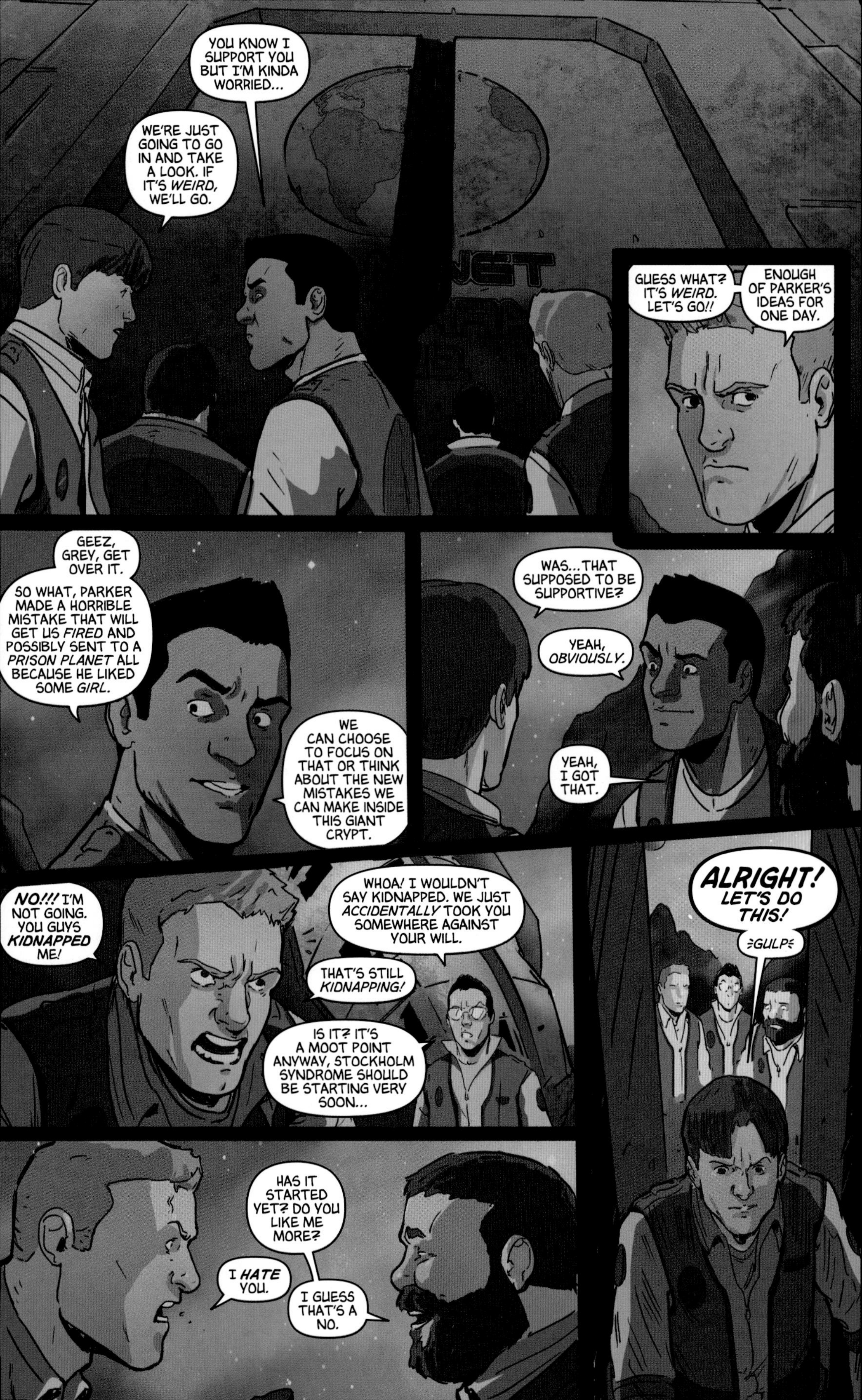

YOU KNOW I SUPPORT YOU BUT I'M KINDA WORRIED...
WE'RE JUST GOING TO GO IN AND TAKE A LOOK. IF IT'S *WEIRD,* WE'LL GO.
GUESS WHAT? IT'S *WEIRD.* LET'S GO!!
ENOUGH OF PARKER'S IDEAS FOR ONE DAY.
GEEZ, GREY, GET OVER IT.
SO WHAT, PARKER MADE A HORRIBLE MISTAKE THAT WILL GET US *FIRED* AND POSSIBLY SENT TO A *PRISON PLANET* ALL BECAUSE HE LIKED SOME *GIRL.*
WE CAN CHOOSE TO FOCUS ON THAT OR THINK ABOUT THE NEW MISTAKES WE CAN MAKE INSIDE THIS GIANT CRYPT.
WAS...THAT SUPPOSED TO BE SUPPORTIVE?
YEAH, *OBVIOUSLY.*
YEAH, I GOT THAT.
NO!!! I'M NOT GOING. YOU GUYS ***KIDNAPPED*** ME!
WHOA! I WOULDN'T SAY KIDNAPPED. WE JUST *ACCIDENTALLY* TOOK YOU SOMEWHERE AGAINST YOUR WILL.
THAT'S STILL *KIDNAPPING!*
IS IT? IT'S A MOOT POINT ANYWAY, STOCKHOLM SYNDROME SHOULD BE STARTING VERY SOON...
HAS IT STARTED YET? DO YOU LIKE ME MORE?
I *HATE* YOU.
I GUESS THAT'S A NO.
***ALRIGHT!* LET'S DO THIS!**
GULP

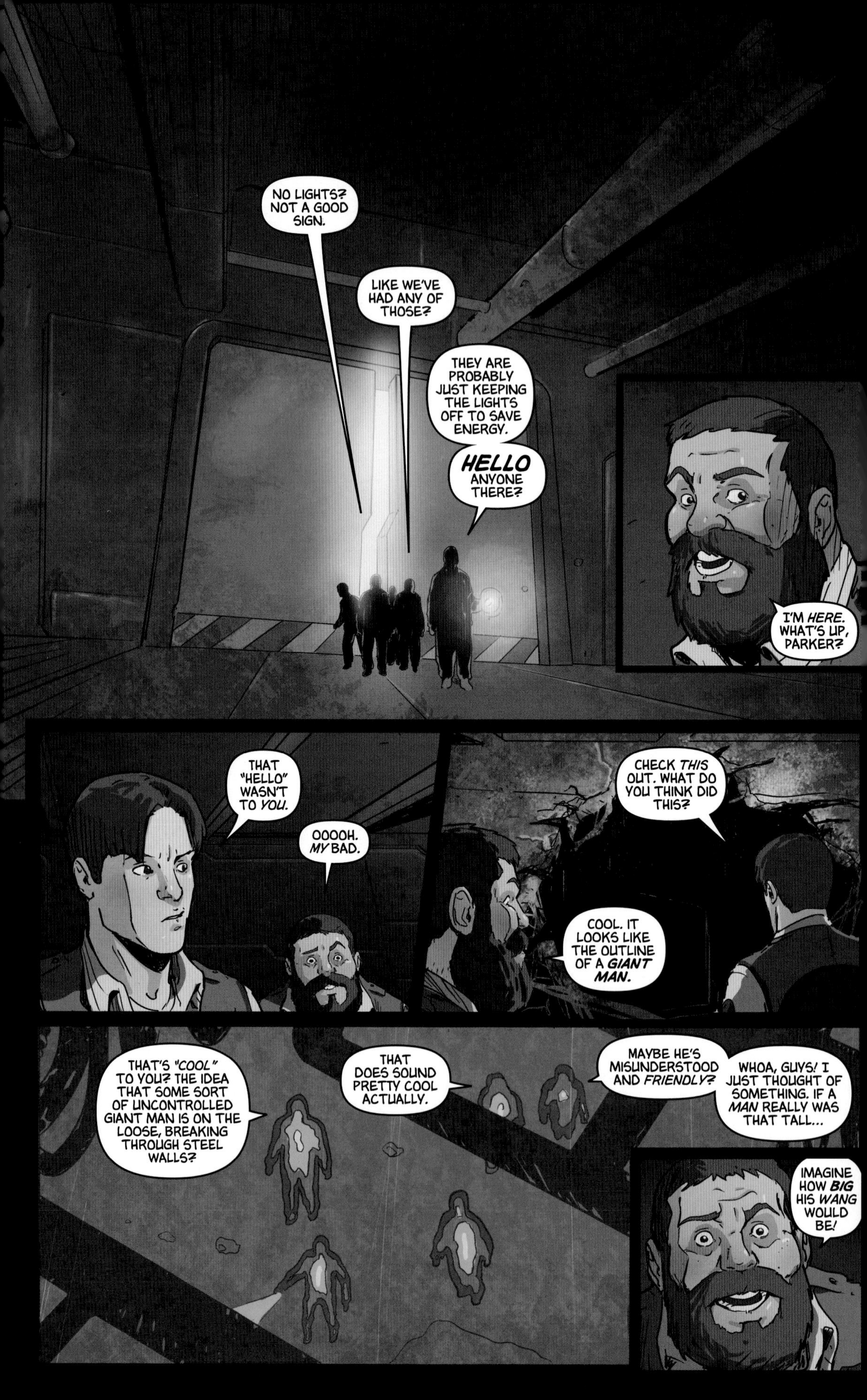
NO LIGHTS? NOT A GOOD SIGN.
LIKE WE'VE HAD ANY OF THOSE?
THEY ARE PROBABLY JUST KEEPING THE LIGHTS OFF TO SAVE ENERGY.
HELLO ANYONE THERE?
I'M HERE. WHAT'S UP, PARKER?
THAT "HELLO" WASN'T TO YOU.
OOOOH. MY BAD.
CHECK THIS OUT. WHAT DO YOU THINK DID THIS?
COOL. IT LOOKS LIKE THE OUTLINE OF A GIANT MAN.
THAT'S "COOL" TO YOU? THE IDEA THAT SOME SORT OF UNCONTROLLED GIANT MAN IS ON THE LOOSE, BREAKING THROUGH STEEL WALLS?
THAT DOES SOUND PRETTY COOL ACTUALLY.
MAYBE HE'S MISUNDERSTOOD AND FRIENDLY?
WHOA, GUYS! I JUST THOUGHT OF SOMETHING. IF A MAN REALLY WAS THAT TALL...
IMAGINE HOW BIG HIS WANG WOULD BE!

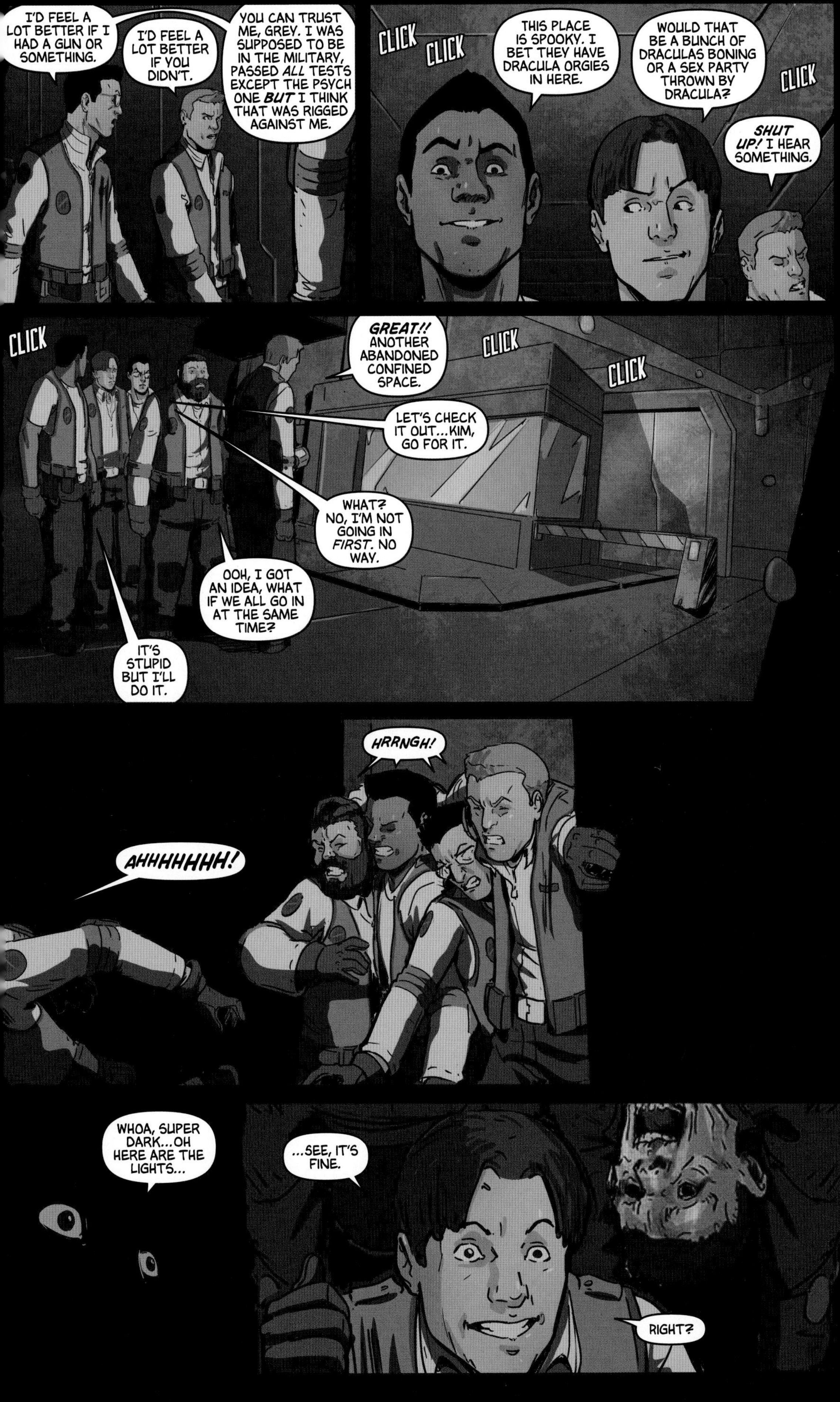
I'D FEEL A LOT BETTER IF I HAD A GUN OR SOMETHING.
I'D FEEL A LOT BETTER IF YOU DIDN'T.
YOU CAN TRUST ME, GREY. I WAS SUPPOSED TO BE IN THE MILITARY, PASSED ALL TESTS EXCEPT THE PSYCH ONE BUT I THINK THAT WAS RIGGED AGAINST ME.
CLICK
CLICK
THIS PLACE IS SPOOKY. I BET THEY HAVE DRACULA ORGIES IN HERE.
WOULD THAT BE A BUNCH OF DRACULAS BONING OR A SEX PARTY THROWN BY DRACULA?
CLICK
SHUT UP! I HEAR SOMETHING.
CLICK
GREAT!! ANOTHER ABANDONED CONFINED SPACE.
CLICK
CLICK
LET'S CHECK IT OUT...KIM, GO FOR IT.
WHAT? NO, I'M NOT GOING IN FIRST. NO WAY.
OOH, I GOT AN IDEA, WHAT IF WE ALL GO IN AT THE SAME TIME?
IT'S STUPID BUT I'LL DO IT.
HRRNGH!
AHHHHHHH!
WHOA, SUPER DARK...OH HERE ARE THE LIGHTS...
...SEE, IT'S FINE.
RIGHT?

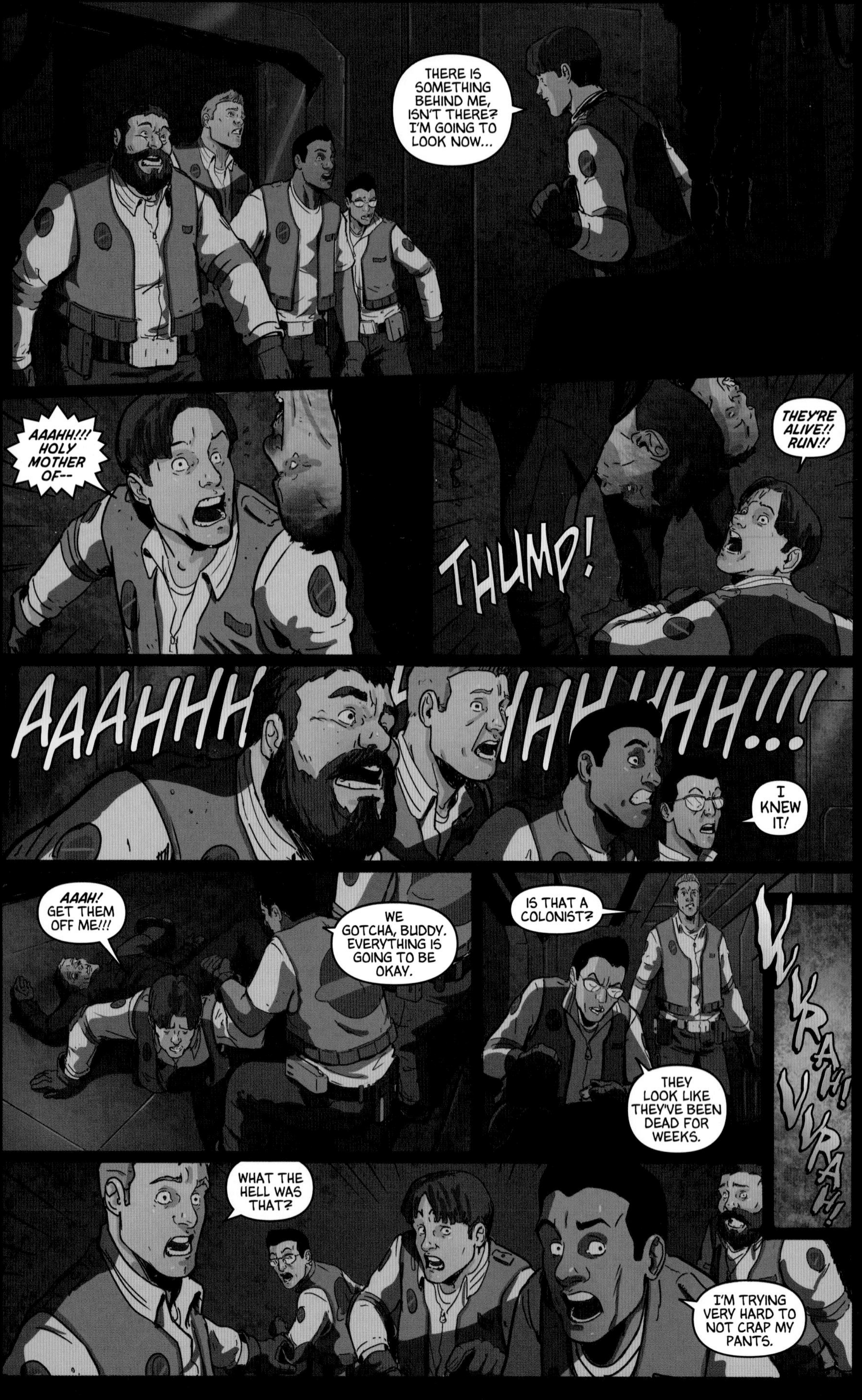
THERE IS SOMETHING BEHIND ME, ISN'T THERE? I'M GOING TO LOOK NOW...
AAAHH!!! HOLY MOTHER OF--
THUMP!
THEY'RE ALIVE!! RUN!!
AAAHHHHHHHH!!!
I KNEW IT!
AAAH! GET THEM OFF ME!!!
WE GOTCHA, BUDDY. EVERYTHING IS GOING TO BE OKAY.
IS THAT A COLONIST?
THEY LOOK LIKE THEY'VE BEEN DEAD FOR WEEKS.
VKRAH! VKRAH!
WHAT THE HELL WAS THAT?
I'M TRYING VERY HARD TO NOT CRAP MY PANTS.

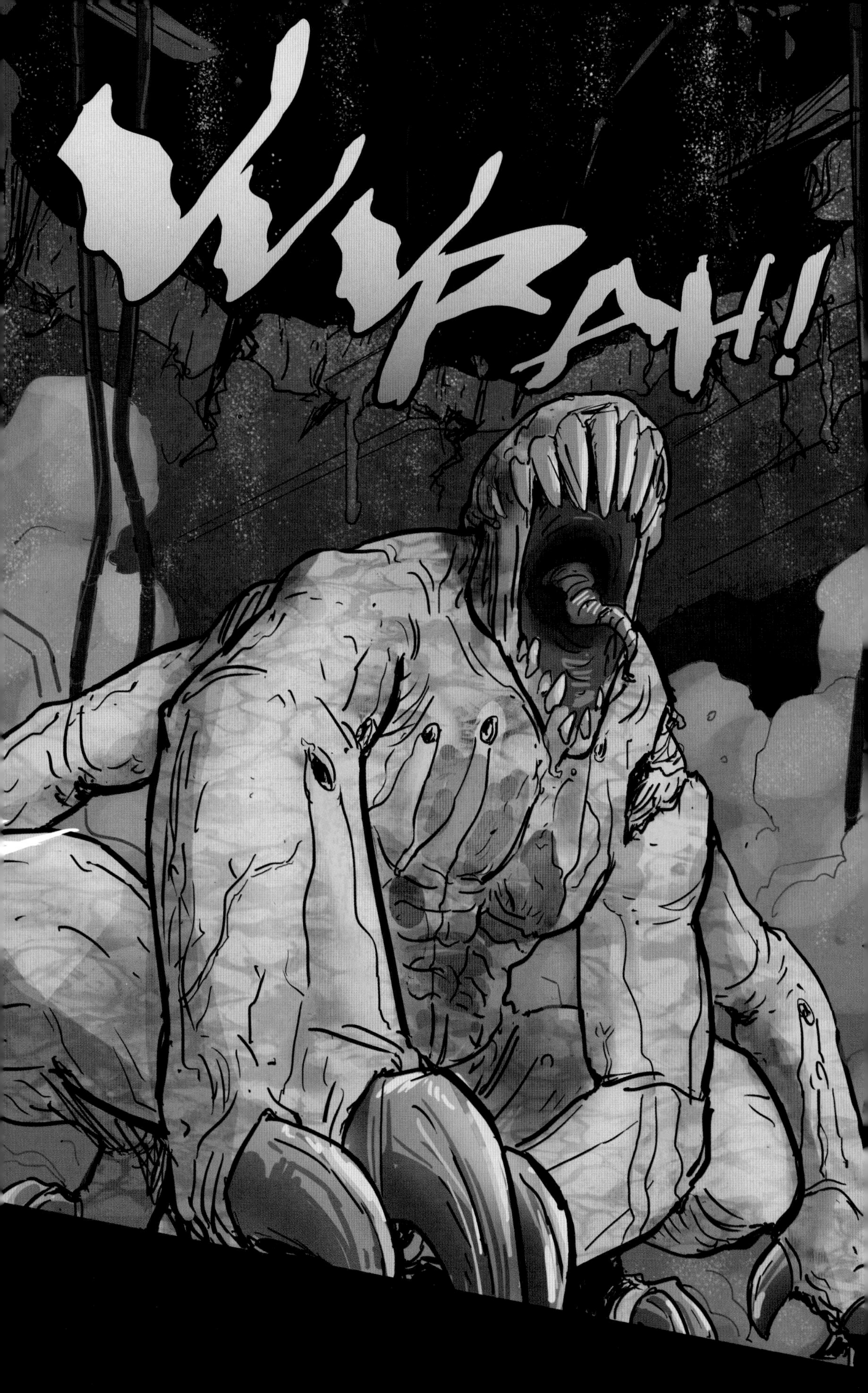
WRAH!

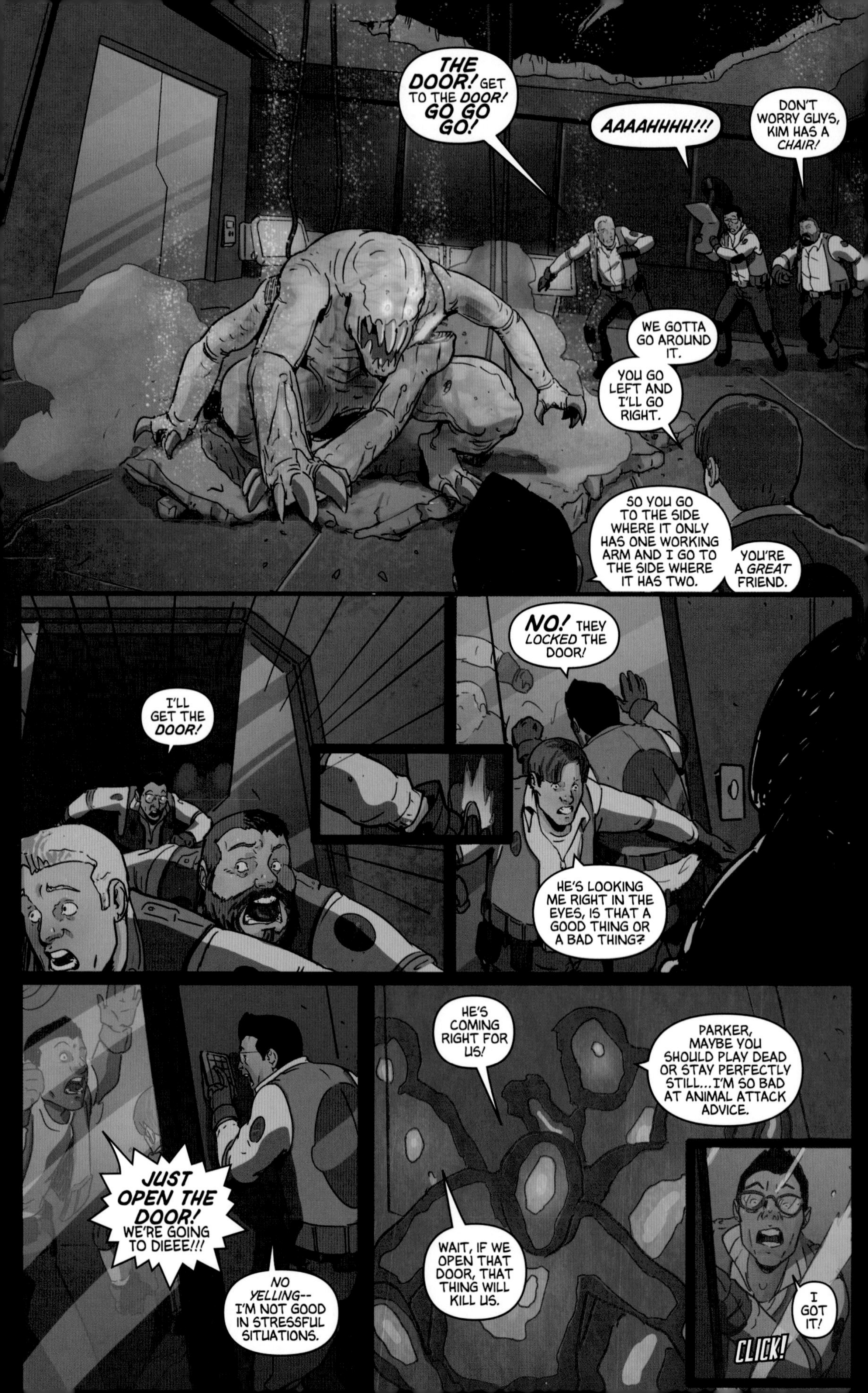
THE DOOR! GET TO THE DOOR! GO GO GO!
AAAAHHHH!!!
DON'T WORRY GUYS, KIM HAS A CHAIR!
WE GOTTA GO AROUND IT.
YOU GO LEFT AND I'LL GO RIGHT.
SO YOU GO TO THE SIDE WHERE IT ONLY HAS ONE WORKING ARM AND I GO TO THE SIDE WHERE IT HAS TWO.
YOU'RE A GREAT FRIEND.
I'LL GET THE DOOR!
NO! THEY LOCKED THE DOOR!
HE'S LOOKING ME RIGHT IN THE EYES, IS THAT A GOOD THING OR A BAD THING?
JUST OPEN THE DOOR! WE'RE GOING TO DIEEE!!!
NO YELLING-- I'M NOT GOOD IN STRESSFUL SITUATIONS.
HE'S COMING RIGHT FOR US!
PARKER, MAYBE YOU SHOULD PLAY DEAD OR STAY PERFECTLY STILL... I'M SO BAD AT ANIMAL ATTACK ADVICE.
WAIT, IF WE OPEN THAT DOOR, THAT THING WILL KILL US.
I GOT IT!
CLICK!

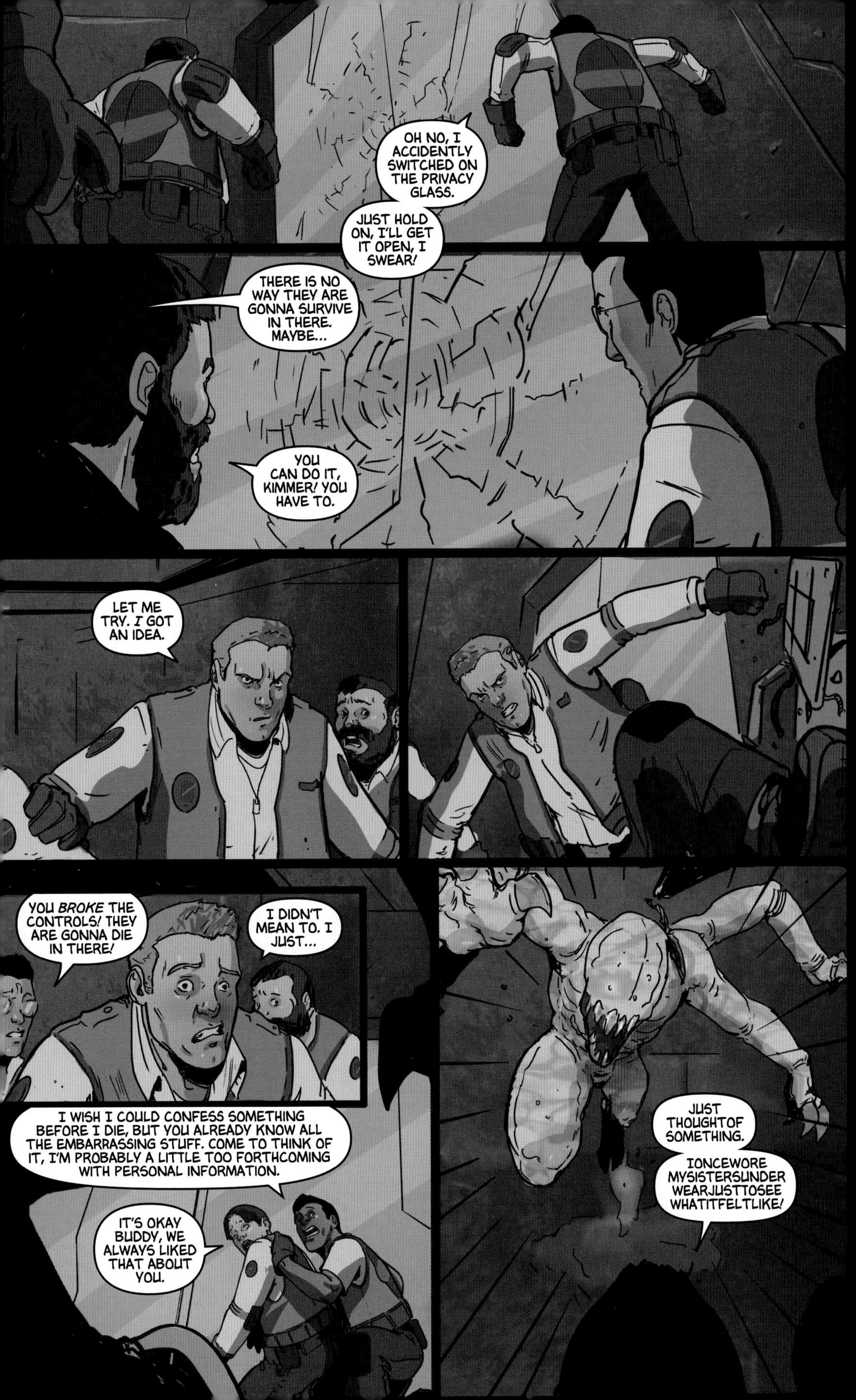
OH NO, I ACCIDENTLY SWITCHED ON THE PRIVACY GLASS.
JUST HOLD ON, I'LL GET IT OPEN, I SWEAR!
THERE IS NO WAY THEY ARE GONNA SURVIVE IN THERE. MAYBE...
YOU CAN DO IT, KIMMER! YOU HAVE TO.
LET ME TRY. *I* GOT AN IDEA.
YOU *BROKE* THE CONTROLS! THEY ARE GONNA DIE IN THERE!
I DIDN'T MEAN TO. I JUST...
I WISH I COULD CONFESS SOMETHING BEFORE I DIE, BUT YOU ALREADY KNOW ALL THE EMBARRASSING STUFF. COME TO THINK OF IT, I'M PROBABLY A LITTLE TOO FORTHCOMING WITH PERSONAL INFORMATION.
IT'S OKAY BUDDY, WE ALWAYS LIKED THAT ABOUT YOU.
JUST THOUGHTOF SOMETHING.
IONCEWORE MYSISTERSUNDER WEARJUSTTOSEE WHATITFELTLIKE!

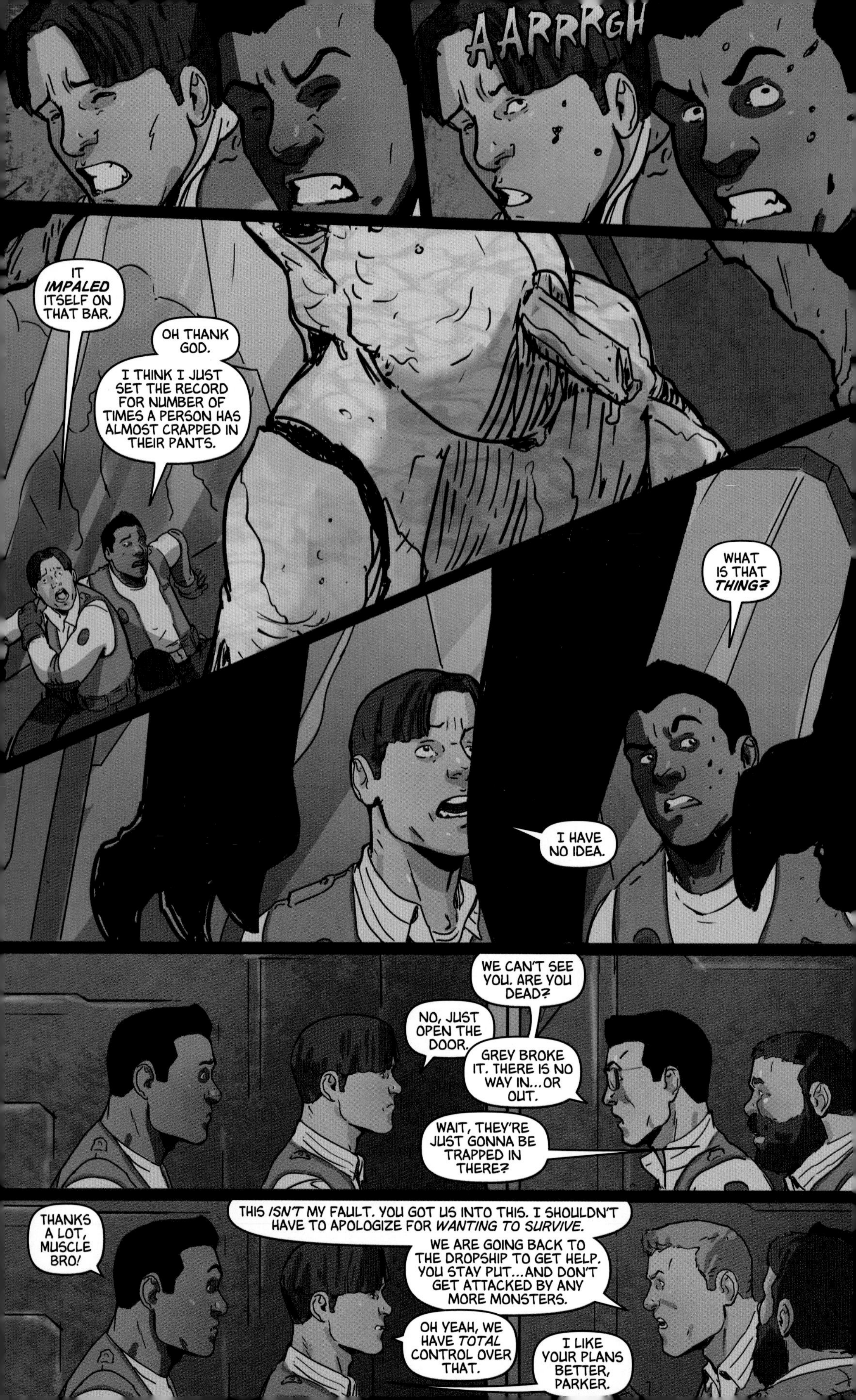
AARRRGH
IT *IMPALED* ITSELF ON THAT BAR.
OH THANK GOD.
I THINK I JUST SET THE RECORD FOR NUMBER OF TIMES A PERSON HAS ALMOST CRAPPED IN THEIR PANTS.
WHAT IS THAT *THING?*
I HAVE NO IDEA.
WE CAN'T SEE YOU. ARE YOU DEAD?
NO, JUST OPEN THE DOOR.
GREY BROKE IT. THERE IS NO WAY IN...OR OUT.
WAIT, THEY'RE JUST GONNA BE TRAPPED IN THERE?
THANKS A LOT, MUSCLE BRO!
THIS *ISN'T* MY FAULT. YOU GOT US INTO THIS. I SHOULDN'T HAVE TO APOLOGIZE FOR *WANTING TO SURVIVE.*
WE ARE GOING BACK TO THE DROPSHIP TO GET HELP. YOU STAY PUT...AND DON'T GET ATTACKED BY ANY MORE MONSTERS.
OH YEAH, WE HAVE *TOTAL* CONTROL OVER THAT.
I LIKE YOUR PLANS BETTER, PARKER.

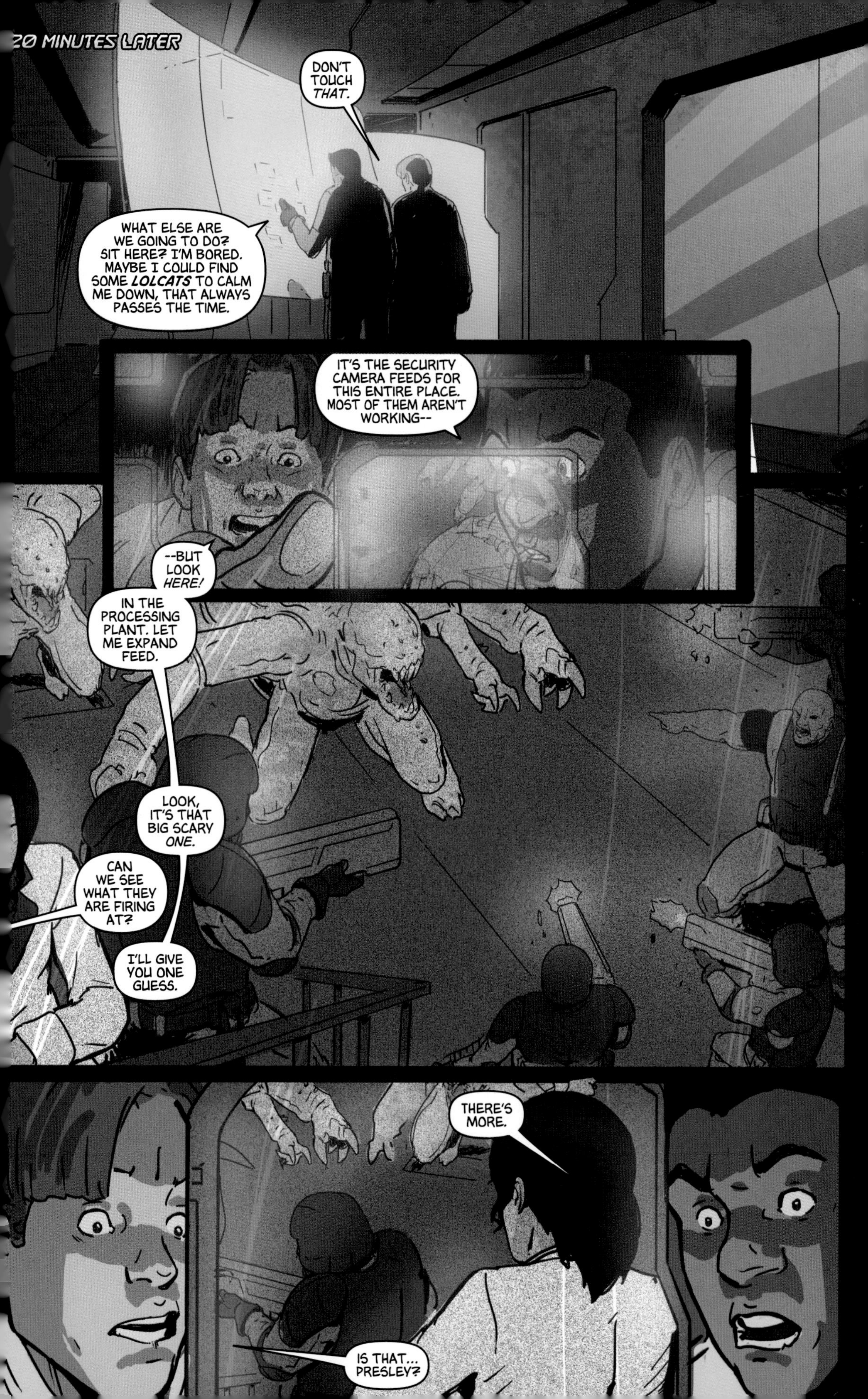
20 MINUTES LATER
DON'T TOUCH THAT.
WHAT ELSE ARE WE GOING TO DO? SIT HERE? I'M BORED. MAYBE I COULD FIND SOME LOLCATS TO CALM ME DOWN, THAT ALWAYS PASSES THE TIME.
IT'S THE SECURITY CAMERA FEEDS FOR THIS ENTIRE PLACE. MOST OF THEM AREN'T WORKING--
--BUT LOOK HERE!
IN THE PROCESSING PLANT. LET ME EXPAND FEED.
LOOK, IT'S THAT BIG SCARY ONE.
CAN WE SEE WHAT THEY ARE FIRING AT?
I'LL GIVE YOU ONE GUESS.
THERE'S MORE.
IS THAT... PRESLEY?

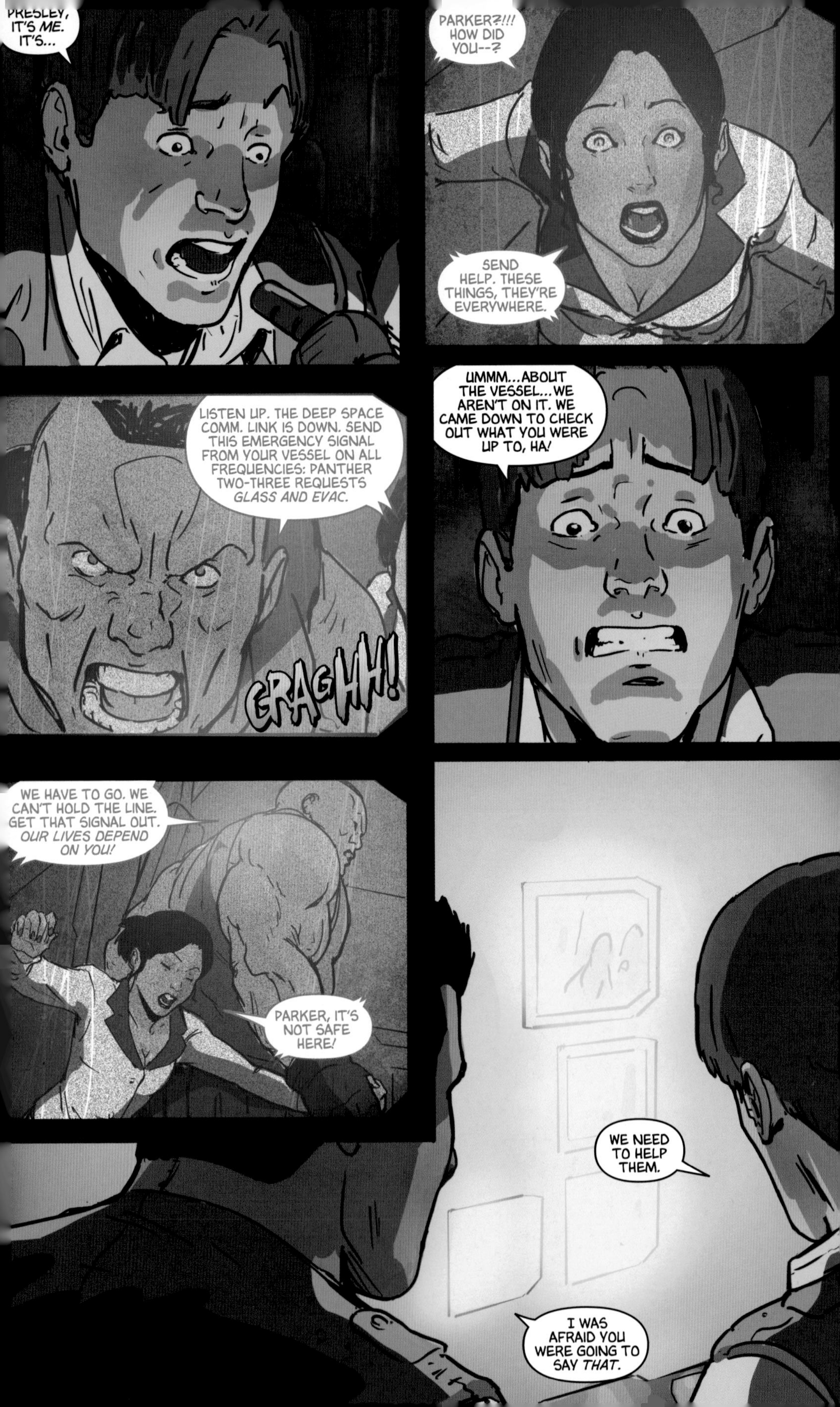
PRESLEY, IT'S ME. IT'S...
PARKER?!!! HOW DID YOU--?
SEND HELP. THESE THINGS, THEY'RE EVERYWHERE.
LISTEN UP. THE DEEP SPACE COMM. LINK IS DOWN. SEND THIS EMERGENCY SIGNAL FROM YOUR VESSEL ON ALL FREQUENCIES: PANTHER TWO-THREE REQUESTS GLASS AND EVAC.
CRAGHH!
UMMM...ABOUT THE VESSEL...WE AREN'T ON IT. WE CAME DOWN TO CHECK OUT WHAT YOU WERE UP TO, HA!
WE HAVE TO GO. WE CAN'T HOLD THE LINE. GET THAT SIGNAL OUT. OUR LIVES DEPEND ON YOU!
PARKER, IT'S NOT SAFE HERE!
WE NEED TO HELP THEM.
I WAS AFRAID YOU WERE GOING TO SAY THAT.

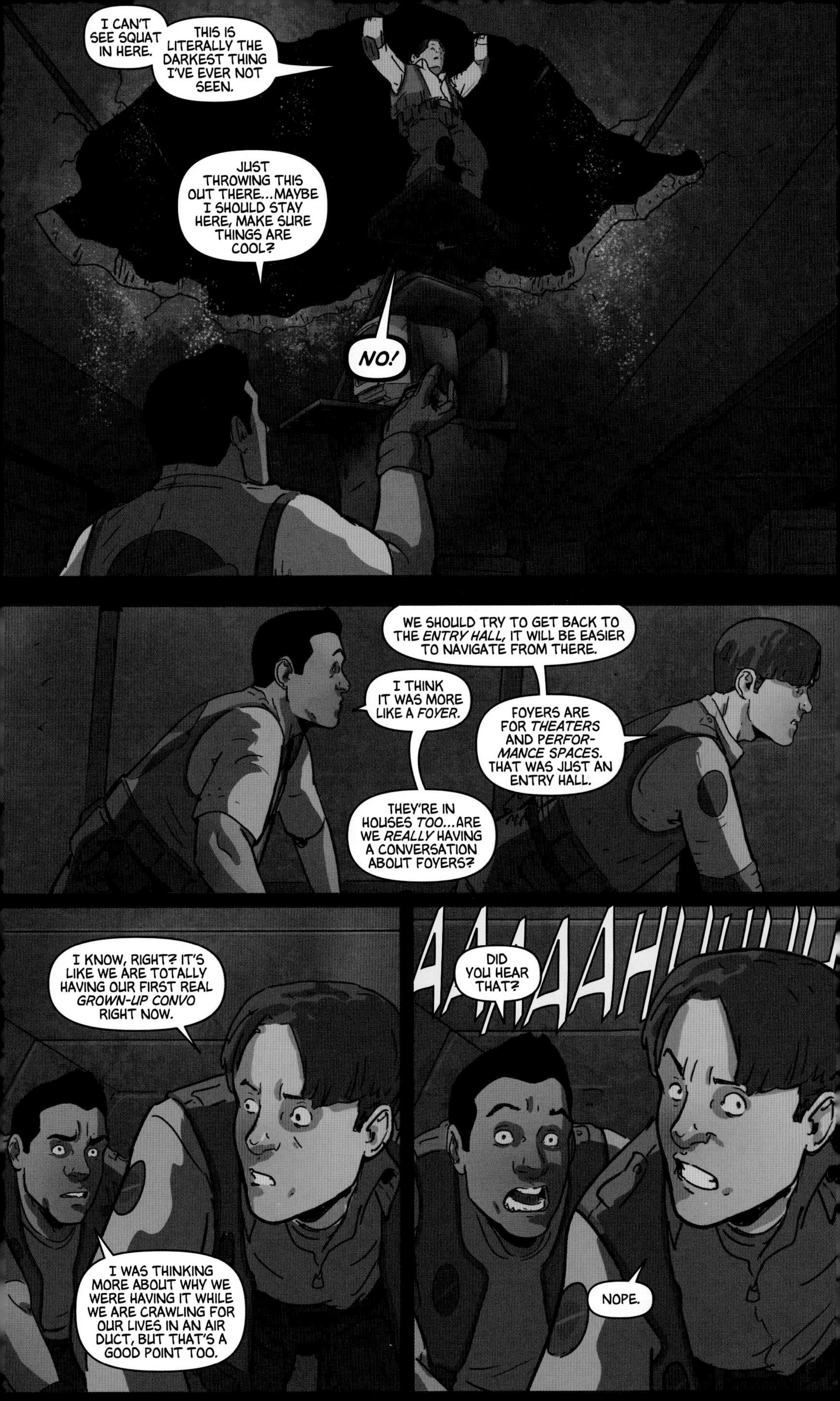

I CAN'T SEE SQUAT IN HERE.
THIS IS LITERALLY THE DARKEST THING I'VE EVER NOT SEEN.
JUST THROWING THIS OUT THERE...MAYBE I SHOULD STAY HERE, MAKE SURE THINGS ARE COOL?
NO!
WE SHOULD TRY TO GET BACK TO THE *ENTRY HALL*, IT WILL BE EASIER TO NAVIGATE FROM THERE.
I THINK IT WAS MORE LIKE A *FOYER*.
FOYERS ARE FOR *THEATERS* AND *PERFORMANCE SPACES*. THAT WAS JUST AN ENTRY HALL.
THEY'RE IN HOUSES *TOO*...ARE WE *REALLY* HAVING A CONVERSATION ABOUT FOYERS?
I KNOW, RIGHT? IT'S LIKE WE ARE TOTALLY HAVING OUR FIRST REAL *GROWN-UP CONVO* RIGHT NOW.
I WAS THINKING MORE ABOUT WHY WE WERE HAVING IT WHILE WE ARE CRAWLING FOR OUR LIVES IN AN AIR DUCT, BUT THAT'S A GOOD POINT TOO.
AAAAAHHUUUU
DID YOU HEAR THAT?
NOPE.

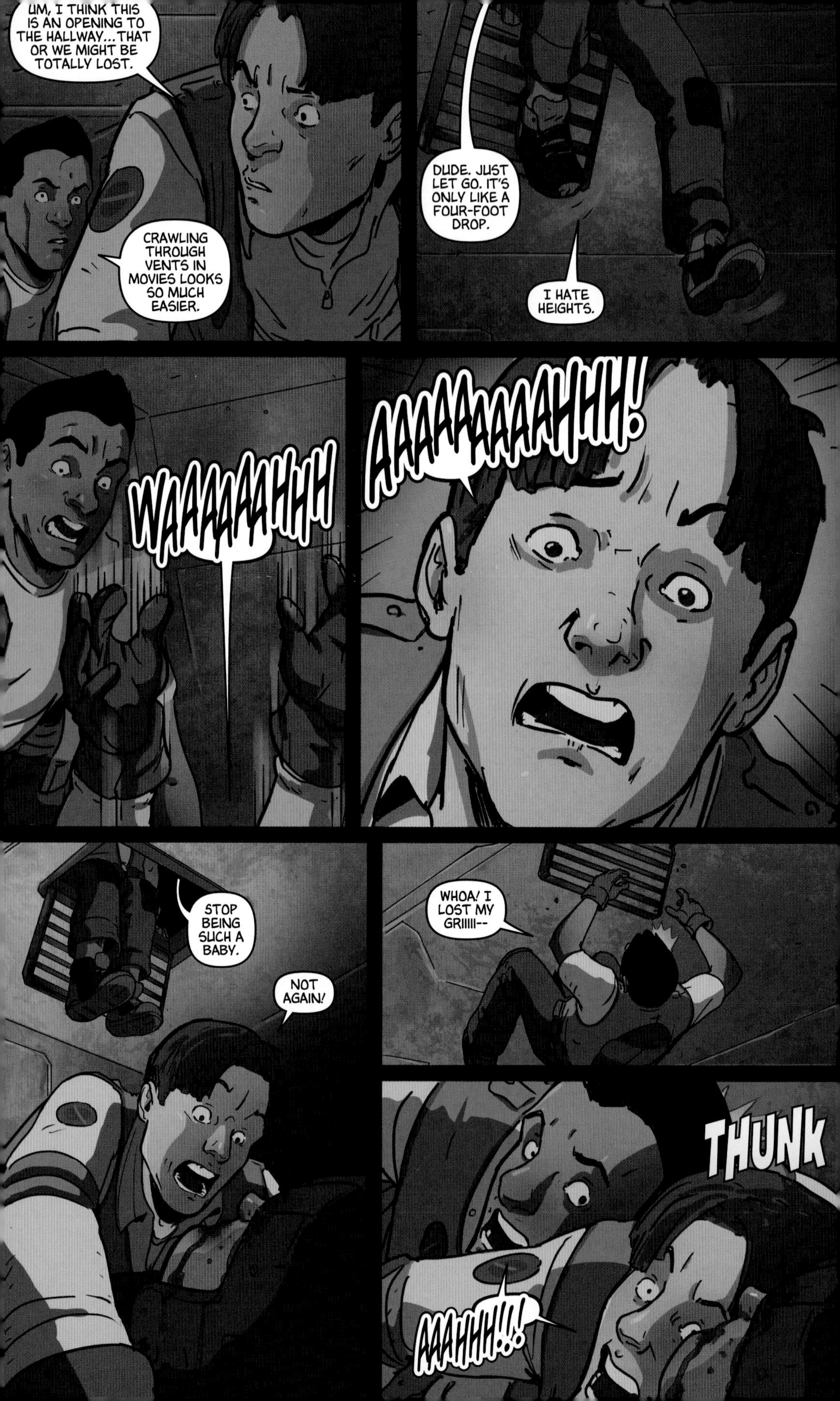
UM, I THINK THIS IS AN OPENING TO THE HALLWAY...THAT OR WE MIGHT BE TOTALLY LOST.
CRAWLING THROUGH VENTS IN MOVIES LOOKS SO MUCH EASIER.
DUDE. JUST LET GO. IT'S ONLY LIKE A FOUR-FOOT DROP.
I HATE HEIGHTS.
WAAAAAAHHH
AAAAAAAAHHH!
STOP BEING SUCH A BABY.
NOT AGAIN!
WHOA! I LOST MY GRIIIII--
THUNK
AAAHHH!!!

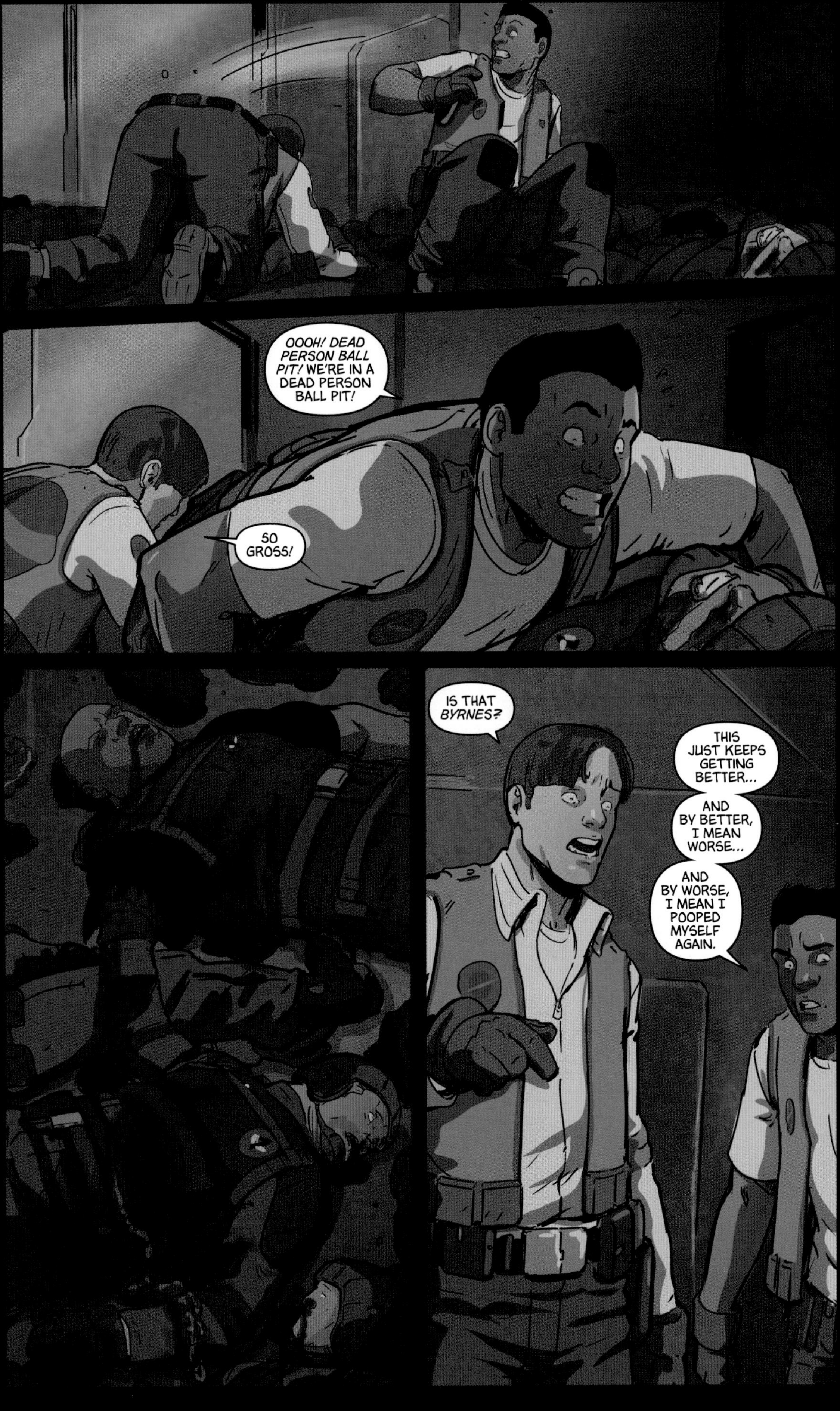
OOOH! DEAD PERSON BALL PIT! WE'RE IN A DEAD PERSON BALL PIT!
SO GROSS!
IS THAT *BYRNES?*
THIS JUST KEEPS GETTING BETTER...
AND BY BETTER, I MEAN WORSE...
AND BY WORSE, I MEAN I POOPED MYSELF AGAIN.

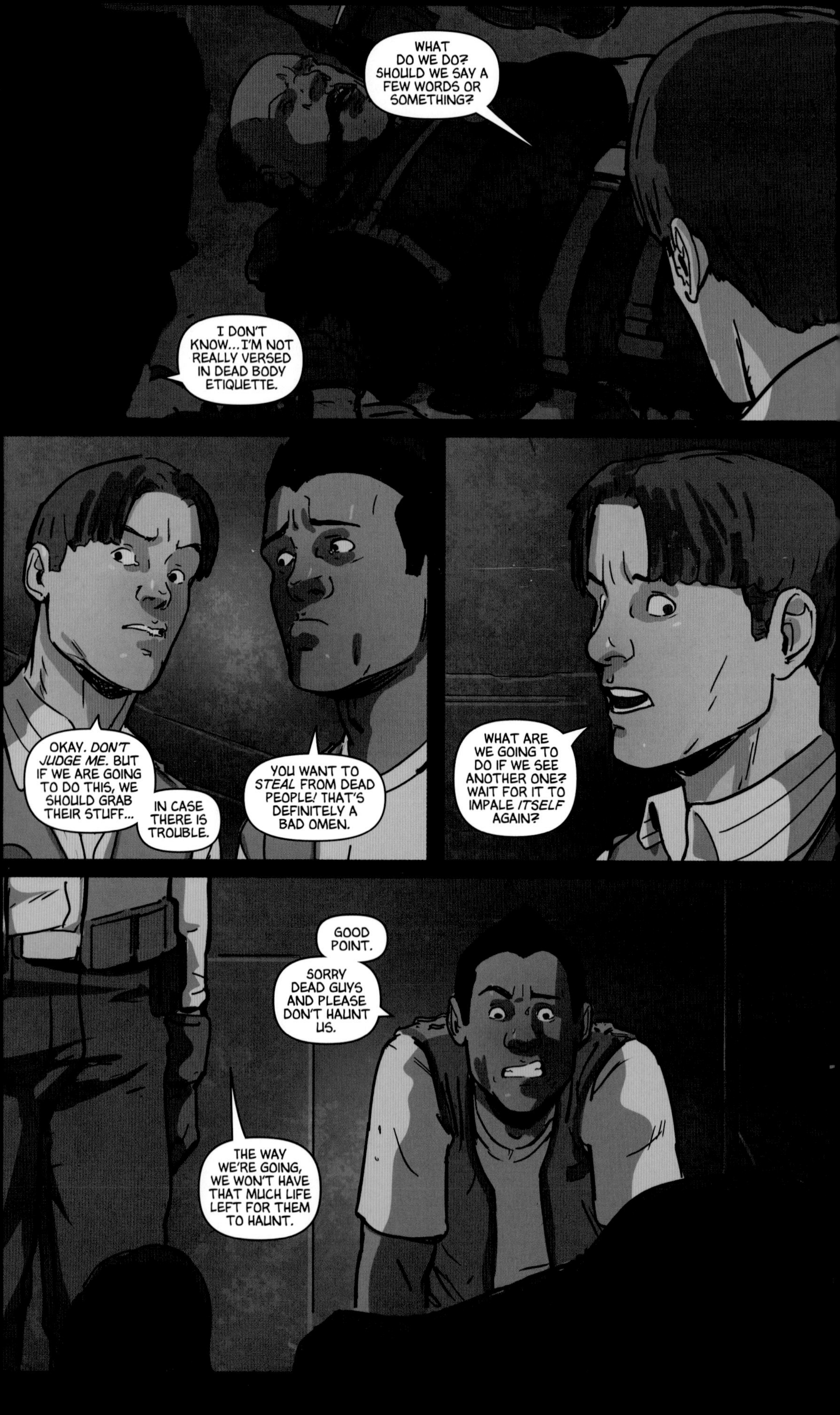
WHAT DO WE DO? SHOULD WE SAY A FEW WORDS OR SOMETHING?
I DON'T KNOW... I'M NOT REALLY VERSED IN DEAD BODY ETIQUETTE.
OKAY. *DON'T JUDGE ME.* BUT IF WE ARE GOING TO DO THIS, WE SHOULD GRAB THEIR STUFF...
IN CASE THERE IS TROUBLE.
YOU WANT TO *STEAL* FROM DEAD PEOPLE! THAT'S DEFINITELY A BAD OMEN.
WHAT ARE WE GOING TO DO IF WE SEE ANOTHER ONE? WAIT FOR IT TO IMPALE *ITSELF* AGAIN?
GOOD POINT.
SORRY DEAD GUYS AND PLEASE DON'T HAUNT US.
THE WAY WE'RE GOING, WE WON'T HAVE THAT MUCH LIFE LEFT FOR THEM TO HAUNT.

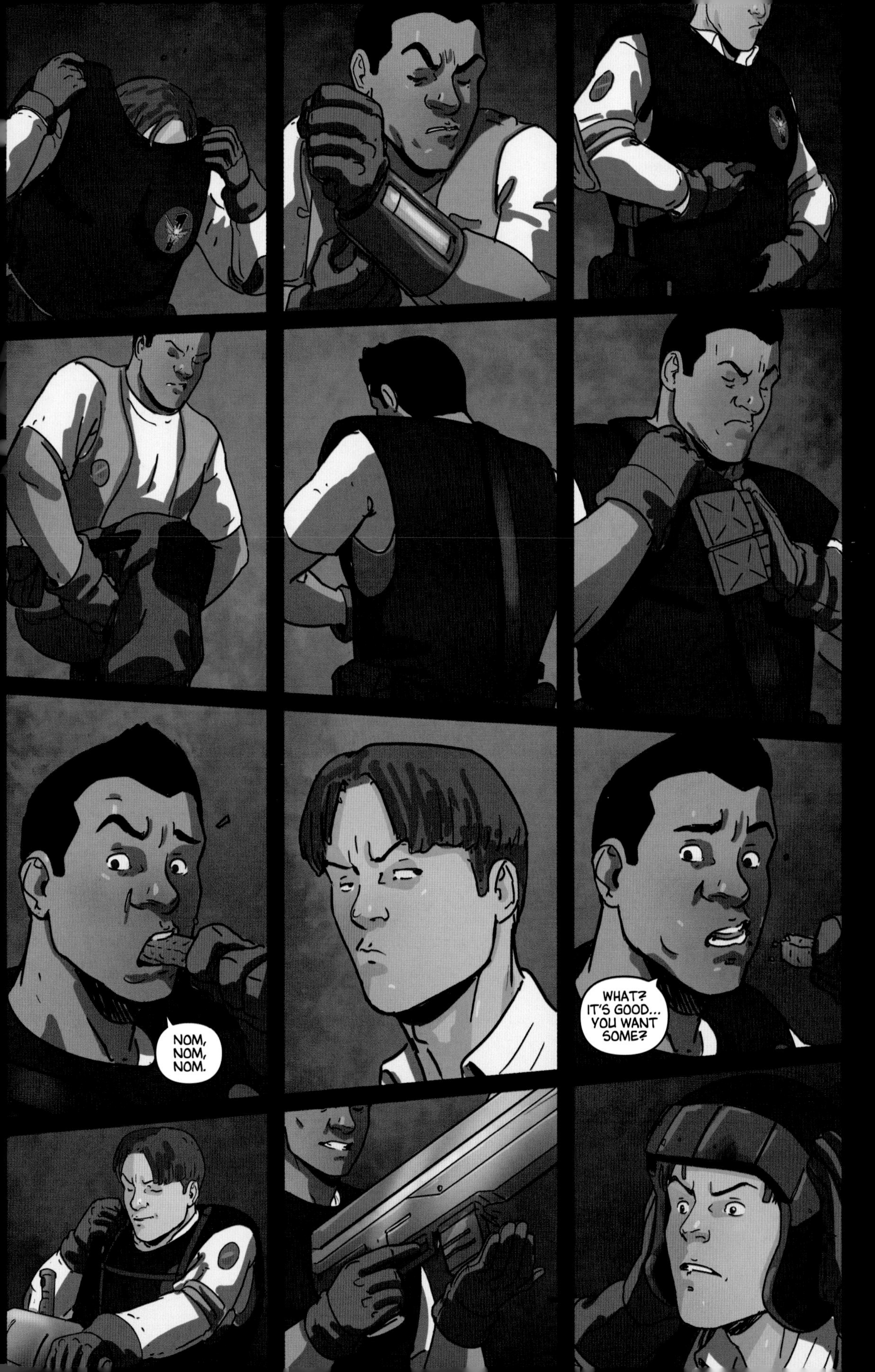
NOM, NOM, NOM.
WHAT? IT'S GOOD... YOU WANT SOME?

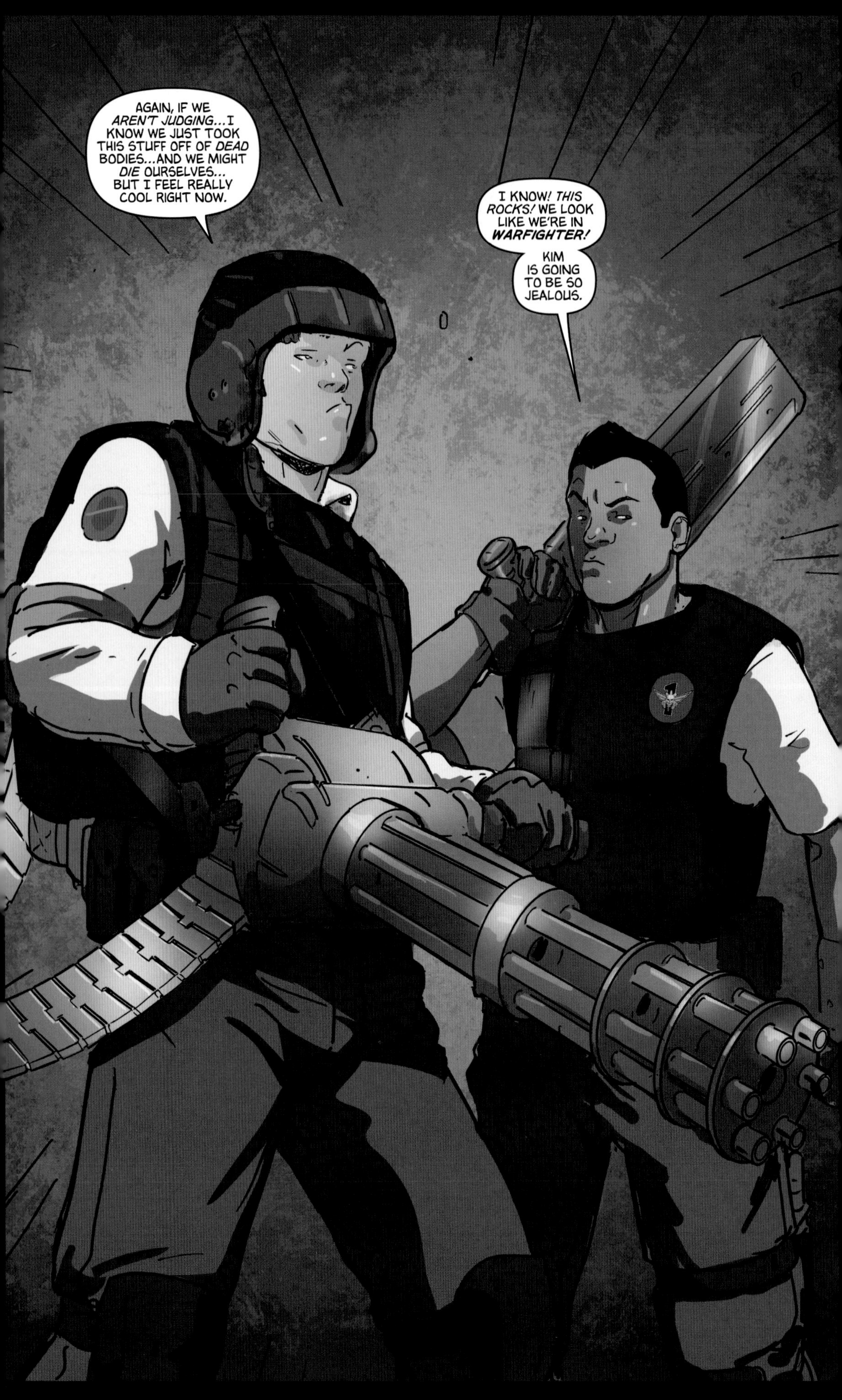
AGAIN, IF WE *AREN'T JUDGING*... I KNOW WE JUST TOOK THIS STUFF OFF OF *DEAD* BODIES...AND WE MIGHT *DIE* OURSELVES... BUT I FEEL REALLY COOL RIGHT NOW.
I KNOW! *THIS ROCKS!* WE LOOK LIKE WE'RE IN ***WARFIGHTER!***
KIM IS GOING TO BE SO JEALOUS.

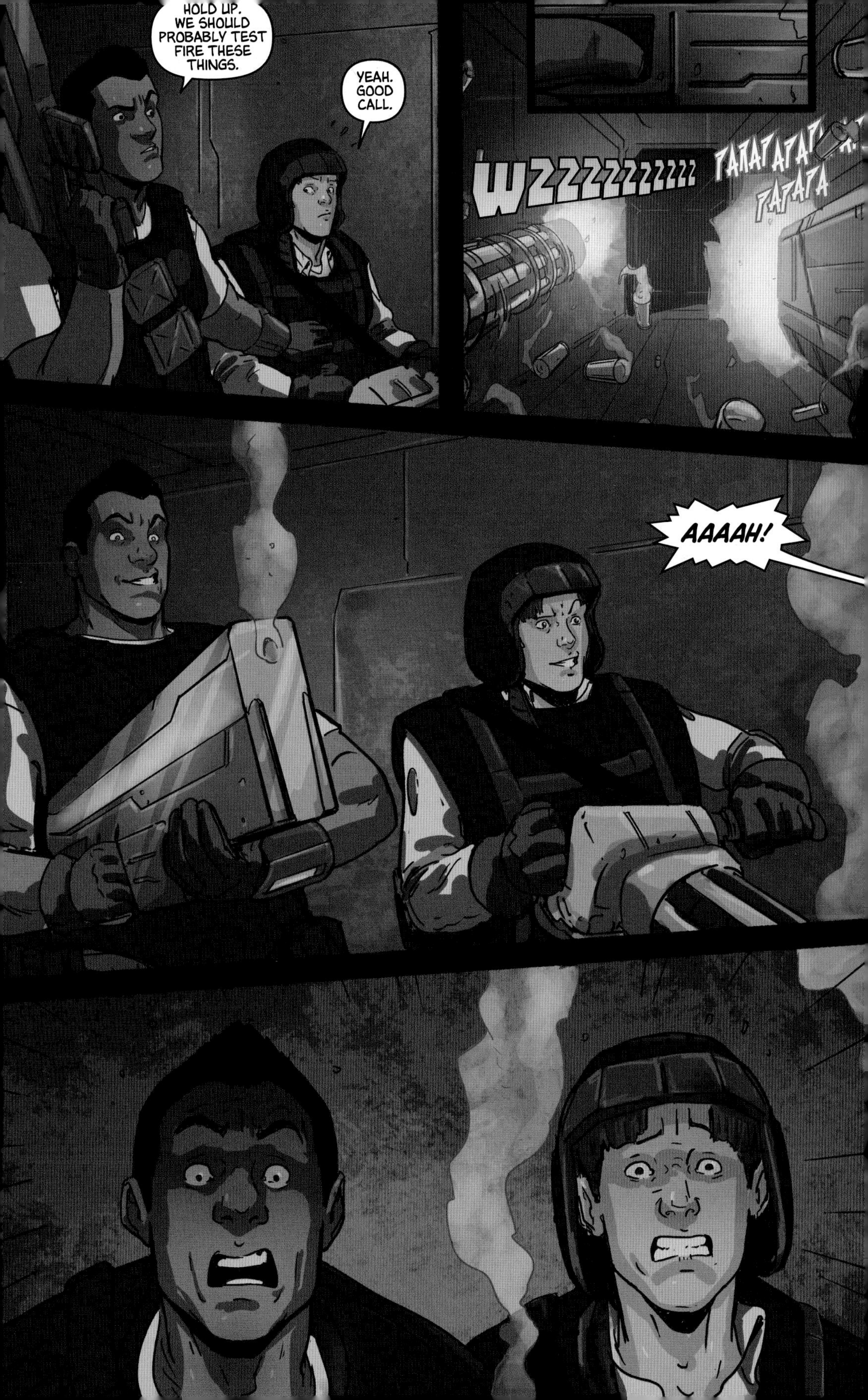
HOLD UP. WE SHOULD PROBABLY TEST FIRE THESE THINGS.
YEAH. GOOD CALL.
WZZZZZZZZZZZ
PARAPAPA
PAPAPA
AAAAH!

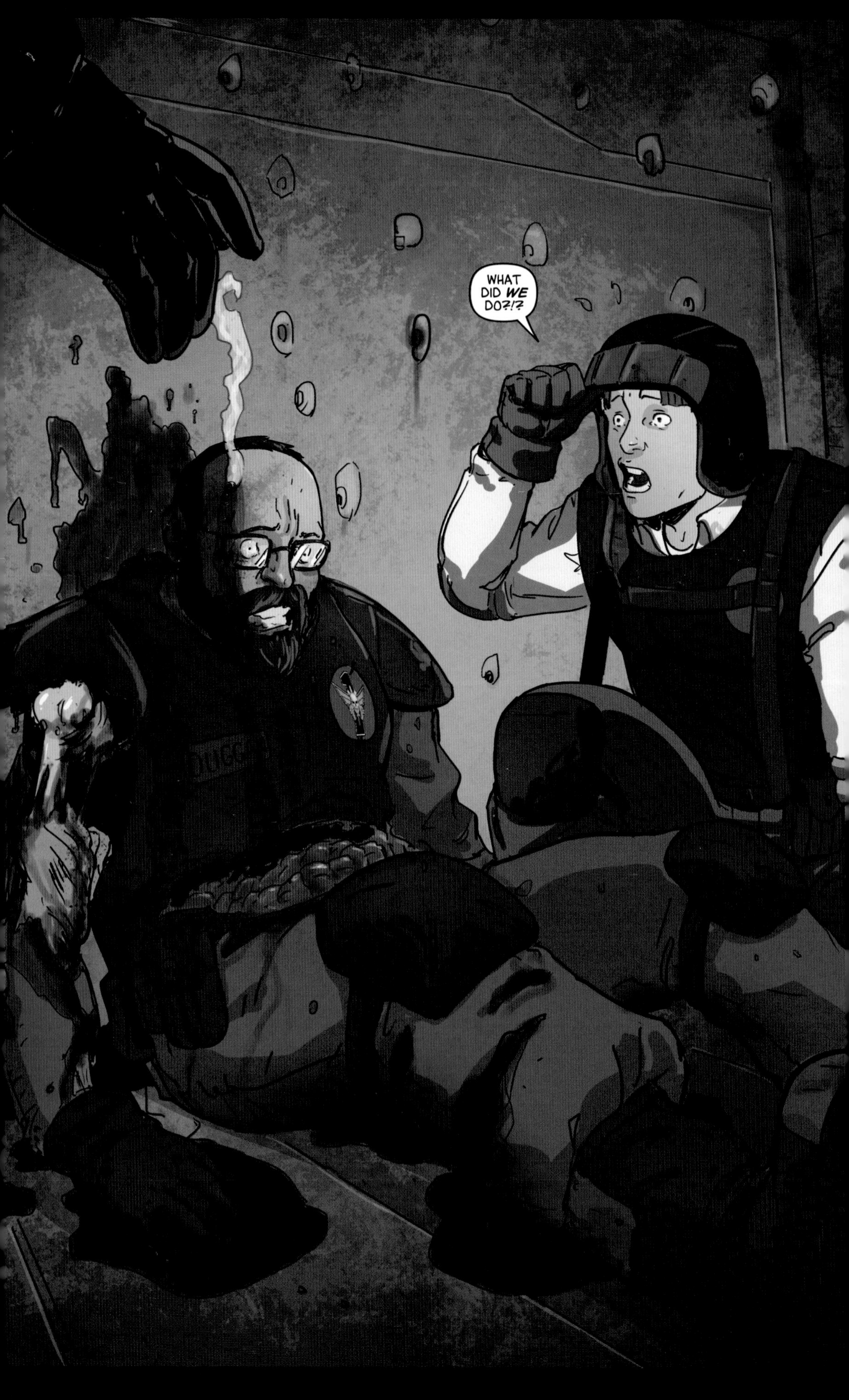
WHAT DID WE DO?!?

SPACE-EX

"We know how to handle your package."

Chapter Three
COVER BY
MANUEL BRACCHI
COLORS BY STEPHEN DOWNER

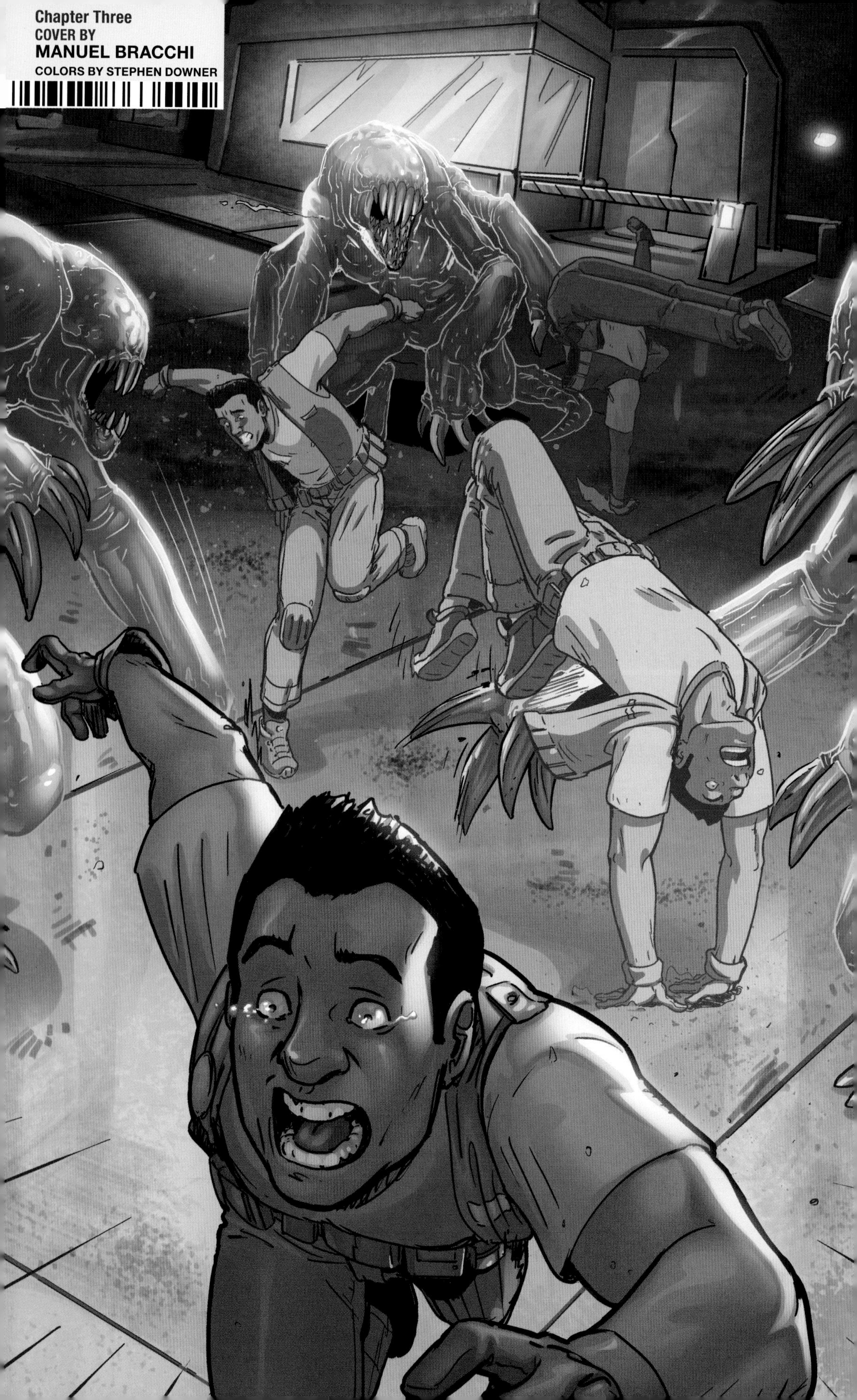

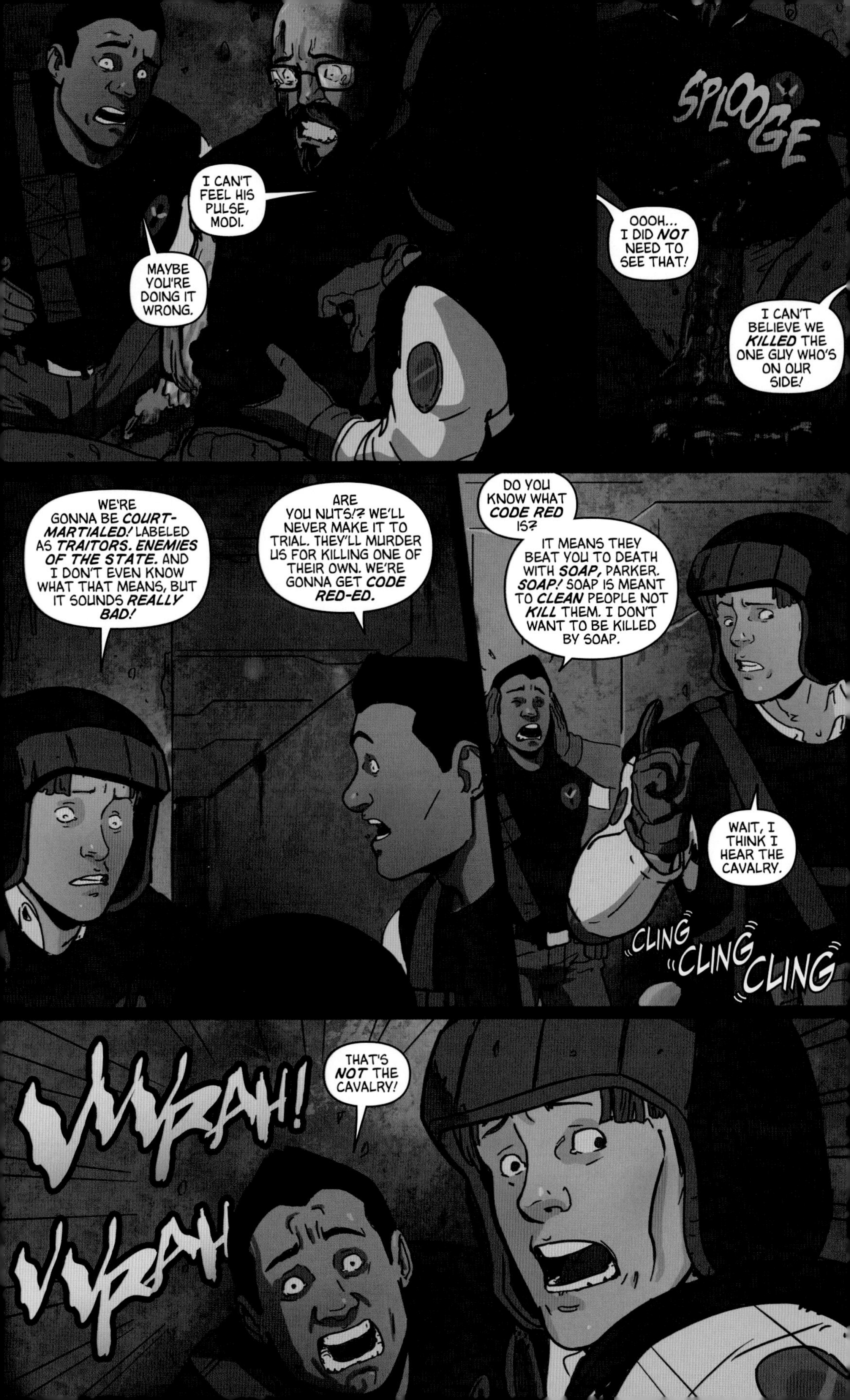
I CAN'T FEEL HIS PULSE, MODI.
MAYBE YOU'RE DOING IT WRONG.
SPLOOGE
OOOH... I DID NOT NEED TO SEE THAT!
I CAN'T BELIEVE WE KILLED THE ONE GUY WHO'S ON OUR SIDE!
WE'RE GONNA BE COURT-MARTIALED! LABELED AS TRAITORS. ENEMIES OF THE STATE. AND I DON'T EVEN KNOW WHAT THAT MEANS, BUT IT SOUNDS REALLY BAD!
ARE YOU NUTS!? WE'LL NEVER MAKE IT TO TRIAL. THEY'LL MURDER US FOR KILLING ONE OF THEIR OWN. WE'RE GONNA GET CODE RED-ED.
DO YOU KNOW WHAT CODE RED IS?
IT MEANS THEY BEAT YOU TO DEATH WITH SOAP, PARKER. SOAP! SOAP IS MEANT TO CLEAN PEOPLE NOT KILL THEM. I DON'T WANT TO BE KILLED BY SOAP.
WAIT, I THINK I HEAR THE CAVALRY.
CLING CLING CLING
VVRAH!
THAT'S NOT THE CAVALRY!
VVRAH

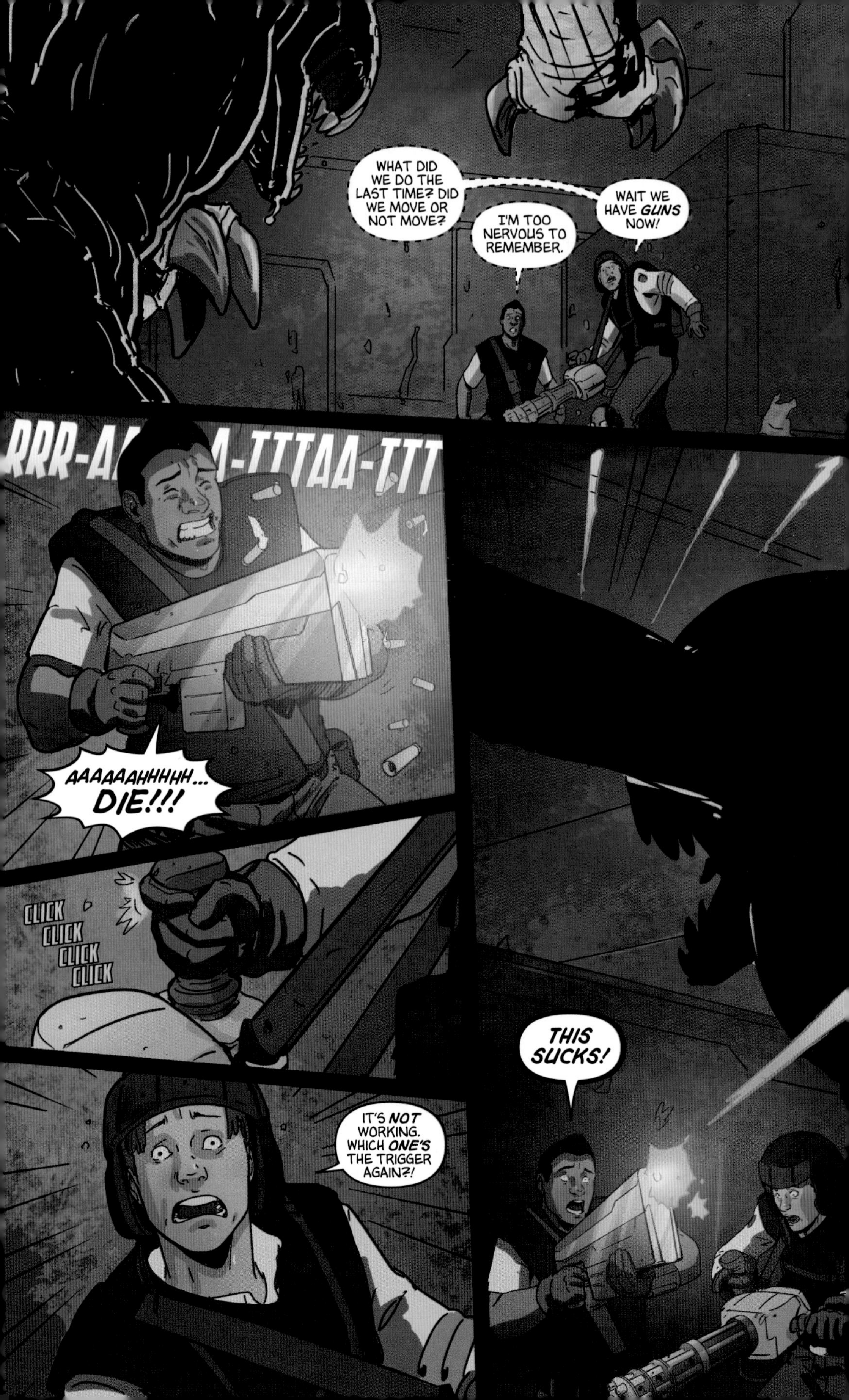

WHAT DID WE DO THE LAST TIME? DID WE MOVE OR NOT MOVE?
I'M TOO NERVOUS TO REMEMBER.
WAIT WE HAVE GUNS NOW!
AAAAAAHHHHH... DIE!!!
CLICK CLICK CLICK CLICK
IT'S NOT WORKING. WHICH ONE'S THE TRIGGER AGAIN?!
THIS SUCKS!

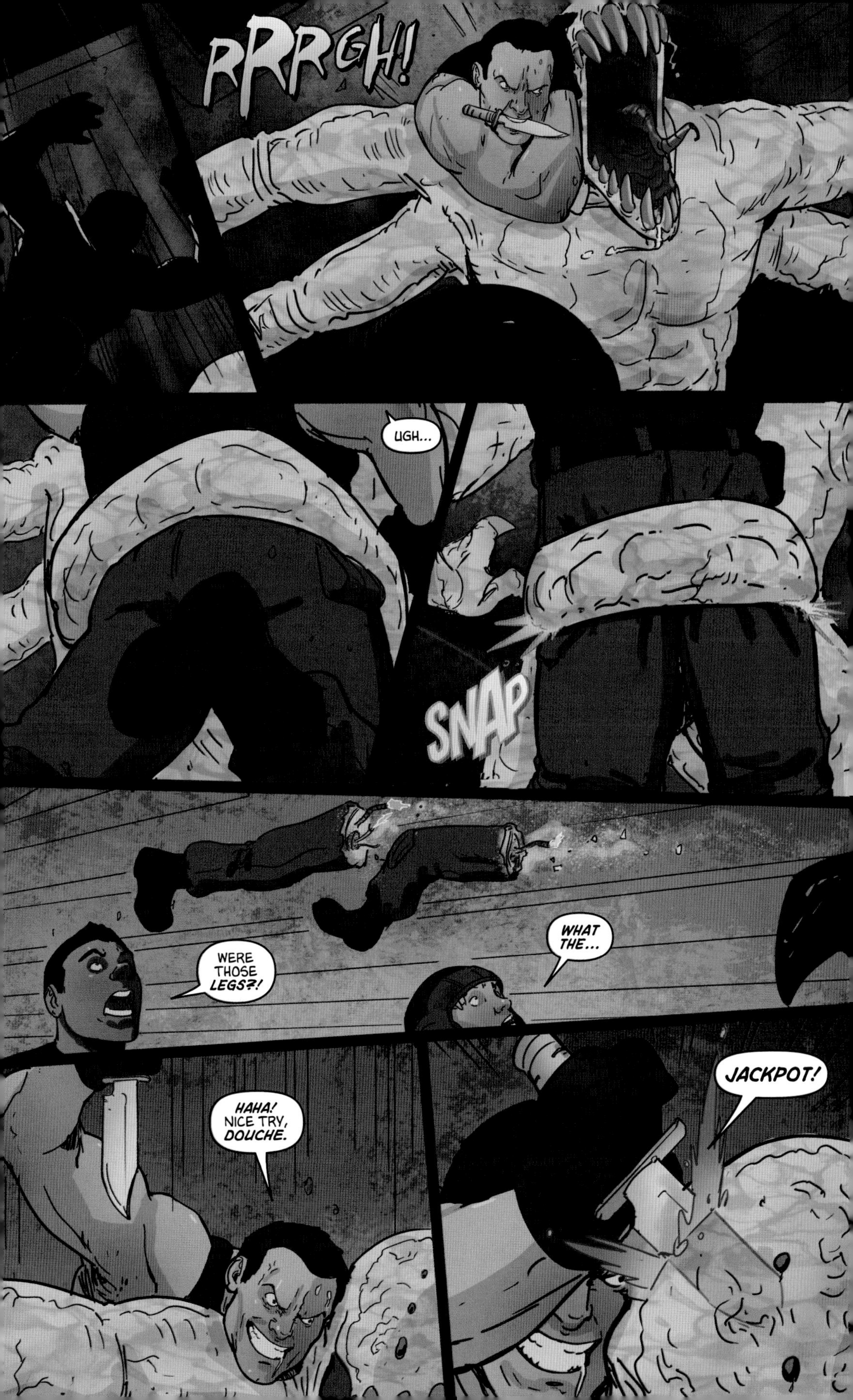
RRRGH!
UGH...
SNAP
WERE THOSE LEGS?!
WHAT THE...
HAHA! NICE TRY, DOUCHE.
JACKPOT!

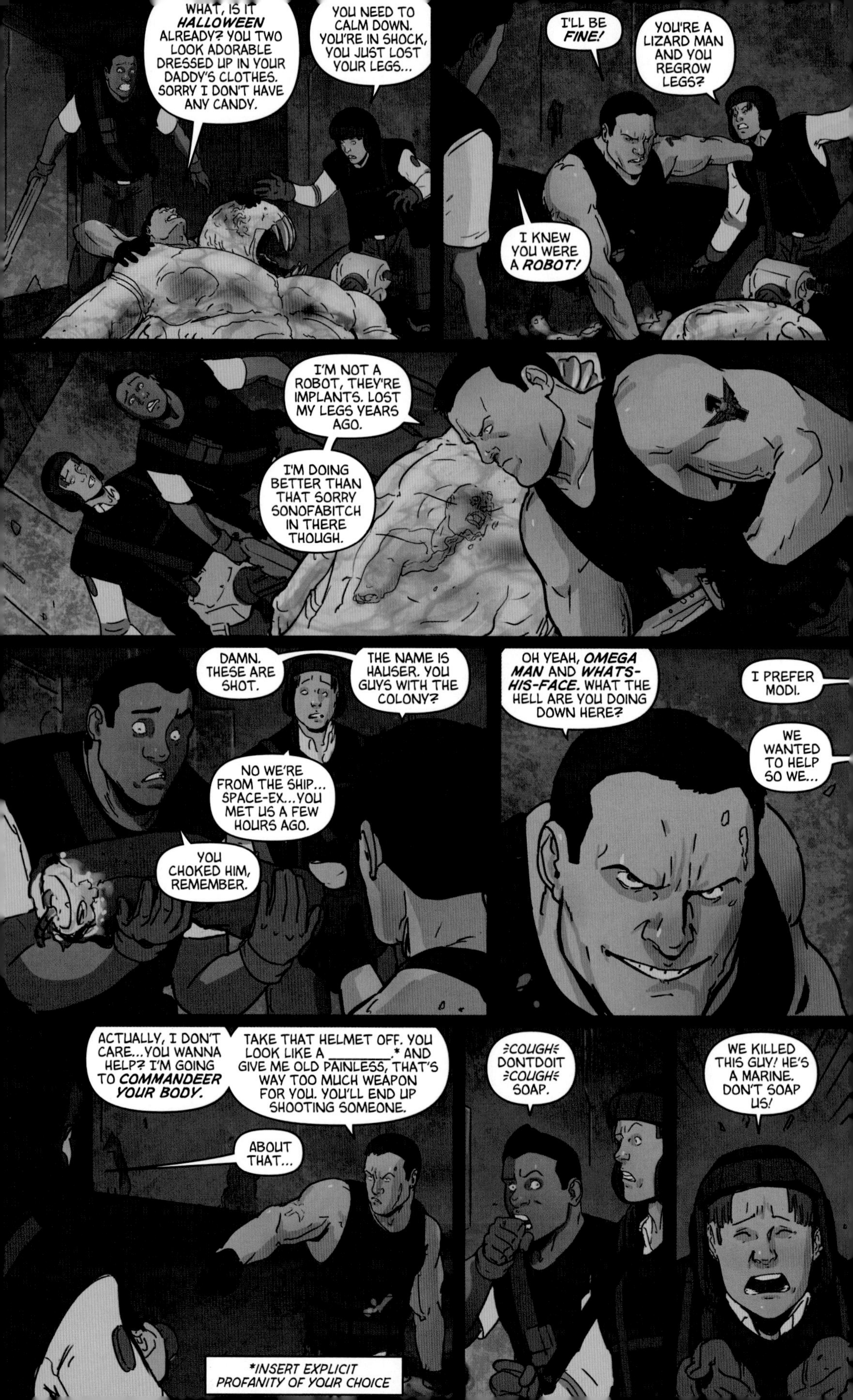
WHAT, IS IT HALLOWEEN ALREADY? YOU TWO LOOK ADORABLE DRESSED UP IN YOUR DADDY'S CLOTHES. SORRY I DON'T HAVE ANY CANDY.
YOU NEED TO CALM DOWN. YOU'RE IN SHOCK, YOU JUST LOST YOUR LEGS...
I'LL BE FINE!
YOU'RE A LIZARD MAN AND YOU REGROW LEGS?
I KNEW YOU WERE A ROBOT!
I'M NOT A ROBOT, THEY'RE IMPLANTS. LOST MY LEGS YEARS AGO.
I'M DOING BETTER THAN THAT SORRY SONOFABITCH IN THERE THOUGH.
DAMN. THESE ARE SHOT.
THE NAME IS HAUSER. YOU GUYS WITH THE COLONY?
NO WE'RE FROM THE SHIP... SPACE-EX...YOU MET US A FEW HOURS AGO.
YOU CHOKED HIM, REMEMBER.
OH YEAH, OMEGA MAN AND WHATS-HIS-FACE. WHAT THE HELL ARE YOU DOING DOWN HERE?
I PREFER MODI.
WE WANTED TO HELP SO WE...
ACTUALLY, I DON'T CARE...YOU WANNA HELP? I'M GOING TO COMMANDEER YOUR BODY.
TAKE THAT HELMET OFF. YOU LOOK LIKE A ________* AND GIVE ME OLD PAINLESS, THAT'S WAY TOO MUCH WEAPON FOR YOU. YOU'LL END UP SHOOTING SOMEONE.
ABOUT THAT...
*INSERT EXPLICIT PROFANITY OF YOUR CHOICE
COUGH DONTDOIT *COUGH* SOAP.
WE KILLED THIS GUY! HE'S A MARINE. DON'T SOAP US!

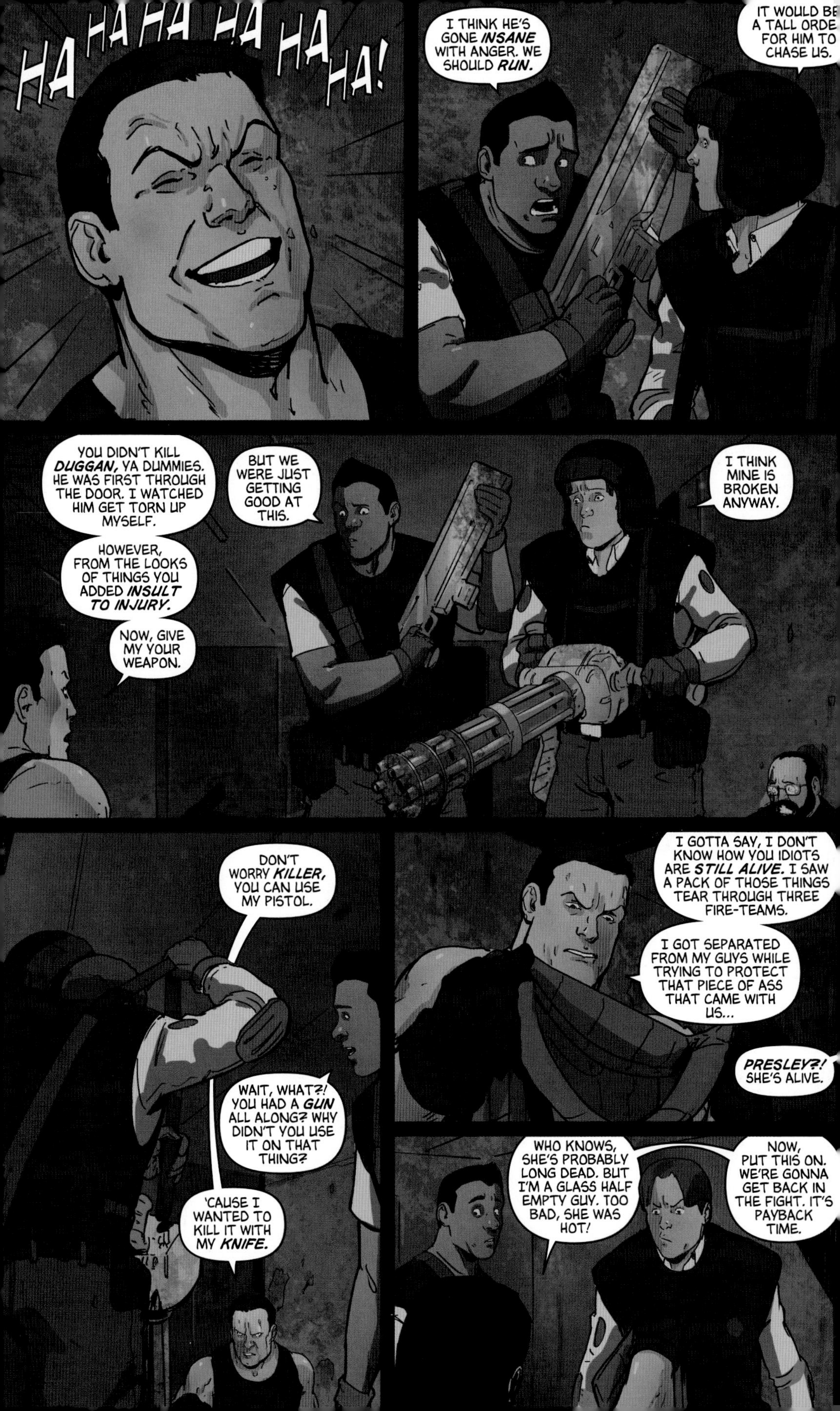
HA HA HA HA HA HA HA HA!
I THINK HE'S GONE INSANE WITH ANGER. WE SHOULD RUN.
IT WOULD BE A TALL ORDE FOR HIM TO CHASE US.
YOU DIDN'T KILL DUGGAN, YA DUMMIES. HE WAS FIRST THROUGH THE DOOR. I WATCHED HIM GET TORN UP MYSELF.
BUT WE WERE JUST GETTING GOOD AT THIS.
I THINK MINE IS BROKEN ANYWAY.
HOWEVER, FROM THE LOOKS OF THINGS YOU ADDED INSULT TO INJURY.
NOW, GIVE MY YOUR WEAPON.
DON'T WORRY KILLER, YOU CAN USE MY PISTOL.
WAIT, WHAT?! YOU HAD A GUN ALL ALONG? WHY DIDN'T YOU USE IT ON THAT THING?
'CAUSE I WANTED TO KILL IT WITH MY KNIFE.
I GOTTA SAY, I DON'T KNOW HOW YOU IDIOTS ARE STILL ALIVE. I SAW A PACK OF THOSE THINGS TEAR THROUGH THREE FIRE-TEAMS.
I GOT SEPARATED FROM MY GUYS WHILE TRYING TO PROTECT THAT PIECE OF ASS THAT CAME WITH US...
PRESLEY?! SHE'S ALIVE.
WHO KNOWS, SHE'S PROBABLY LONG DEAD. BUT I'M A GLASS HALF EMPTY GUY. TOO BAD, SHE WAS HOT!
NOW, PUT THIS ON. WE'RE GONNA GET BACK IN THE FIGHT. IT'S PAYBACK TIME.

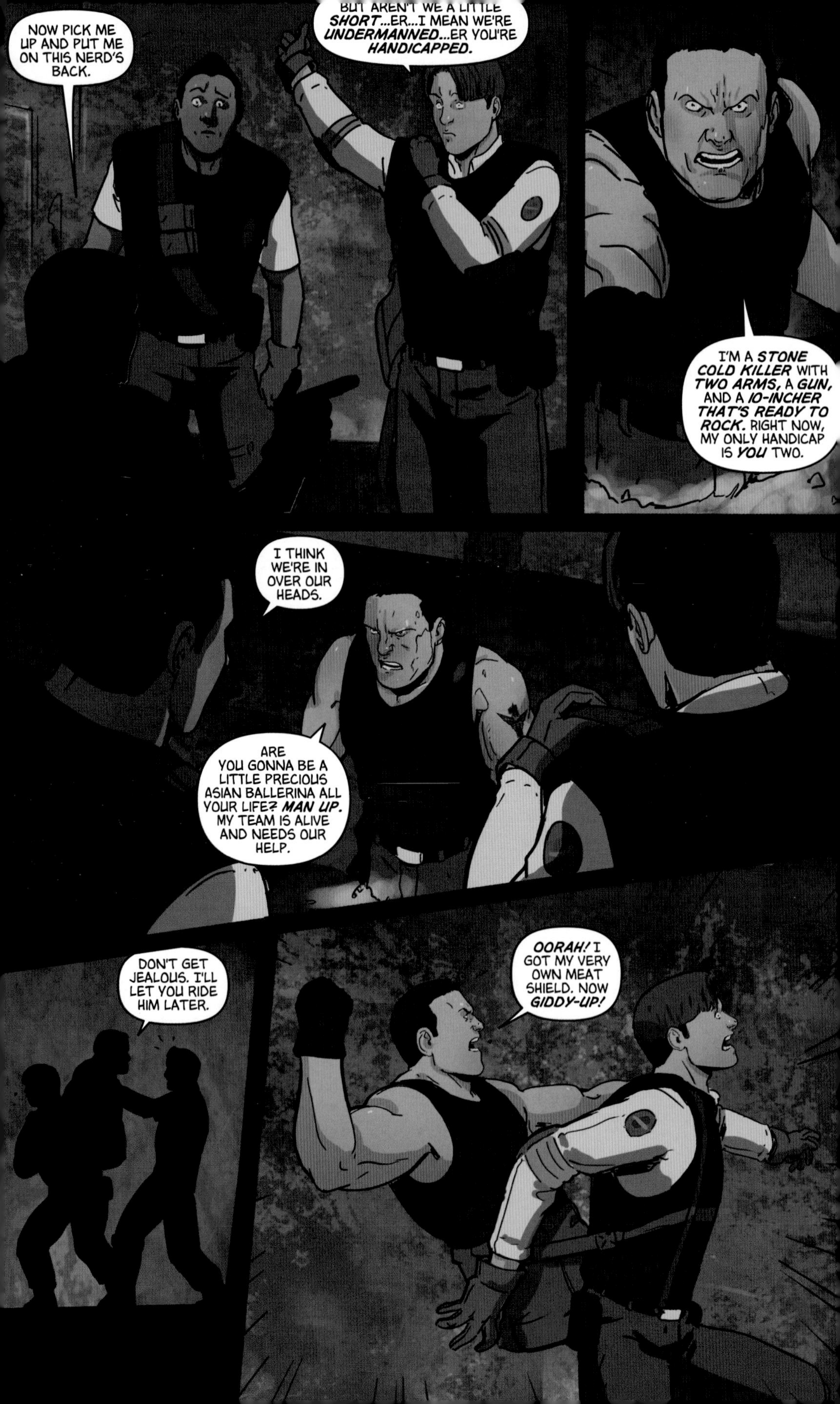
NOW PICK ME UP AND PUT ME ON THIS NERD'S BACK.
BUT AREN'T WE A LITTLE SHORT...ER...I MEAN WE'RE UNDERMANNED...ER YOU'RE HANDICAPPED.
I'M A STONE COLD KILLER WITH TWO ARMS, A GUN, AND A 10-INCHER THAT'S READY TO ROCK. RIGHT NOW, MY ONLY HANDICAP IS YOU TWO.
I THINK WE'RE IN OVER OUR HEADS.
ARE YOU GONNA BE A LITTLE PRECIOUS ASIAN BALLERINA ALL YOUR LIFE? MAN UP. MY TEAM IS ALIVE AND NEEDS OUR HELP.
DON'T GET JEALOUS. I'LL LET YOU RIDE HIM LATER.
OORAH! I GOT MY VERY OWN MEAT SHIELD. NOW GIDDY-UP!

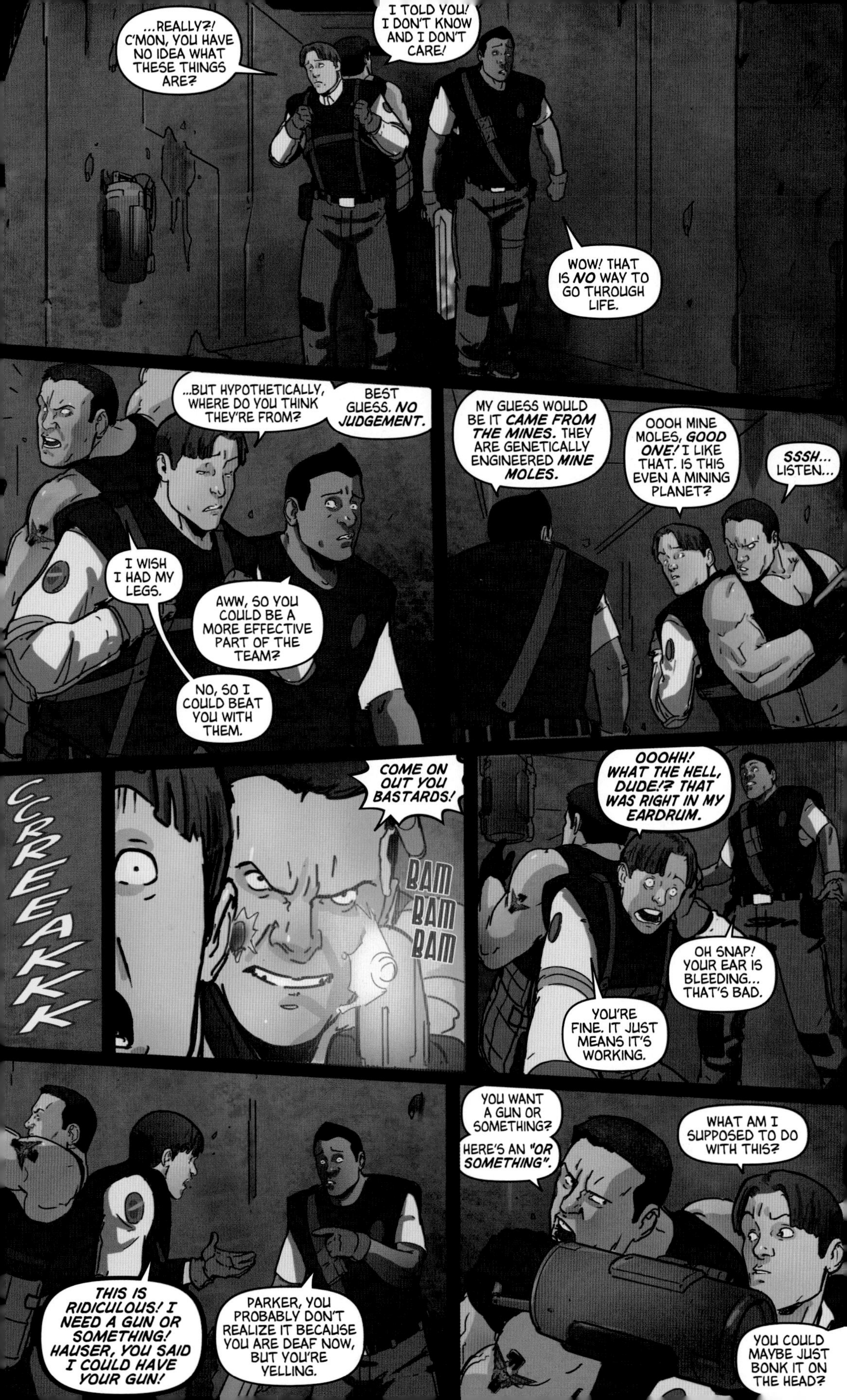
...REALLY?! C'MON, YOU HAVE NO IDEA WHAT THESE THINGS ARE?
I TOLD YOU! I DON'T KNOW AND I DON'T CARE!
WOW! THAT IS NO WAY TO GO THROUGH LIFE.
...BUT HYPOTHETICALLY, WHERE DO YOU THINK THEY'RE FROM?
BEST GUESS. NO JUDGEMENT.
I WISH I HAD MY LEGS.
AWW, SO YOU COULD BE A MORE EFFECTIVE PART OF THE TEAM?
NO, SO I COULD BEAT YOU WITH THEM.
MY GUESS WOULD BE IT CAME FROM THE MINES. THEY ARE GENETICALLY ENGINEERED MINE MOLES.
OOOH MINE MOLES, GOOD ONE! I LIKE THAT. IS THIS EVEN A MINING PLANET?
SSSH... LISTEN...
CCRREEEAKKK
COME ON OUT YOU BASTARDS!
BAM BAM BAM
OOOHH! WHAT THE HELL, DUDE!? THAT WAS RIGHT IN MY EARDRUM.
OH SNAP! YOUR EAR IS BLEEDING... THAT'S BAD.
YOU'RE FINE. IT JUST MEANS IT'S WORKING.
THIS IS RIDICULOUS! I NEED A GUN OR SOMETHING! HAUSER, YOU SAID I COULD HAVE YOUR GUN!
PARKER, YOU PROBABLY DON'T REALIZE IT BECAUSE YOU ARE DEAF NOW, BUT YOU'RE YELLING.
YOU WANT A GUN OR SOMETHING?
HERE'S AN "OR SOMETHING".
WHAT AM I SUPPOSED TO DO WITH THIS?
YOU COULD MAYBE JUST BONK IT ON THE HEAD?

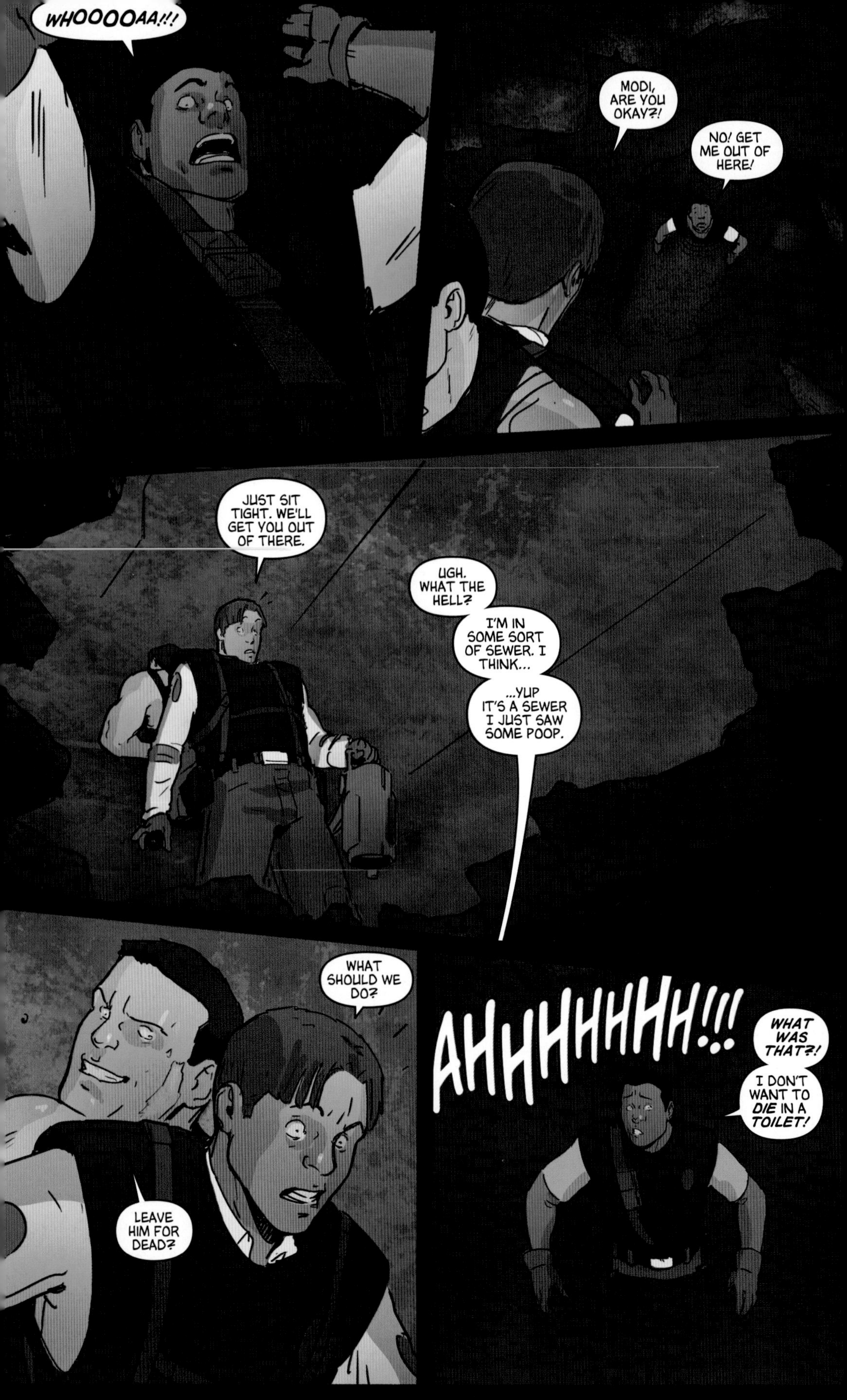
WHOOOOAA!!!
MODI, ARE YOU OKAY?!
NO! GET ME OUT OF HERE!
JUST SIT TIGHT. WE'LL GET YOU OUT OF THERE.
UGH. WHAT THE HELL?
I'M IN SOME SORT OF SEWER. I THINK...
...YUP IT'S A SEWER I JUST SAW SOME POOP.
WHAT SHOULD WE DO?
LEAVE HIM FOR DEAD?
AHHHHHHH!!!
WHAT WAS THAT?!
I DON'T WANT TO DIE IN A TOILET!

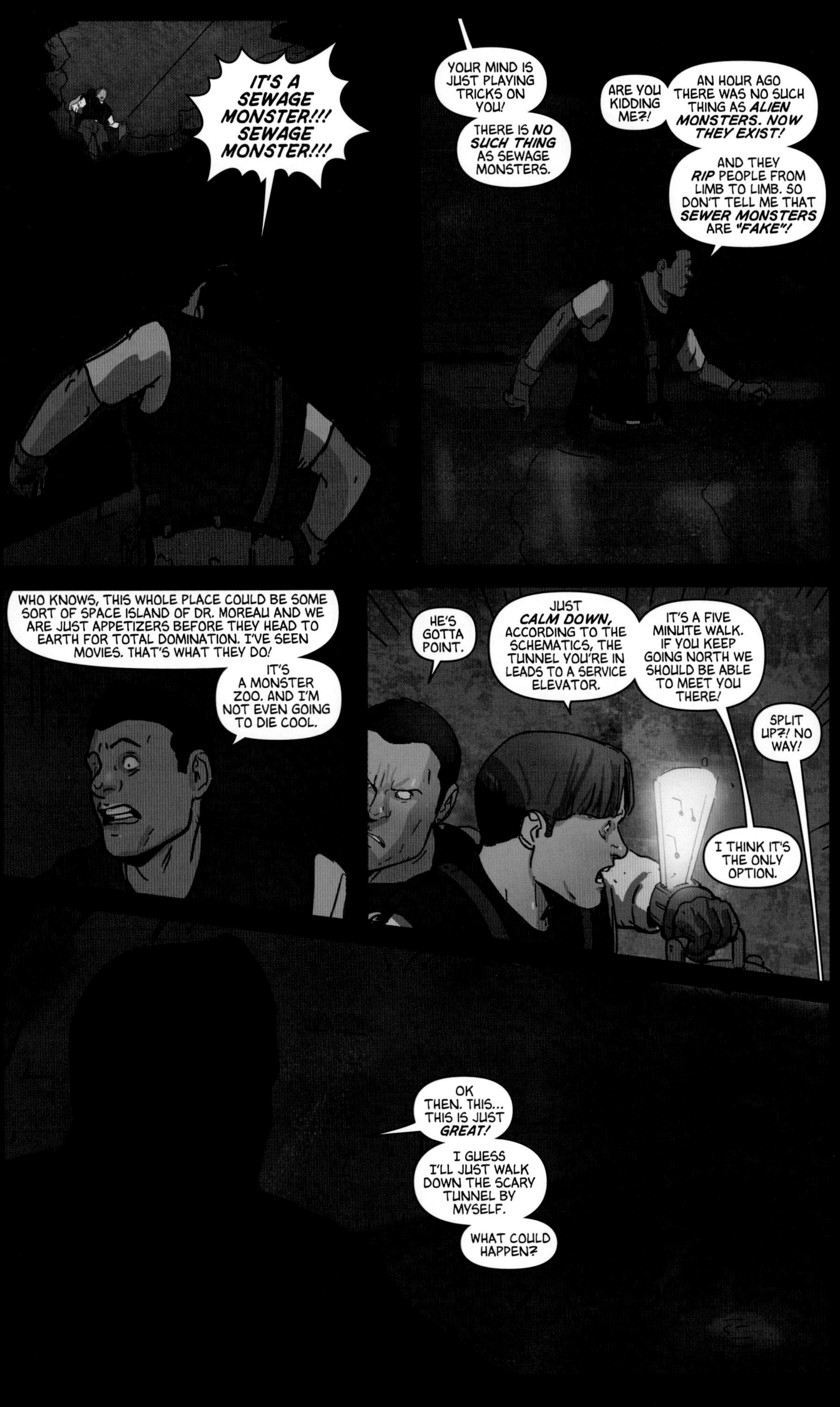
IT'S A SEWAGE MONSTER!!! SEWAGE MONSTER!!!
YOUR MIND IS JUST PLAYING TRICKS ON YOU!
THERE IS NO SUCH THING AS SEWAGE MONSTERS.
ARE YOU KIDDING ME?!
AN HOUR AGO THERE WAS NO SUCH THING AS ALIEN MONSTERS. NOW THEY EXIST!
AND THEY RIP PEOPLE FROM LIMB TO LIMB. SO DON'T TELL ME THAT SEWER MONSTERS ARE "FAKE"!
WHO KNOWS, THIS WHOLE PLACE COULD BE SOME SORT OF SPACE ISLAND OF DR. MOREAU AND WE ARE JUST APPETIZERS BEFORE THEY HEAD TO EARTH FOR TOTAL DOMINATION. I'VE SEEN MOVIES. THAT'S WHAT THEY DO!
IT'S A MONSTER ZOO. AND I'M NOT EVEN GOING TO DIE COOL.
HE'S GOTTA POINT.
JUST CALM DOWN, ACCORDING TO THE SCHEMATICS, THE TUNNEL YOU'RE IN LEADS TO A SERVICE ELEVATOR.
IT'S A FIVE MINUTE WALK. IF YOU KEEP GOING NORTH WE SHOULD BE ABLE TO MEET YOU THERE!
SPLIT UP?! NO WAY!
I THINK IT'S THE ONLY OPTION.
OK THEN. THIS... THIS IS JUST GREAT!
I GUESS I'LL JUST WALK DOWN THE SCARY TUNNEL BY MYSELF.
WHAT COULD HAPPEN?

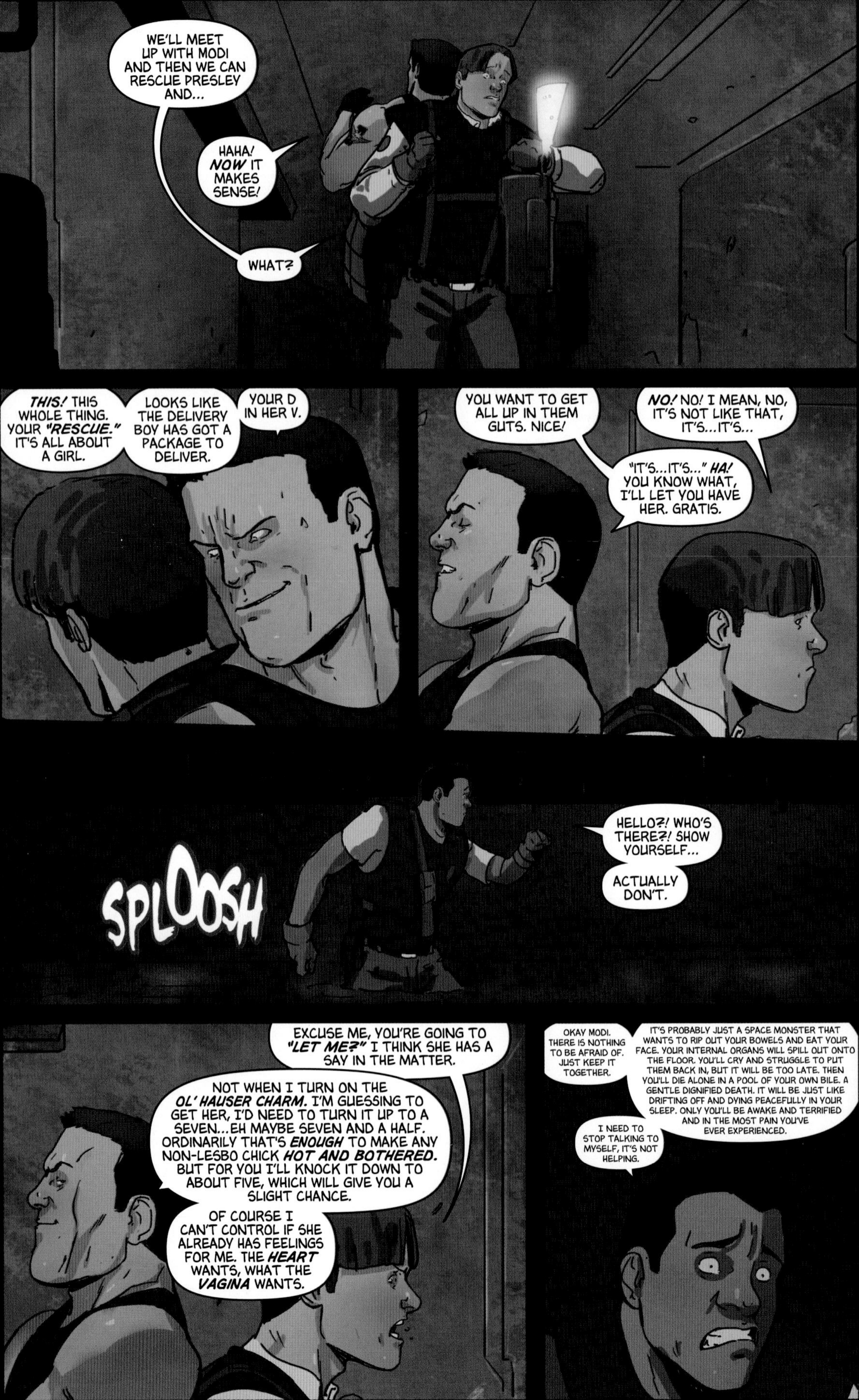
WE'LL MEET UP WITH MODI AND THEN WE CAN RESCUE PRESLEY AND...
HAHA! NOW IT MAKES SENSE!
WHAT?
THIS! THIS WHOLE THING. YOUR "RESCUE." IT'S ALL ABOUT A GIRL.
LOOKS LIKE THE DELIVERY BOY HAS GOT A PACKAGE TO DELIVER.
YOUR D IN HER V.
YOU WANT TO GET ALL UP IN THEM GUTS. NICE!
NO! NO! I MEAN, NO, IT'S NOT LIKE THAT, IT'S...IT'S...
"IT'S...IT'S..." HA! YOU KNOW WHAT, I'LL LET YOU HAVE HER. GRATIS.
SPLOOSH
HELLO?! WHO'S THERE?! SHOW YOURSELF...
ACTUALLY DON'T.
EXCUSE ME, YOU'RE GOING TO "LET ME?" I THINK SHE HAS A SAY IN THE MATTER.
NOT WHEN I TURN ON THE OL' HAUSER CHARM. I'M GUESSING TO GET HER, I'D NEED TO TURN IT UP TO A SEVEN...EH MAYBE SEVEN AND A HALF. ORDINARILY THAT'S ENOUGH TO MAKE ANY NON-LESBO CHICK HOT AND BOTHERED. BUT FOR YOU I'LL KNOCK IT DOWN TO ABOUT FIVE, WHICH WILL GIVE YOU A SLIGHT CHANCE.
OF COURSE I CAN'T CONTROL IF SHE ALREADY HAS FEELINGS FOR ME. THE HEART WANTS, WHAT THE VAGINA WANTS.
OKAY MODI. THERE IS NOTHING TO BE AFRAID OF. JUST KEEP IT TOGETHER.
IT'S PROBABLY JUST A SPACE MONSTER THAT WANTS TO RIP OUT YOUR BOWELS AND EAT YOUR FACE. YOUR INTERNAL ORGANS WILL SPILL OUT ONTO THE FLOOR. YOU'LL CRY AND STRUGGLE TO PUT THEM BACK IN, BUT IT WILL BE TOO LATE. THEN YOU'LL DIE ALONE IN A POOL OF YOUR OWN BILE. A GENTLE DIGNIFIED DEATH. IT WILL BE JUST LIKE DRIFTING OFF AND DYING PEACEFULLY IN YOUR SLEEP. ONLY YOU'LL BE AWAKE AND TERRIFIED AND IN THE MOST PAIN YOU'VE EVER EXPERIENCED.
I NEED TO STOP TALKING TO MYSELF, IT'S NOT HELPING.

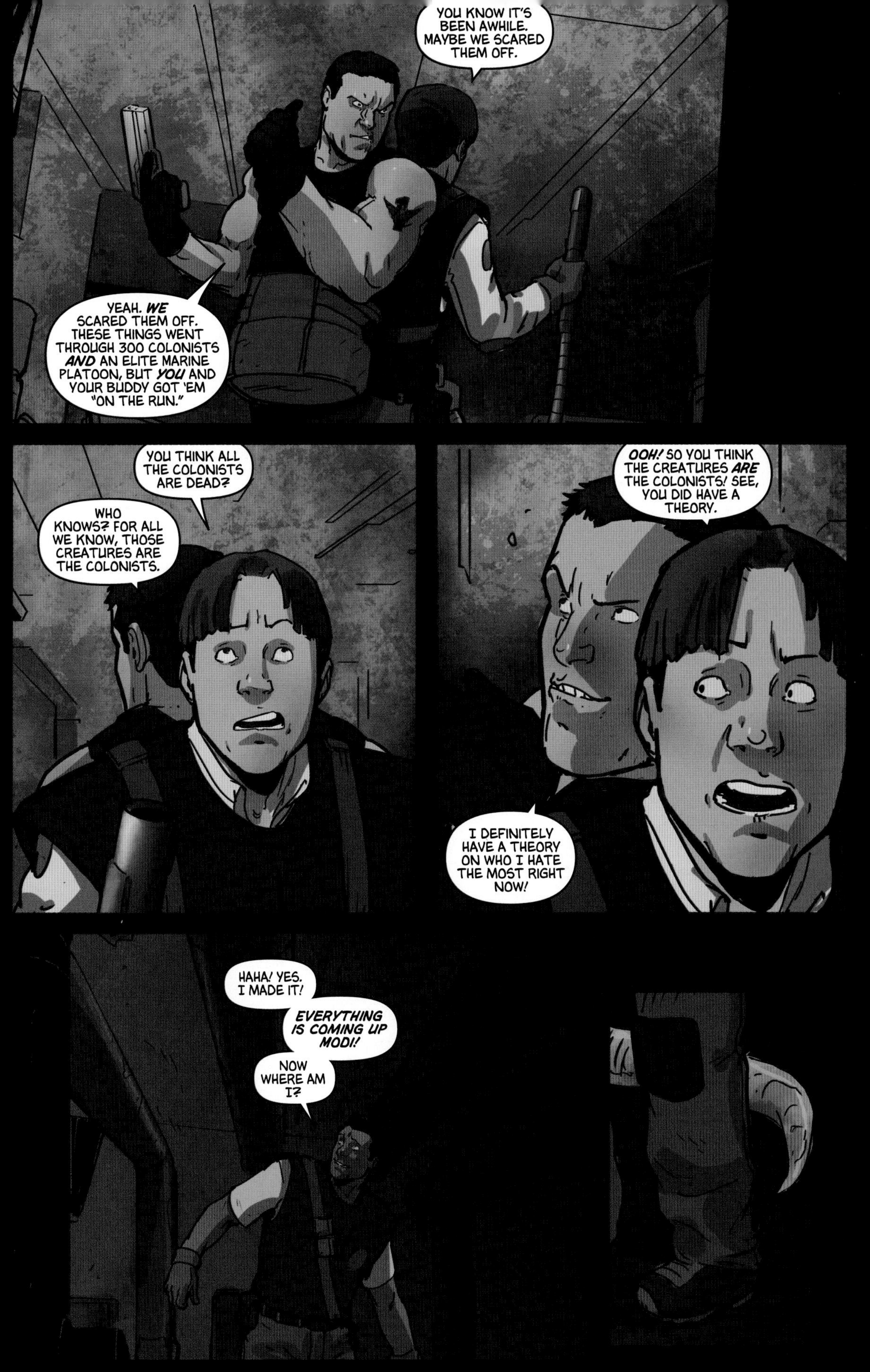
YOU KNOW IT'S BEEN AWHILE. MAYBE WE SCARED THEM OFF.
YEAH. ***WE*** SCARED THEM OFF. THESE THINGS WENT THROUGH 300 COLONISTS ***AND*** AN ELITE MARINE PLATOON, BUT ***YOU*** AND YOUR BUDDY GOT 'EM "ON THE RUN."
YOU THINK ALL THE COLONISTS ARE DEAD?
WHO KNOWS? FOR ALL WE KNOW, THOSE CREATURES ARE THE COLONISTS.
OOH! SO YOU THINK THE CREATURES ***ARE*** THE COLONISTS! SEE, YOU DID HAVE A THEORY.
I DEFINITELY HAVE A THEORY ON WHO I HATE THE MOST RIGHT NOW!
HAHA! YES. I MADE IT!
EVERYTHING IS COMING UP MODI!
NOW WHERE AM I?

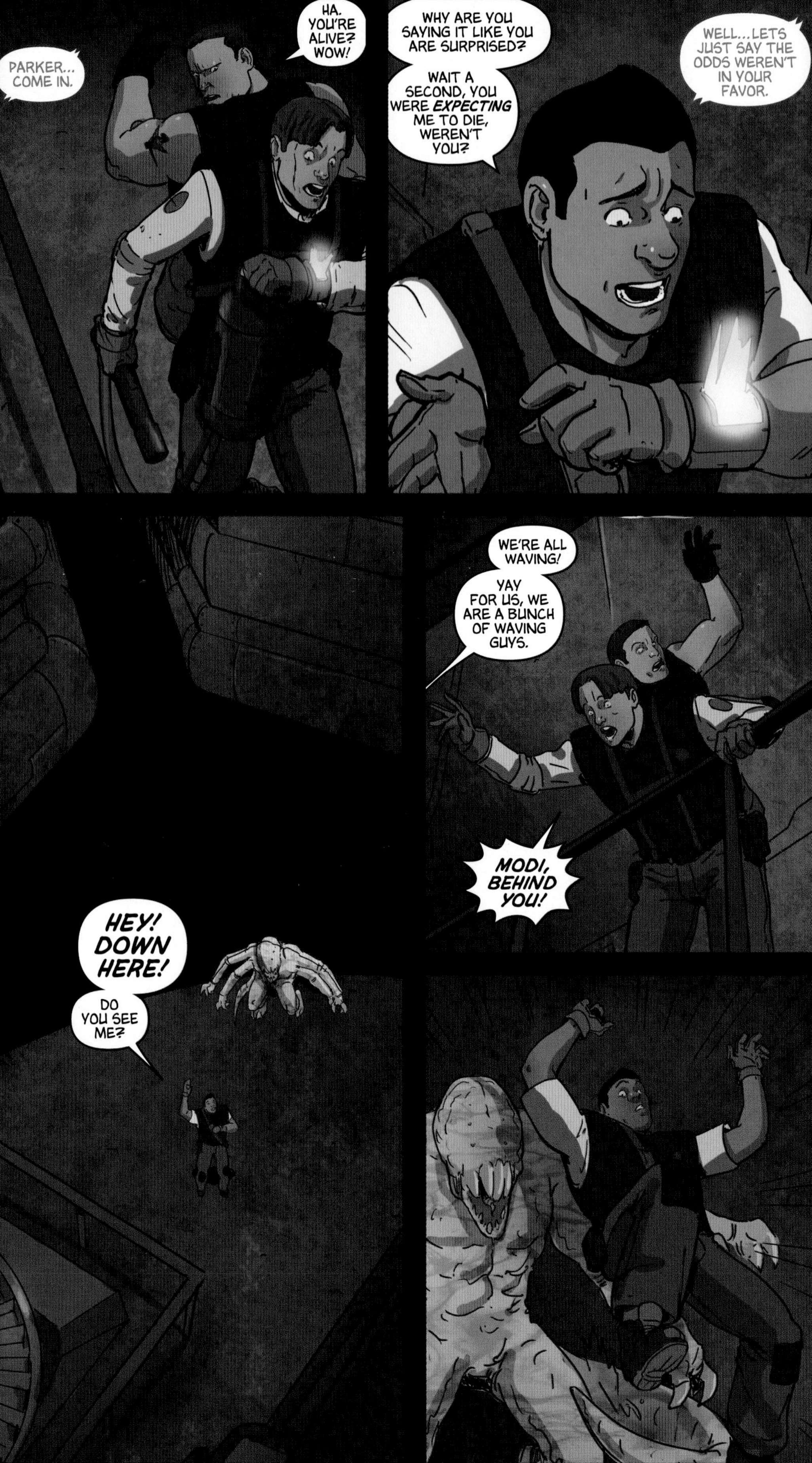
PARKER... COME IN.
HA. YOU'RE ALIVE? WOW!
WHY ARE YOU SAYING IT LIKE YOU ARE SURPRISED?
WAIT A SECOND, YOU WERE *EXPECTING* ME TO DIE, WEREN'T YOU?
WELL...LETS JUST SAY THE ODDS WEREN'T IN YOUR FAVOR.
HEY! DOWN HERE!
DO YOU SEE ME?
WE'RE ALL WAVING!
YAY FOR US, WE ARE A BUNCH OF WAVING GUYS.
MODI, BEHIND YOU!

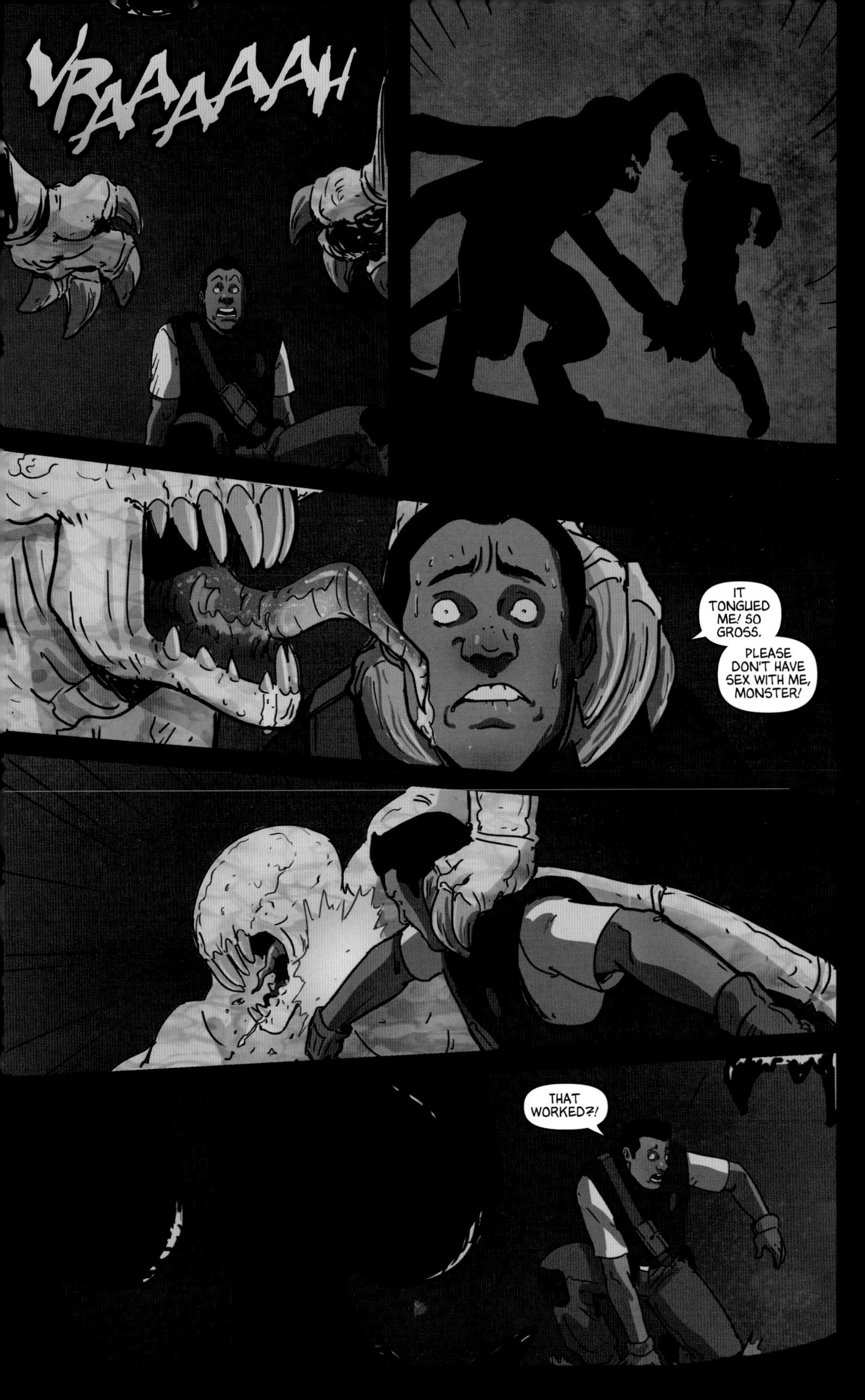
VRAAAAAH
IT TONGUED ME! SO GROSS.
PLEASE DON'T HAVE SEX WITH ME, MONSTER!
THAT WORKED?!

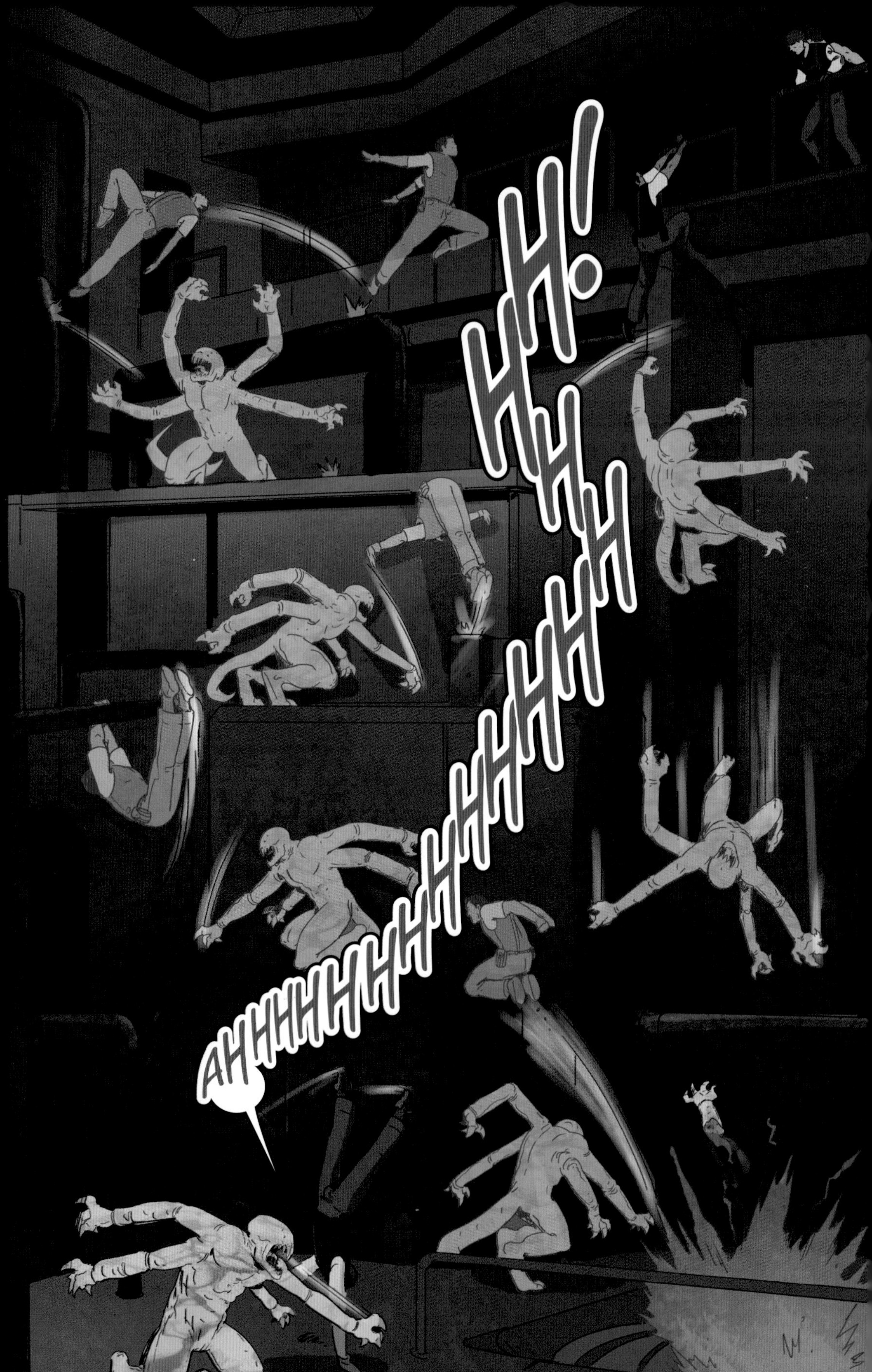
AHHHHHHHHHHHHHHHHHHHH!

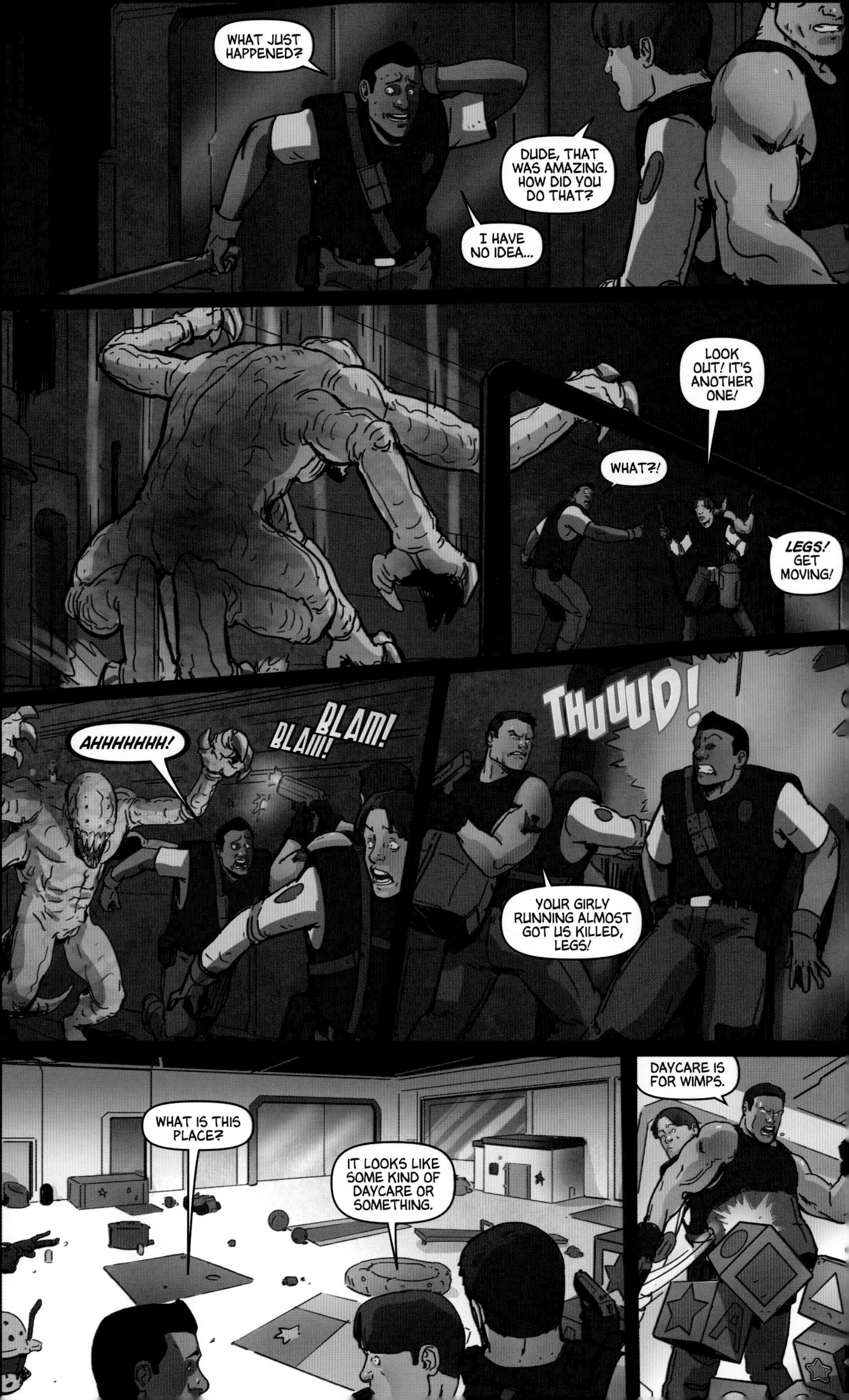
WHAT JUST HAPPENED?
DUDE, THAT WAS AMAZING. HOW DID YOU DO THAT?
I HAVE NO IDEA...
LOOK OUT! IT'S ANOTHER ONE!
WHAT?!
LEGS! GET MOVING!
BLAM! BLAM!
AHHHHHHH!
THUUUD!
YOUR GIRLY RUNNING ALMOST GOT US KILLED, LEGS!
WHAT IS THIS PLACE?
IT LOOKS LIKE SOME KIND OF DAYCARE OR SOMETHING.
DAYCARE IS FOR WIMPS.

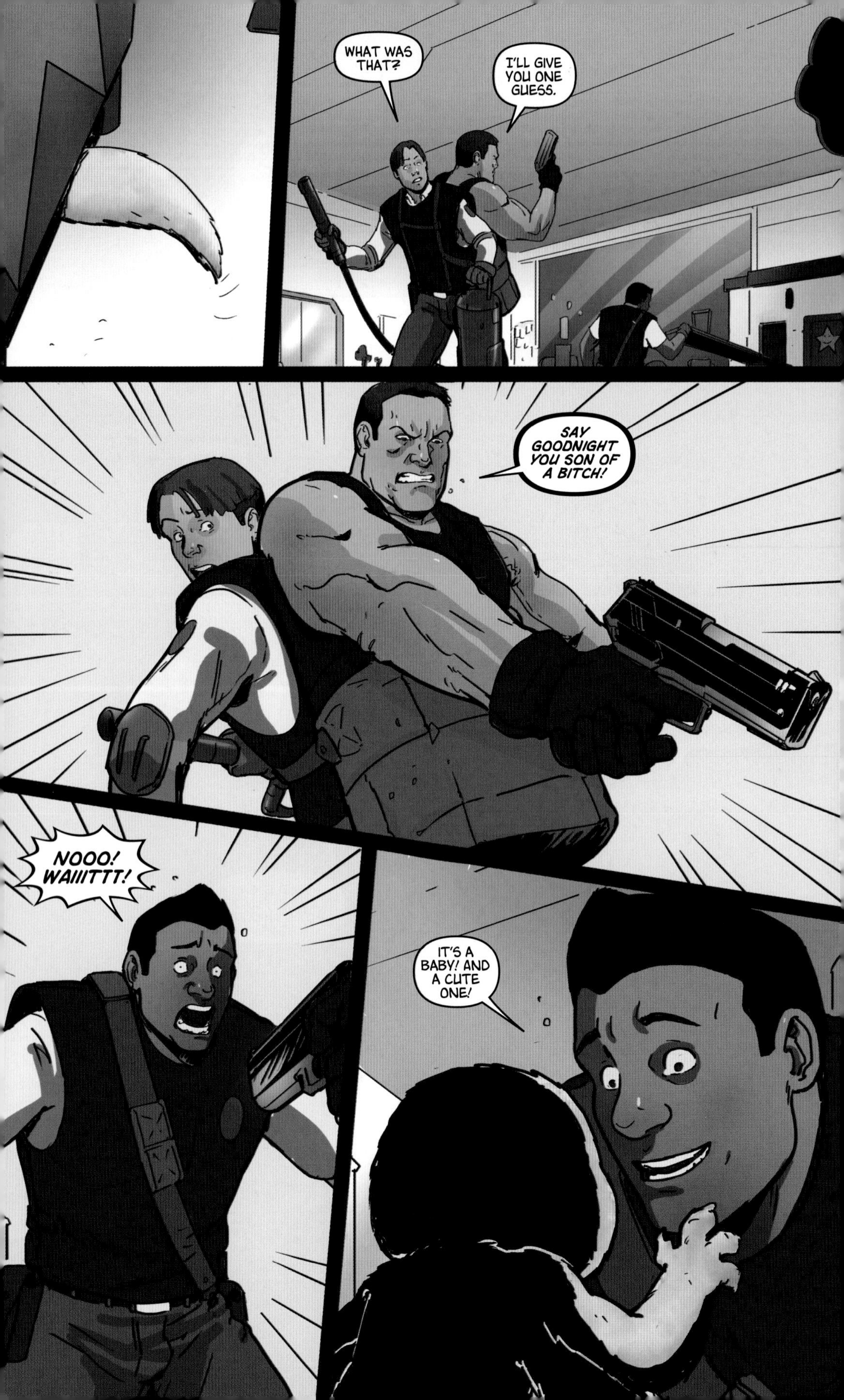
WHAT WAS THAT?
I'LL GIVE YOU ONE GUESS.
SAY GOODNIGHT YOU SON OF A BITCH!
NOOO! WAIIITTT!
IT'S A BABY! AND A CUTE ONE!

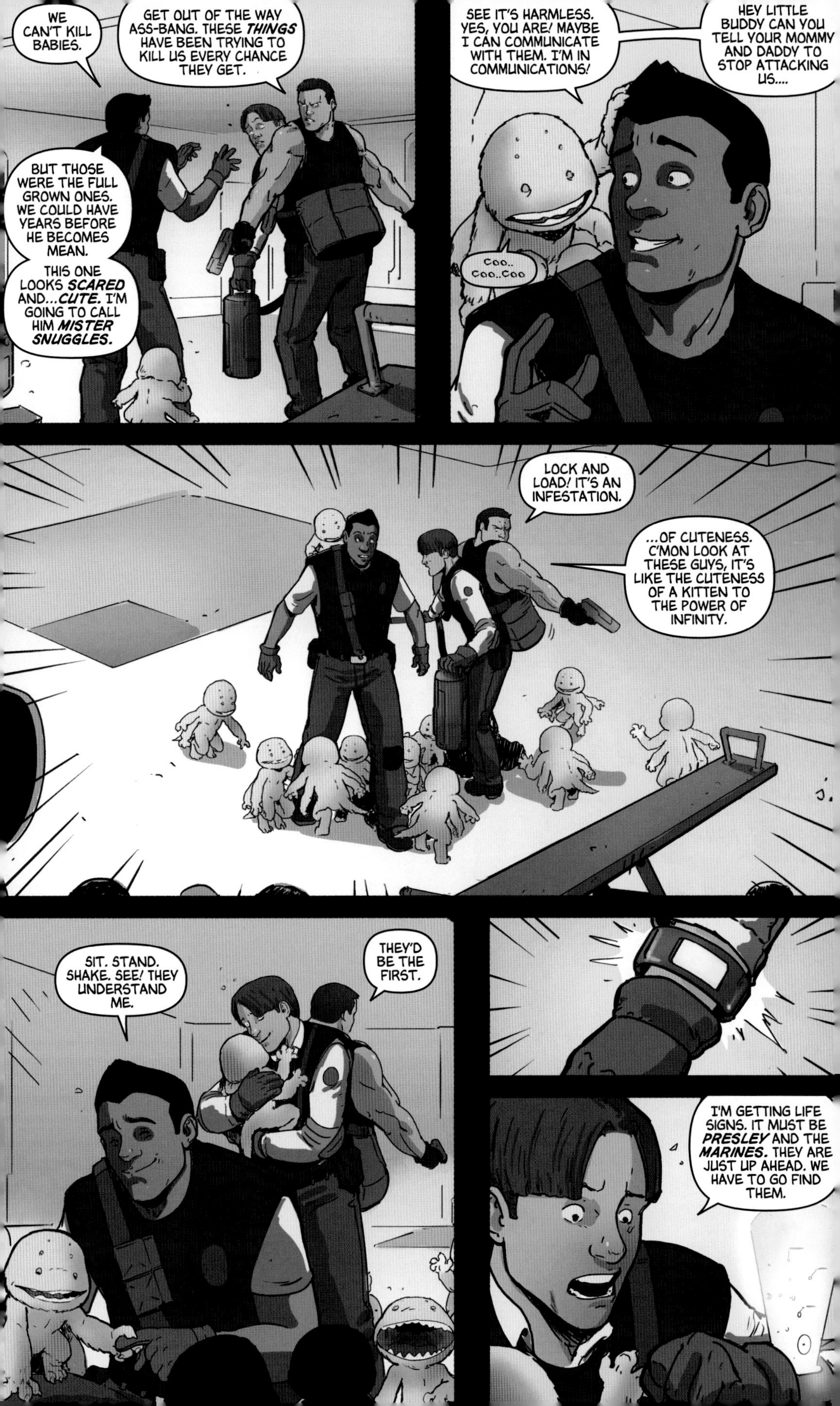
WE CAN'T KILL BABIES.
GET OUT OF THE WAY ASS-BANG. THESE THINGS HAVE BEEN TRYING TO KILL US EVERY CHANCE THEY GET.
BUT THOSE WERE THE FULL GROWN ONES. WE COULD HAVE YEARS BEFORE HE BECOMES MEAN.
THIS ONE LOOKS SCARED AND...CUTE. I'M GOING TO CALL HIM MISTER SNUGGLES.
SEE IT'S HARMLESS. YES, YOU ARE! MAYBE I CAN COMMUNICATE WITH THEM. I'M IN COMMUNICATIONS!
HEY LITTLE BUDDY CAN YOU TELL YOUR MOMMY AND DADDY TO STOP ATTACKING US....
COO.. COO..COO
LOCK AND LOAD! IT'S AN INFESTATION.
...OF CUTENESS. C'MON LOOK AT THESE GUYS, IT'S LIKE THE CUTENESS OF A KITTEN TO THE POWER OF INFINITY.
SIT. STAND. SHAKE. SEE! THEY UNDERSTAND ME.
THEY'D BE THE FIRST.
I'M GETTING LIFE SIGNS. IT MUST BE PRESLEY AND THE MARINES. THEY ARE JUST UP AHEAD. WE HAVE TO GO FIND THEM.

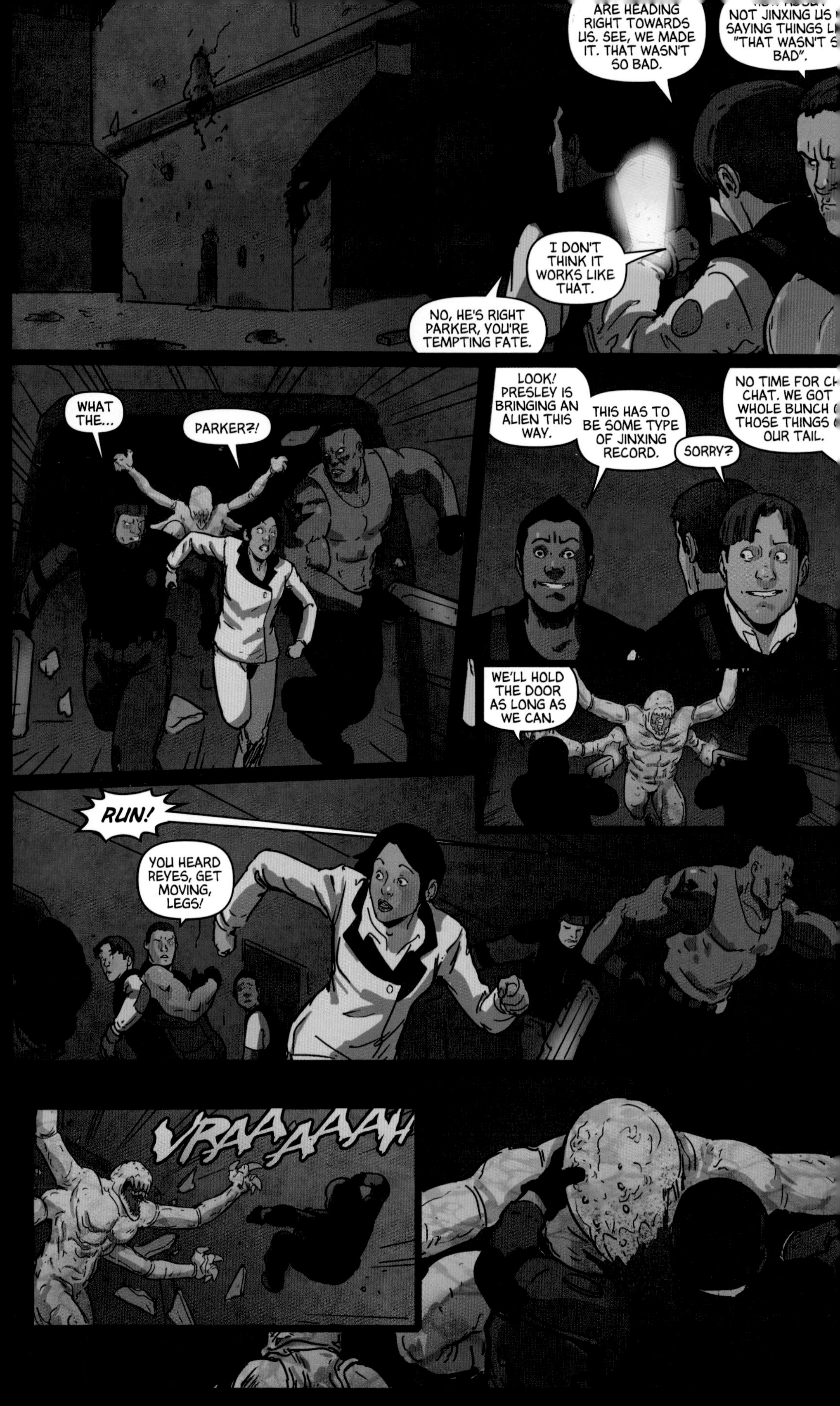

ARE HEADING RIGHT TOWARDS US. SEE, WE MADE IT. THAT WASN'T SO BAD.
NOT JINXING US SAYING THINGS LI "THAT WASN'T S BAD".
I DON'T THINK IT WORKS LIKE THAT.
NO, HE'S RIGHT PARKER, YOU'RE TEMPTING FATE.
WHAT THE...
PARKER?!
LOOK! PRESLEY IS BRINGING AN ALIEN THIS WAY.
THIS HAS TO BE SOME TYPE OF JINXING RECORD.
SORRY?
NO TIME FOR CH CHAT. WE GOT WHOLE BUNCH THOSE THINGS OUR TAIL.
WE'LL HOLD THE DOOR AS LONG AS WE CAN.
RUN!
YOU HEARD REYES, GET MOVING, LEGS!
VRAAAAAAH

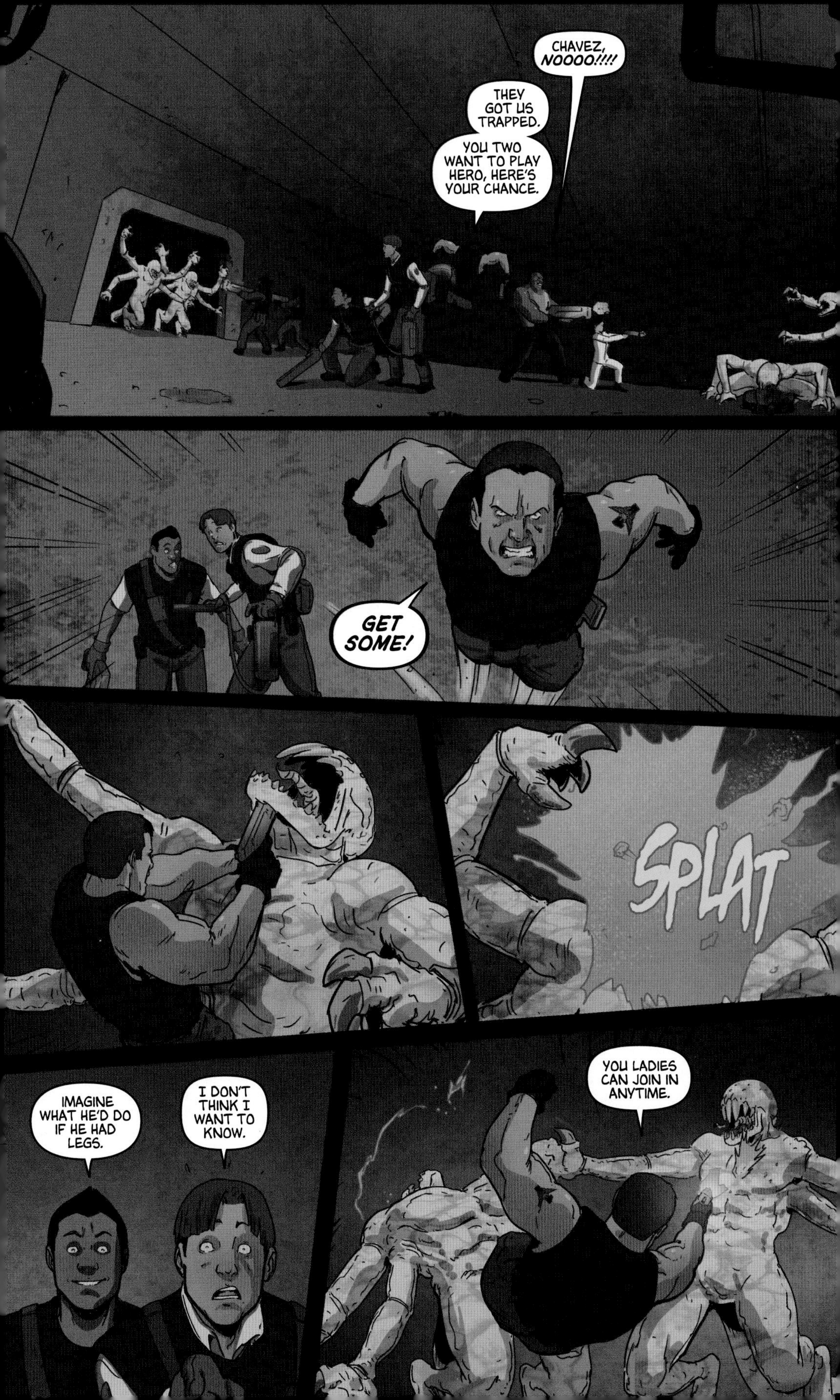
CHAVEZ, NOOOO!!!!
THEY GOT US TRAPPED.
YOU TWO WANT TO PLAY HERO, HERE'S YOUR CHANCE.
GET SOME!
SPLAT
IMAGINE WHAT HE'D DO IF HE HAD LEGS.
I DON'T THINK I WANT TO KNOW.
YOU LADIES CAN JOIN IN ANYTIME.

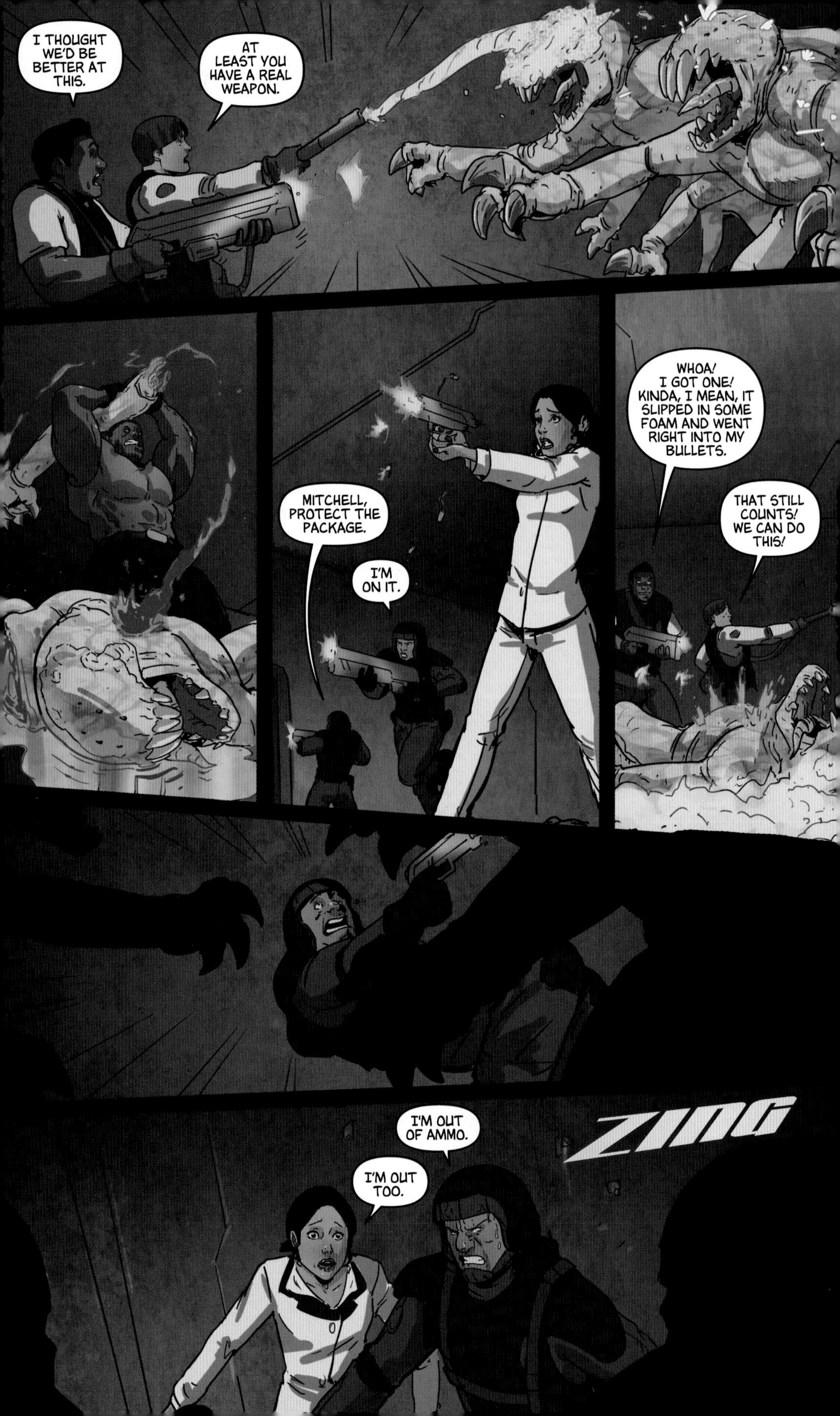
I THOUGHT WE'D BE BETTER AT THIS.
AT LEAST YOU HAVE A REAL WEAPON.
MITCHELL, PROTECT THE PACKAGE.
I'M ON IT.
WHOA! I GOT ONE! KINDA, I MEAN, IT SLIPPED IN SOME FOAM AND WENT RIGHT INTO MY BULLETS.
THAT STILL COUNTS! WE CAN DO THIS!
ZING
I'M OUT OF AMMO.
I'M OUT TOO.

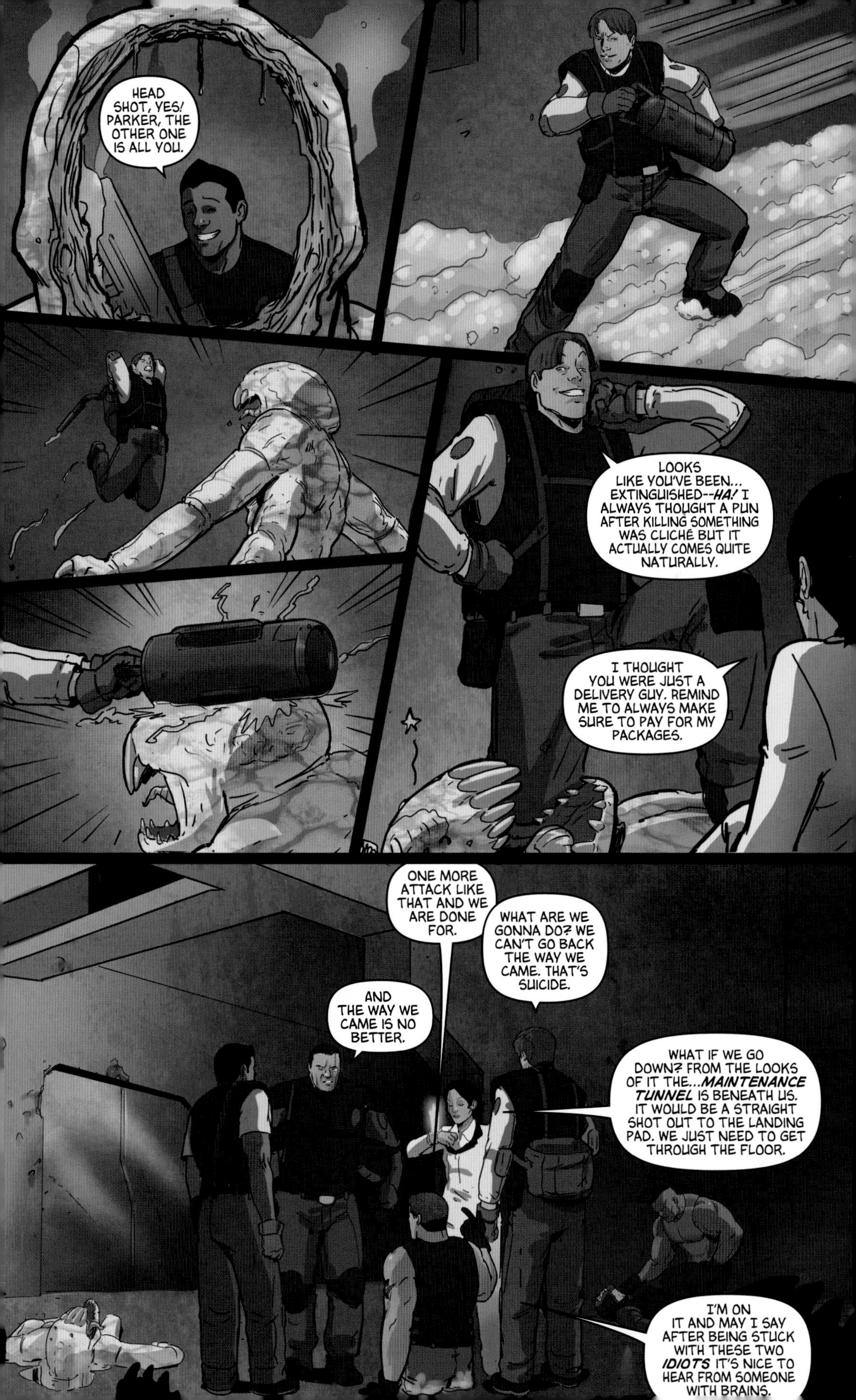
HEAD SHOT, YES! PARKER, THE OTHER ONE IS ALL YOU.
LOOKS LIKE YOU'VE BEEN... EXTINGUISHED--*HA!* I ALWAYS THOUGHT A PUN AFTER KILLING SOMETHING WAS CLICHÉ BUT IT ACTUALLY COMES QUITE NATURALLY.
I THOUGHT YOU WERE JUST A DELIVERY GUY. REMIND ME TO ALWAYS MAKE SURE TO PAY FOR MY PACKAGES.
ONE MORE ATTACK LIKE THAT AND WE ARE DONE FOR.
WHAT ARE WE GONNA DO? WE CAN'T GO BACK THE WAY WE CAME. THAT'S SUICIDE.
AND THE WAY WE CAME IS NO BETTER.
WHAT IF WE GO DOWN? FROM THE LOOKS OF IT THE... *MAINTENANCE TUNNEL* IS BENEATH US. IT WOULD BE A STRAIGHT SHOT OUT TO THE LANDING PAD. WE JUST NEED TO GET THROUGH THE FLOOR.
I'M ON IT AND MAY I SAY AFTER BEING STUCK WITH THESE TWO *IDIOTS* IT'S NICE TO HEAR FROM SOMEONE WITH BRAINS.

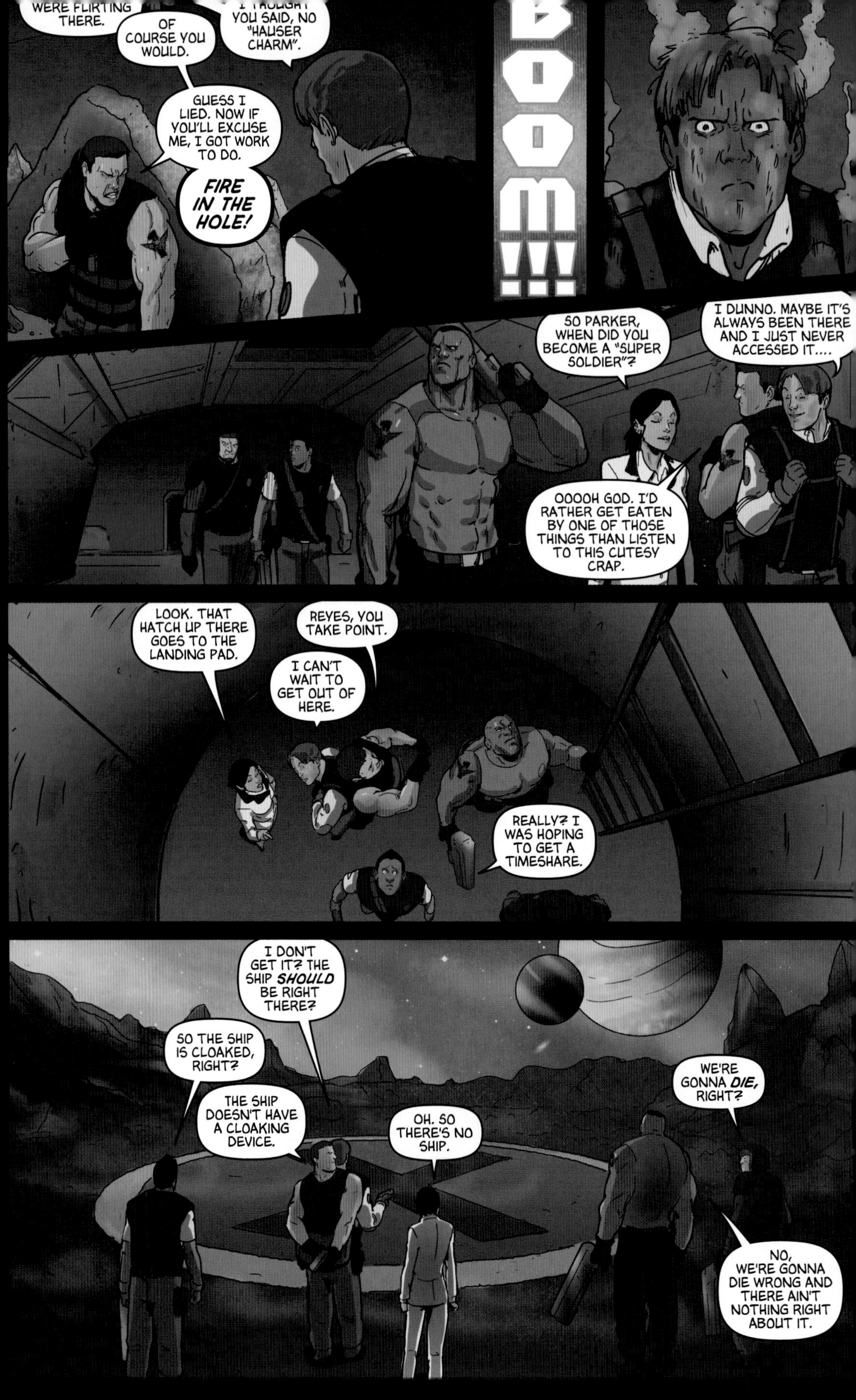
WERE FLIRTING THERE.
OF COURSE YOU WOULD.
I THOUGHT YOU SAID, NO "HAUSER CHARM".
GUESS I LIED. NOW IF YOU'LL EXCUSE ME, I GOT WORK TO DO.
FIRE IN THE HOLE!
BOOOM!!!
SO PARKER, WHEN DID YOU BECOME A "SUPER SOLDIER"?
I DUNNO. MAYBE IT'S ALWAYS BEEN THERE AND I JUST NEVER ACCESSED IT....
OOOOH GOD. I'D RATHER GET EATEN BY ONE OF THOSE THINGS THAN LISTEN TO THIS CUTESY CRAP.
LOOK. THAT HATCH UP THERE GOES TO THE LANDING PAD.
REYES, YOU TAKE POINT.
I CAN'T WAIT TO GET OUT OF HERE.
REALLY? I WAS HOPING TO GET A TIMESHARE.
I DON'T GET IT? THE SHIP SHOULD BE RIGHT THERE?
SO THE SHIP IS CLOAKED, RIGHT?
THE SHIP DOESN'T HAVE A CLOAKING DEVICE.
OH. SO THERE'S NO SHIP.
WE'RE GONNA DIE, RIGHT?
NO, WE'RE GONNA DIE WRONG AND THERE AIN'T NOTHING RIGHT ABOUT IT.

SPACE-EX

"We know how to handle your package."

Chapter Four
COVER BY
JOSHUA COVEY

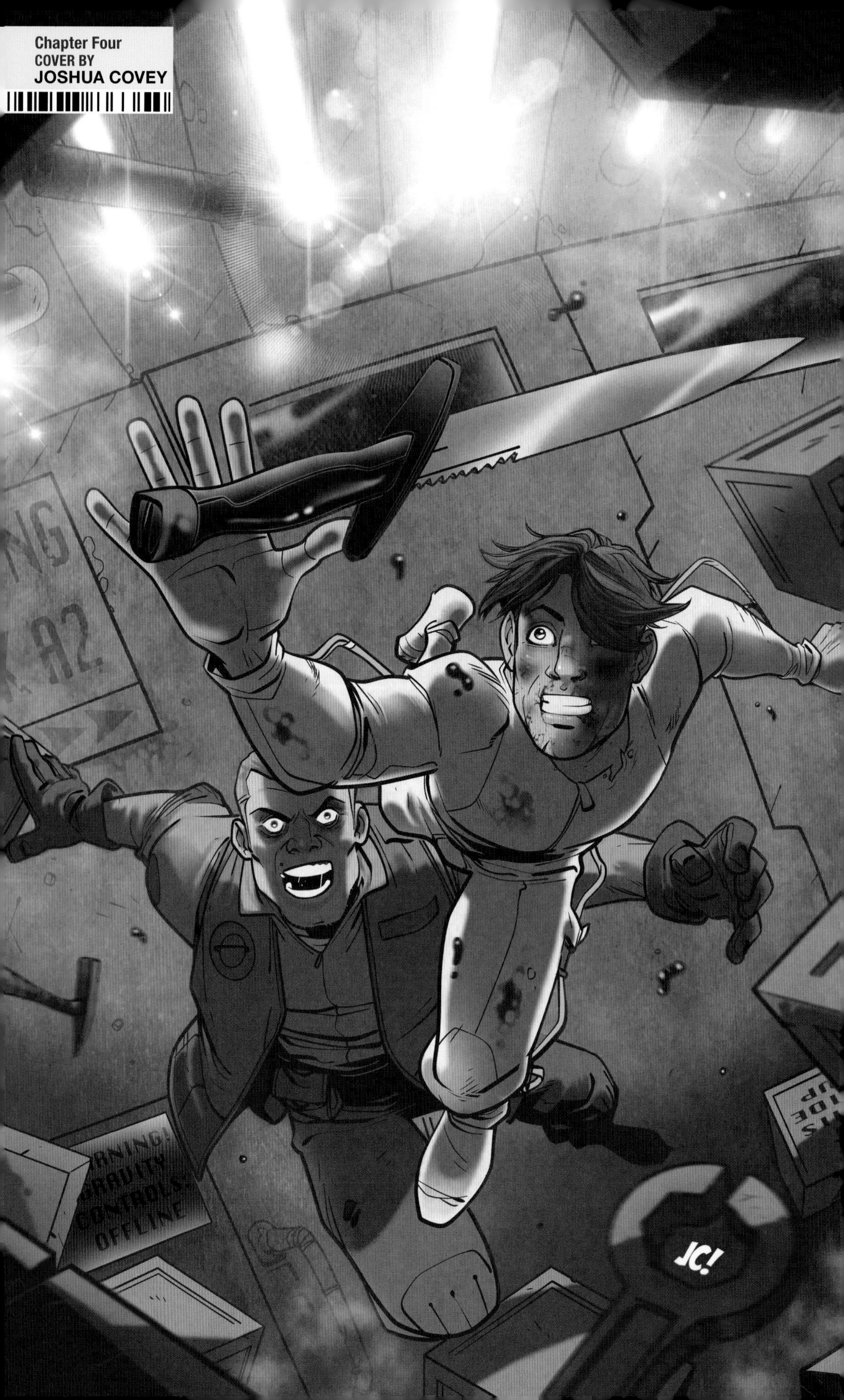
GRAVITY
CONTROLS
OFFLINE
JC!

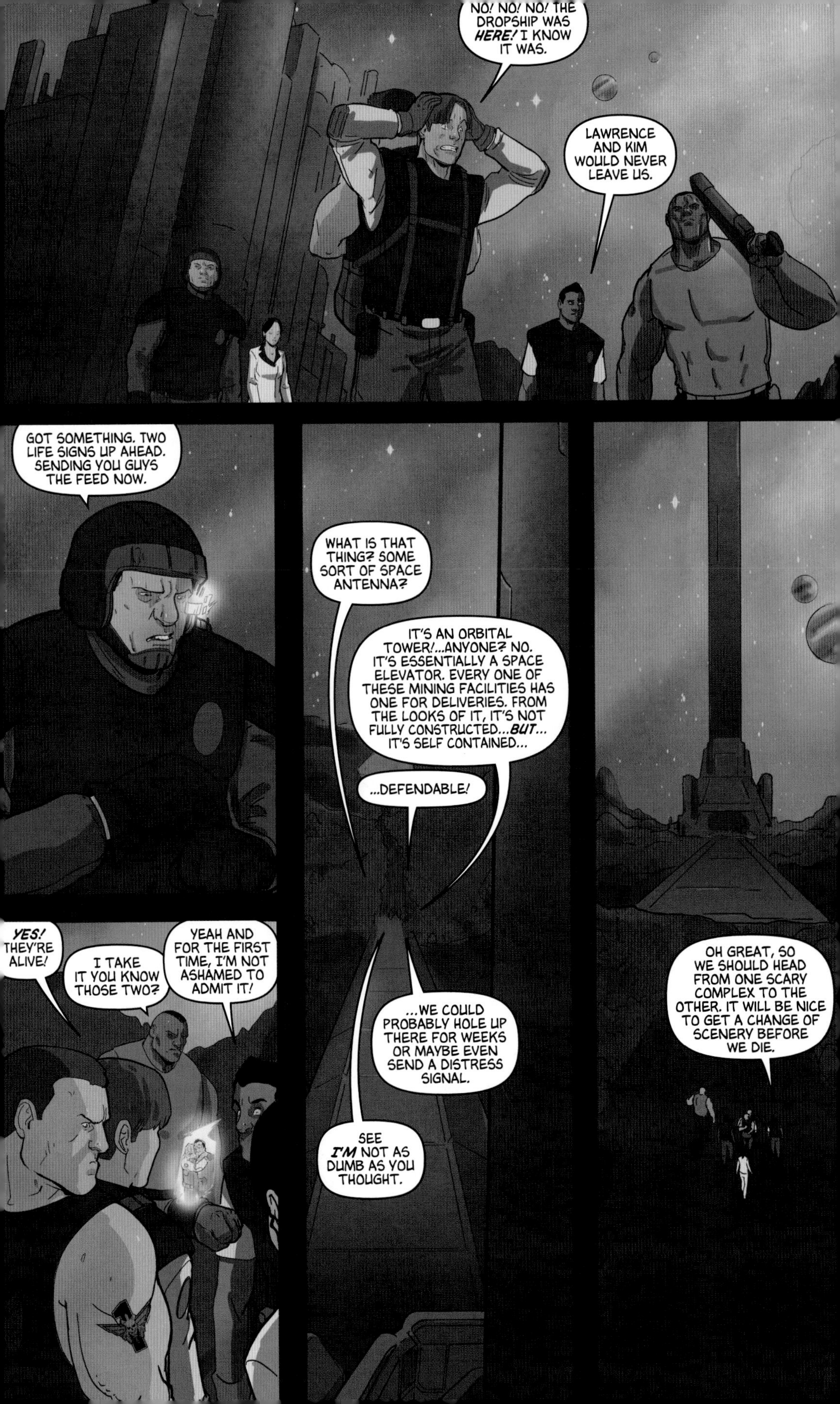
NO! NO! NO! THE DROPSHIP WAS HERE! I KNOW IT WAS.
LAWRENCE AND KIM WOULD NEVER LEAVE US.
GOT SOMETHING. TWO LIFE SIGNS UP AHEAD. SENDING YOU GUYS THE FEED NOW.
WHAT IS THAT THING? SOME SORT OF SPACE ANTENNA?
IT'S AN ORBITAL TOWER!...ANYONE? NO. IT'S ESSENTIALLY A SPACE ELEVATOR. EVERY ONE OF THESE MINING FACILITIES HAS ONE FOR DELIVERIES. FROM THE LOOKS OF IT, IT'S NOT FULLY CONSTRUCTED...BUT... IT'S SELF CONTAINED...
...DEFENDABLE!
...WE COULD PROBABLY HOLE UP THERE FOR WEEKS OR MAYBE EVEN SEND A DISTRESS SIGNAL.
SEE I'M NOT AS DUMB AS YOU THOUGHT.
OH GREAT, SO WE SHOULD HEAD FROM ONE SCARY COMPLEX TO THE OTHER. IT WILL BE NICE TO GET A CHANGE OF SCENERY BEFORE WE DIE.
YES! THEY'RE ALIVE!
I TAKE IT YOU KNOW THOSE TWO?
YEAH AND FOR THE FIRST TIME, I'M NOT ASHAMED TO ADMIT IT!

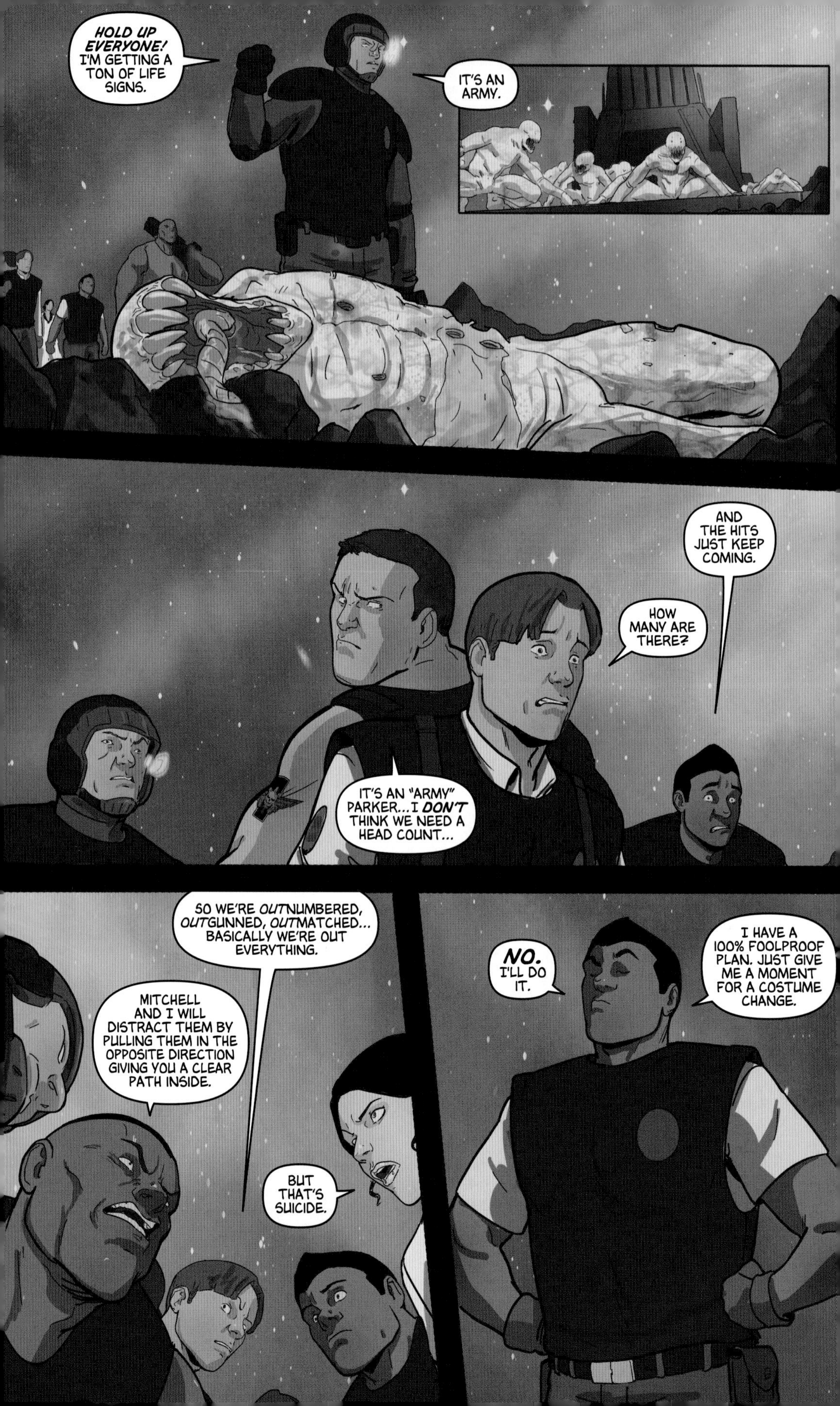
HOLD UP EVERYONE! I'M GETTING A TON OF LIFE SIGNS.
IT'S AN ARMY.
HOW MANY ARE THERE?
AND THE HITS JUST KEEP COMING.
IT'S AN "ARMY" PARKER... I DON'T THINK WE NEED A HEAD COUNT...
SO WE'RE OUTNUMBERED, OUTGUNNED, OUTMATCHED... BASICALLY WE'RE OUT EVERYTHING.
MITCHELL AND I WILL DISTRACT THEM BY PULLING THEM IN THE OPPOSITE DIRECTION GIVING YOU A CLEAR PATH INSIDE.
BUT THAT'S SUICIDE.
NO. I'LL DO IT.
I HAVE A 100% FOOLPROOF PLAN. JUST GIVE ME A MOMENT FOR A COSTUME CHANGE.

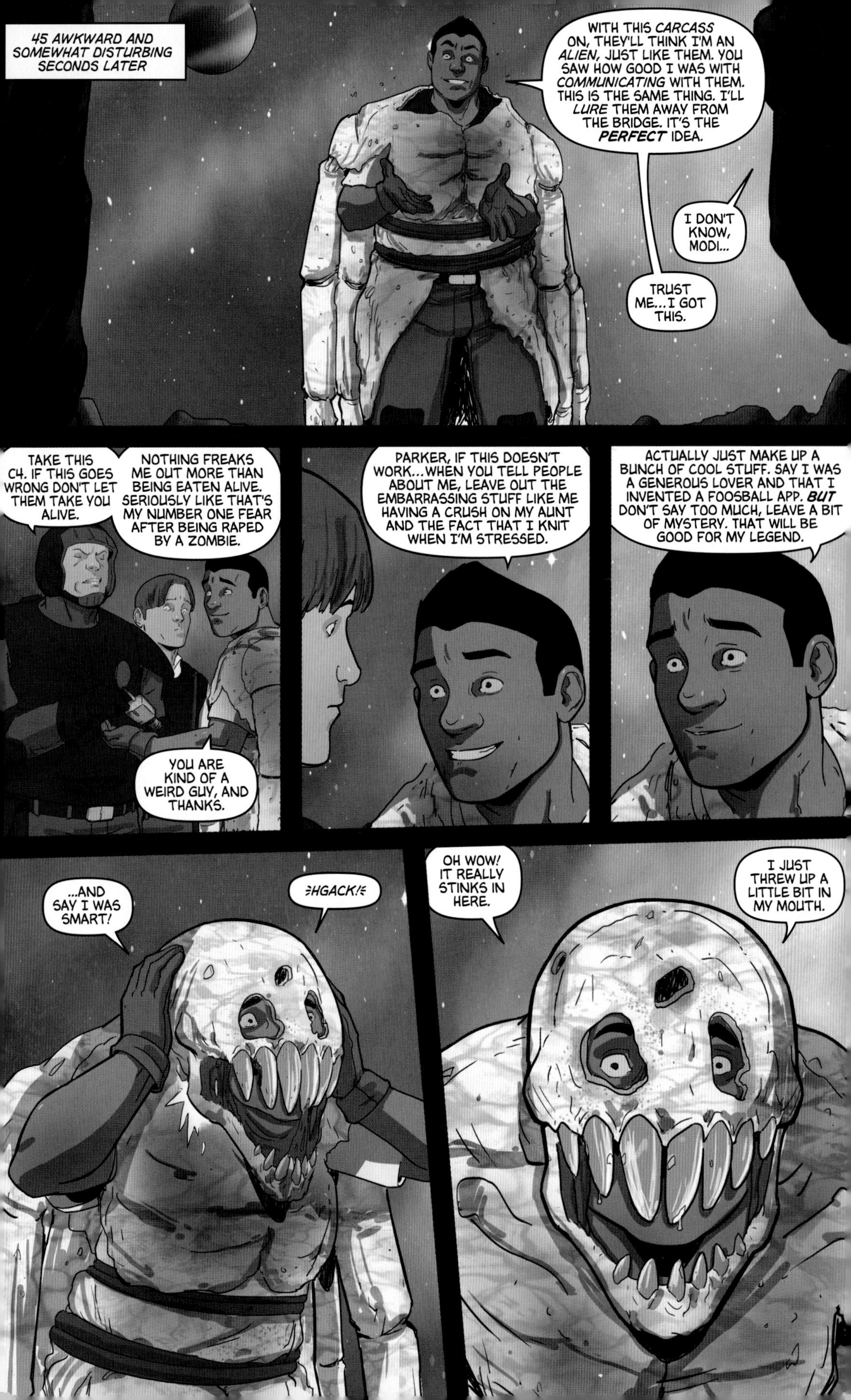
45 AWKWARD AND SOMEWHAT DISTURBING SECONDS LATER
WITH THIS CARCASS ON, THEY'LL THINK I'M AN ALIEN, JUST LIKE THEM. YOU SAW HOW GOOD I WAS WITH COMMUNICATING WITH THEM. THIS IS THE SAME THING. I'LL LURE THEM AWAY FROM THE BRIDGE. IT'S THE PERFECT IDEA.
I DON'T KNOW, MODI...
TRUST ME...I GOT THIS.
TAKE THIS C4. IF THIS GOES WRONG DON'T LET THEM TAKE YOU ALIVE.
NOTHING FREAKS ME OUT MORE THAN BEING EATEN ALIVE. SERIOUSLY LIKE THAT'S MY NUMBER ONE FEAR AFTER BEING RAPED BY A ZOMBIE.
YOU ARE KIND OF A WEIRD GUY, AND THANKS.
PARKER, IF THIS DOESN'T WORK...WHEN YOU TELL PEOPLE ABOUT ME, LEAVE OUT THE EMBARRASSING STUFF LIKE ME HAVING A CRUSH ON MY AUNT AND THE FACT THAT I KNIT WHEN I'M STRESSED.
ACTUALLY JUST MAKE UP A BUNCH OF COOL STUFF. SAY I WAS A GENEROUS LOVER AND THAT I INVENTED A FOOSBALL APP. BUT DON'T SAY TOO MUCH, LEAVE A BIT OF MYSTERY. THAT WILL BE GOOD FOR MY LEGEND.
...AND SAY I WAS SMART!
HGACK!
OH WOW! IT REALLY STINKS IN HERE.
I JUST THREW UP A LITTLE BIT IN MY MOUTH.

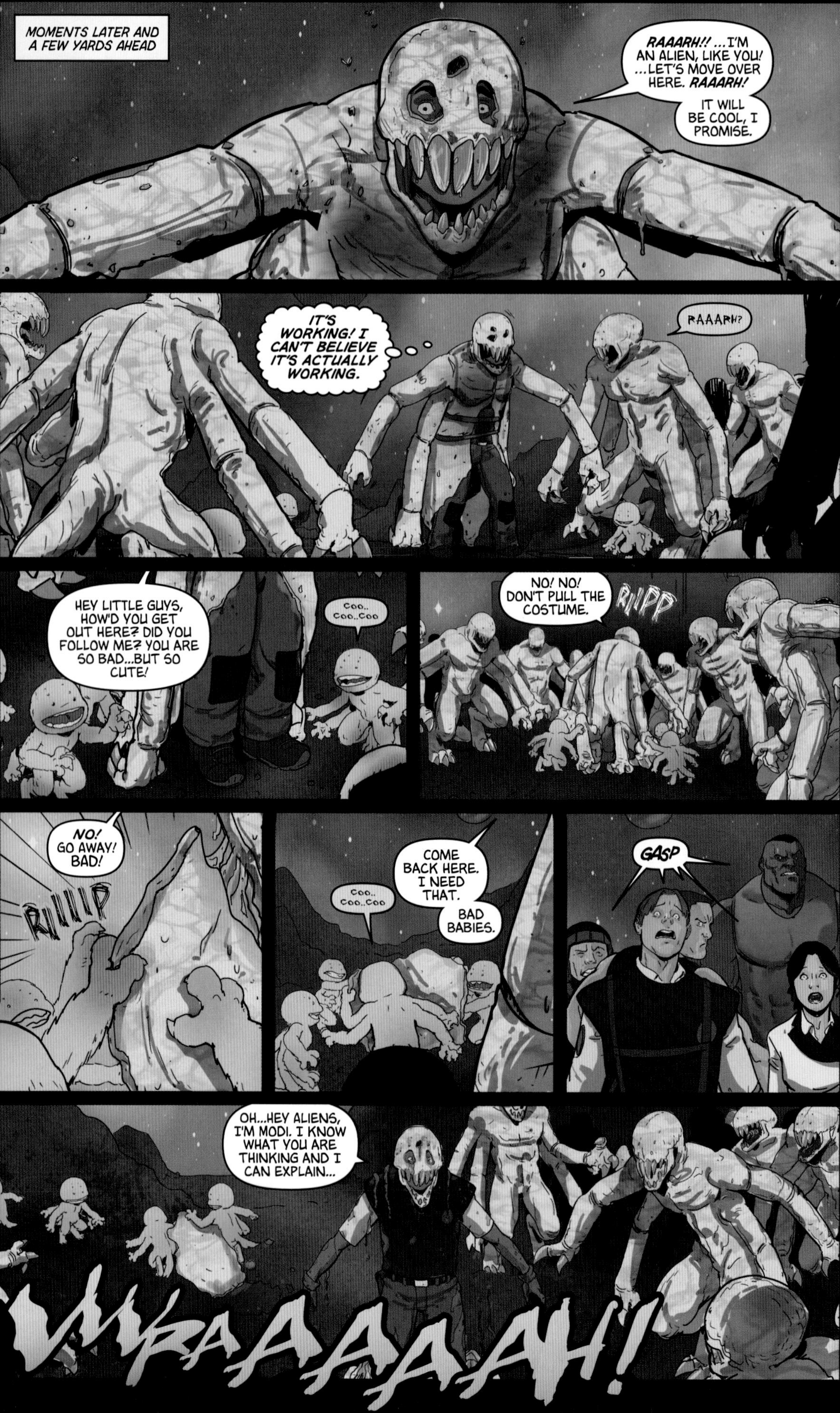
MOMENTS LATER AND A FEW YARDS AHEAD
RAAARH!! ...I'M AN ALIEN, LIKE YOU! ...LET'S MOVE OVER HERE. RAAARH!
IT WILL BE COOL, I PROMISE.
IT'S WORKING! I CAN'T BELIEVE IT'S ACTUALLY WORKING.
RAAARH?
HEY LITTLE GUYS, HOW'D YOU GET OUT HERE? DID YOU FOLLOW ME? YOU ARE SO BAD...BUT SO CUTE!
COO.. COO..COO
NO! NO! DON'T PULL THE COSTUME.
RIIIPP
NO! GO AWAY! BAD!
RIIIIP
COO.. COO..COO
COME BACK HERE. I NEED THAT.
BAD BABIES.
GASP
OH...HEY ALIENS, I'M MODI. I KNOW WHAT YOU ARE THINKING AND I CAN EXPLAIN...
WRAAAAAH!

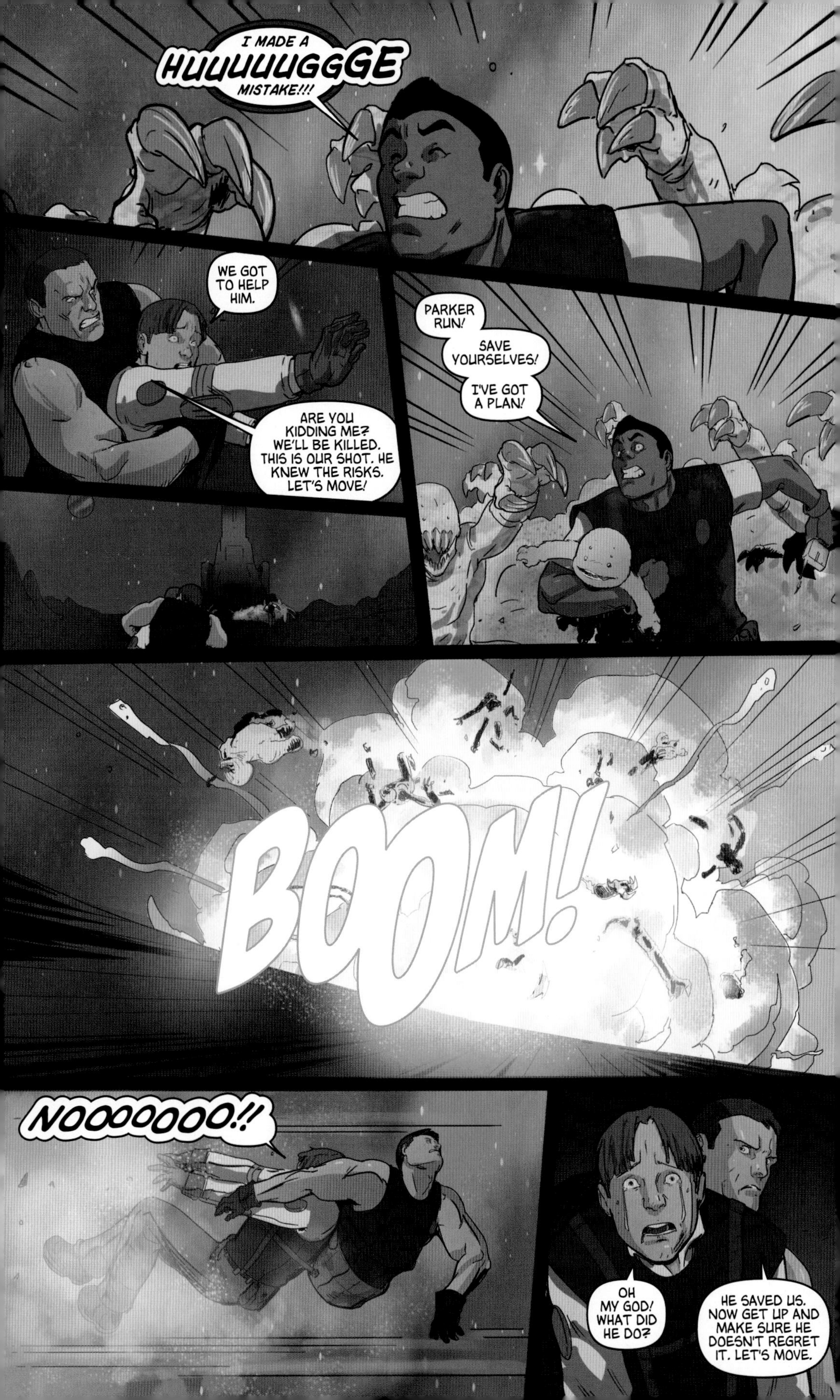

I MADE A HUUUUUUGGGE MISTAKE!!!
WE GOT TO HELP HIM.
ARE YOU KIDDING ME? WE'LL BE KILLED. THIS IS OUR SHOT. HE KNEW THE RISKS. LET'S MOVE!
PARKER RUN!
SAVE YOURSELVES!
I'VE GOT A PLAN!
BOOM!
NOOOOOOO!!
OH MY GOD! WHAT DID HE DO?
HE SAVED US. NOW GET UP AND MAKE SURE HE DOESN'T REGRET IT. LET'S MOVE.

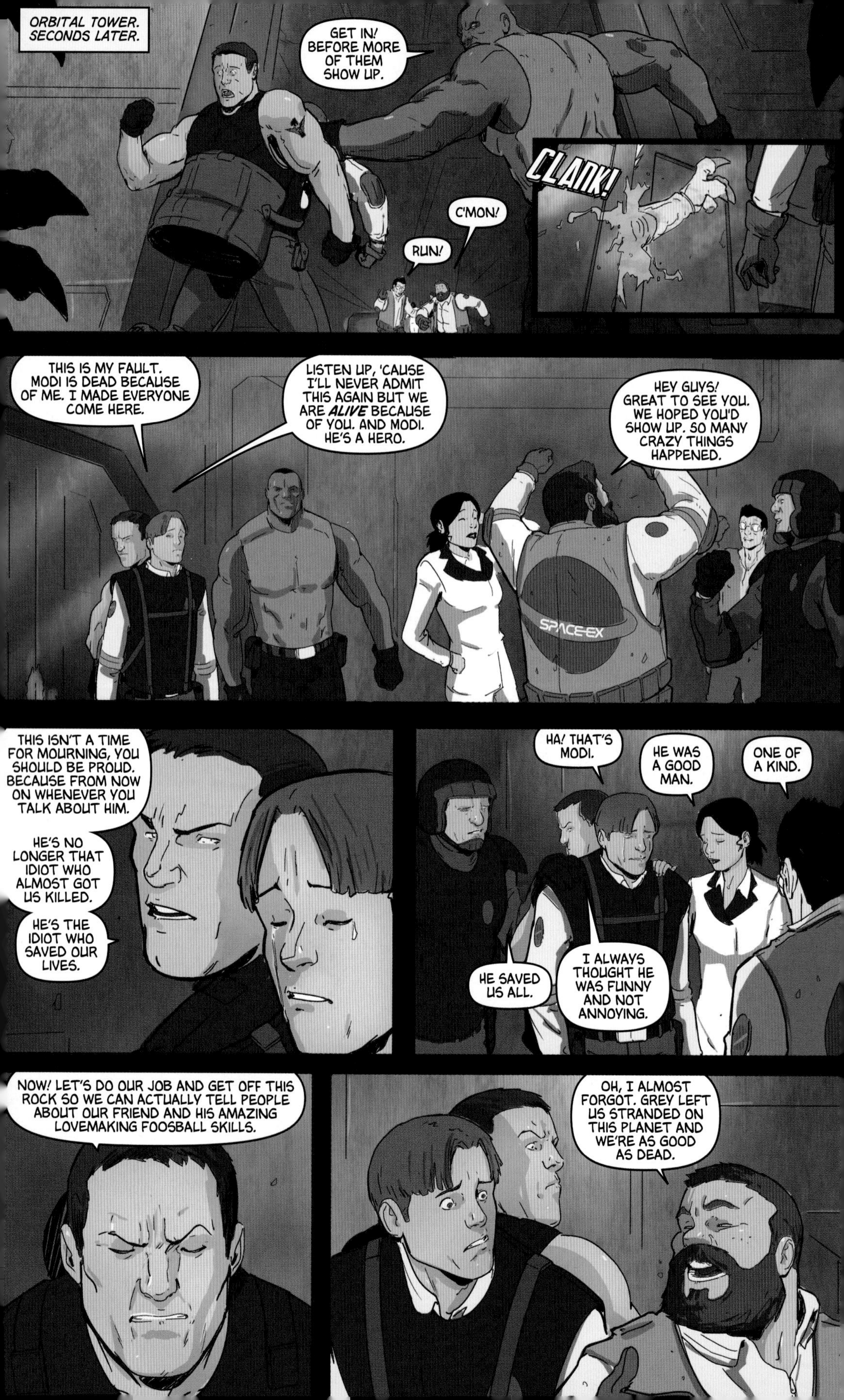
ORBITAL TOWER. SECONDS LATER.
GET IN! BEFORE MORE OF THEM SHOW UP.
CLANK!
C'MON!
RUN!
THIS IS MY FAULT. MODI IS DEAD BECAUSE OF ME. I MADE EVERYONE COME HERE.
LISTEN UP, 'CAUSE I'LL NEVER ADMIT THIS AGAIN BUT WE ARE ALIVE BECAUSE OF YOU. AND MODI. HE'S A HERO.
HEY GUYS! GREAT TO SEE YOU. WE HOPED YOU'D SHOW UP. SO MANY CRAZY THINGS HAPPENED.
SPACE-EX
THIS ISN'T A TIME FOR MOURNING, YOU SHOULD BE PROUD. BECAUSE FROM NOW ON WHENEVER YOU TALK ABOUT HIM.
HE'S NO LONGER THAT IDIOT WHO ALMOST GOT US KILLED.
HE'S THE IDIOT WHO SAVED OUR LIVES.
HA! THAT'S MODI.
HE WAS A GOOD MAN.
ONE OF A KIND.
HE SAVED US ALL.
I ALWAYS THOUGHT HE WAS FUNNY AND NOT ANNOYING.
NOW! LET'S DO OUR JOB AND GET OFF THIS ROCK SO WE CAN ACTUALLY TELL PEOPLE ABOUT OUR FRIEND AND HIS AMAZING LOVEMAKING FOOSBALL SKILLS.
OH, I ALMOST FORGOT. GREY LEFT US STRANDED ON THIS PLANET AND WE'RE AS GOOD AS DEAD.

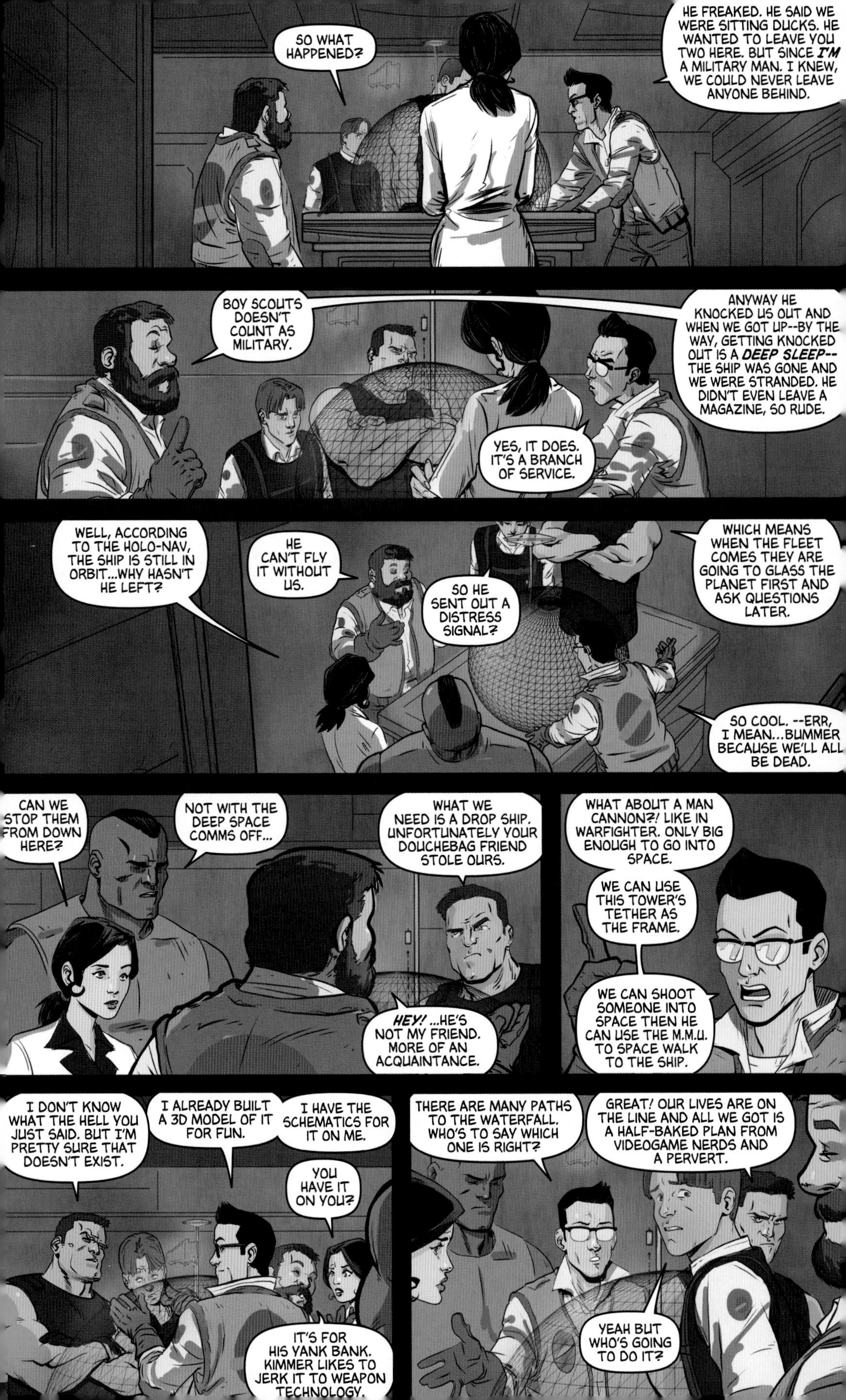
SO WHAT HAPPENED?
HE FREAKED. HE SAID WE WERE SITTING DUCKS. HE WANTED TO LEAVE YOU TWO HERE. BUT SINCE I'M A MILITARY MAN. I KNEW, WE COULD NEVER LEAVE ANYONE BEHIND.
BOY SCOUTS DOESN'T COUNT AS MILITARY.
ANYWAY HE KNOCKED US OUT AND WHEN WE GOT UP--BY THE WAY, GETTING KNOCKED OUT IS A DEEP SLEEP-- THE SHIP WAS GONE AND WE WERE STRANDED. HE DIDN'T EVEN LEAVE A MAGAZINE, SO RUDE.
YES, IT DOES. IT'S A BRANCH OF SERVICE.
WELL, ACCORDING TO THE HOLO-NAV, THE SHIP IS STILL IN ORBIT...WHY HASN'T HE LEFT?
HE CAN'T FLY IT WITHOUT US.
SO HE SENT OUT A DISTRESS SIGNAL?
WHICH MEANS WHEN THE FLEET COMES THEY ARE GOING TO GLASS THE PLANET FIRST AND ASK QUESTIONS LATER.
SO COOL. --ERR, I MEAN...BUMMER BECAUSE WE'LL ALL BE DEAD.
CAN WE STOP THEM FROM DOWN HERE?
NOT WITH THE DEEP SPACE COMMS OFF...
WHAT WE NEED IS A DROP SHIP. UNFORTUNATELY YOUR DOUCHEBAG FRIEND STOLE OURS.
HEY! ...HE'S NOT MY FRIEND. MORE OF AN ACQUAINTANCE.
WHAT ABOUT A MAN CANNON?! LIKE IN WARFIGHTER. ONLY BIG ENOUGH TO GO INTO SPACE.
WE CAN USE THIS TOWER'S TETHER AS THE FRAME.
WE CAN SHOOT SOMEONE INTO SPACE THEN HE CAN USE THE M.M.U. TO SPACE WALK TO THE SHIP.
I DON'T KNOW WHAT THE HELL YOU JUST SAID. BUT I'M PRETTY SURE THAT DOESN'T EXIST.
I ALREADY BUILT A 3D MODEL OF IT FOR FUN.
I HAVE THE SCHEMATICS FOR IT ON ME.
YOU HAVE IT ON YOU?
IT'S FOR HIS YANK BANK. KIMMER LIKES TO JERK IT TO WEAPON TECHNOLOGY.
THERE ARE MANY PATHS TO THE WATERFALL. WHO'S TO SAY WHICH ONE IS RIGHT?
GREAT! OUR LIVES ARE ON THE LINE AND ALL WE GOT IS A HALF-BAKED PLAN FROM VIDEOGAME NERDS AND A PERVERT.
YEAH BUT WHO'S GOING TO DO IT?

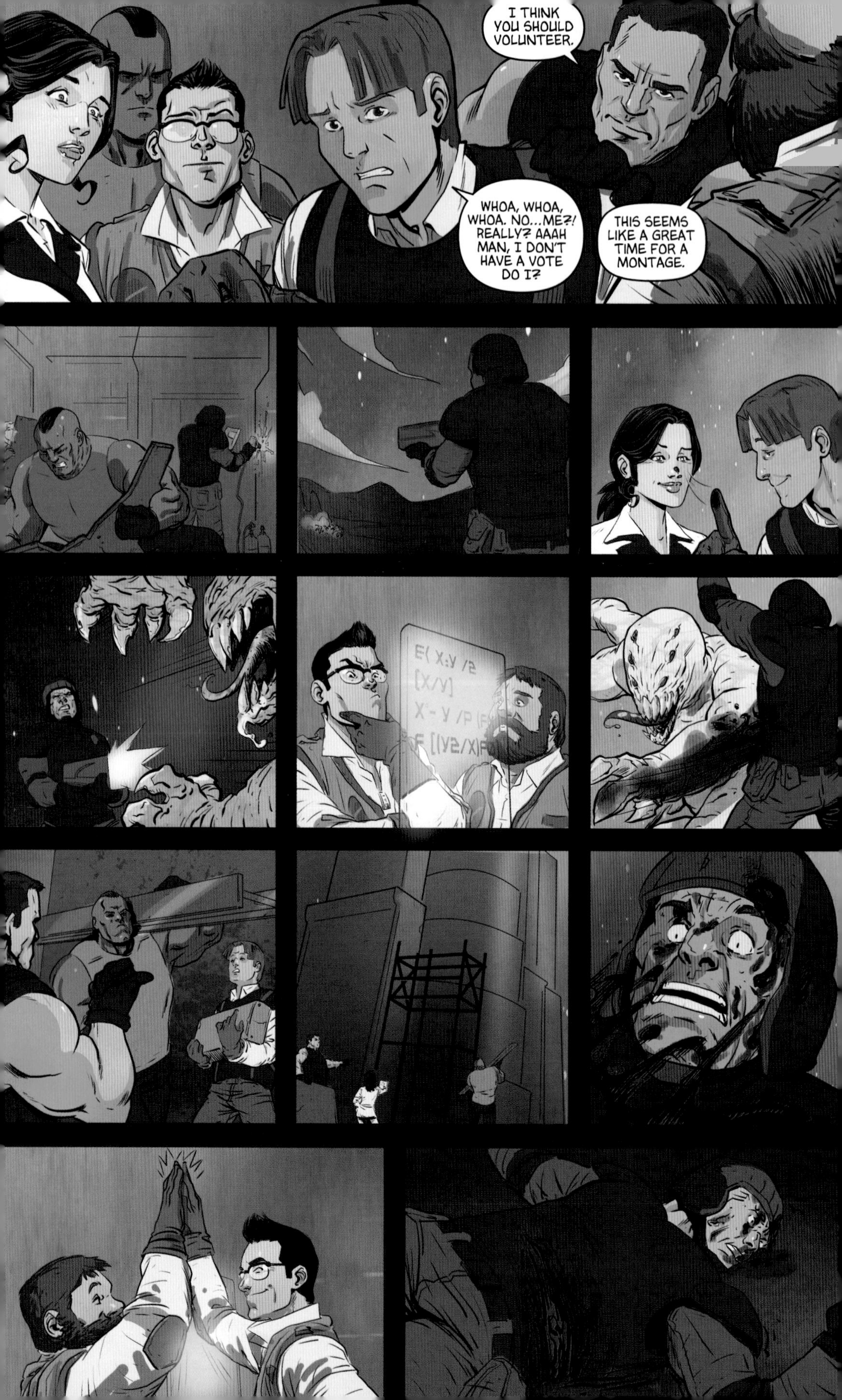
I THINK YOU SHOULD VOLUNTEER.
WHOA, WHOA, WHOA. NO...ME?! REALLY? AAAH MAN, I DON'T HAVE A VOTE DO I?
THIS SEEMS LIKE A GREAT TIME FOR A MONTAGE.

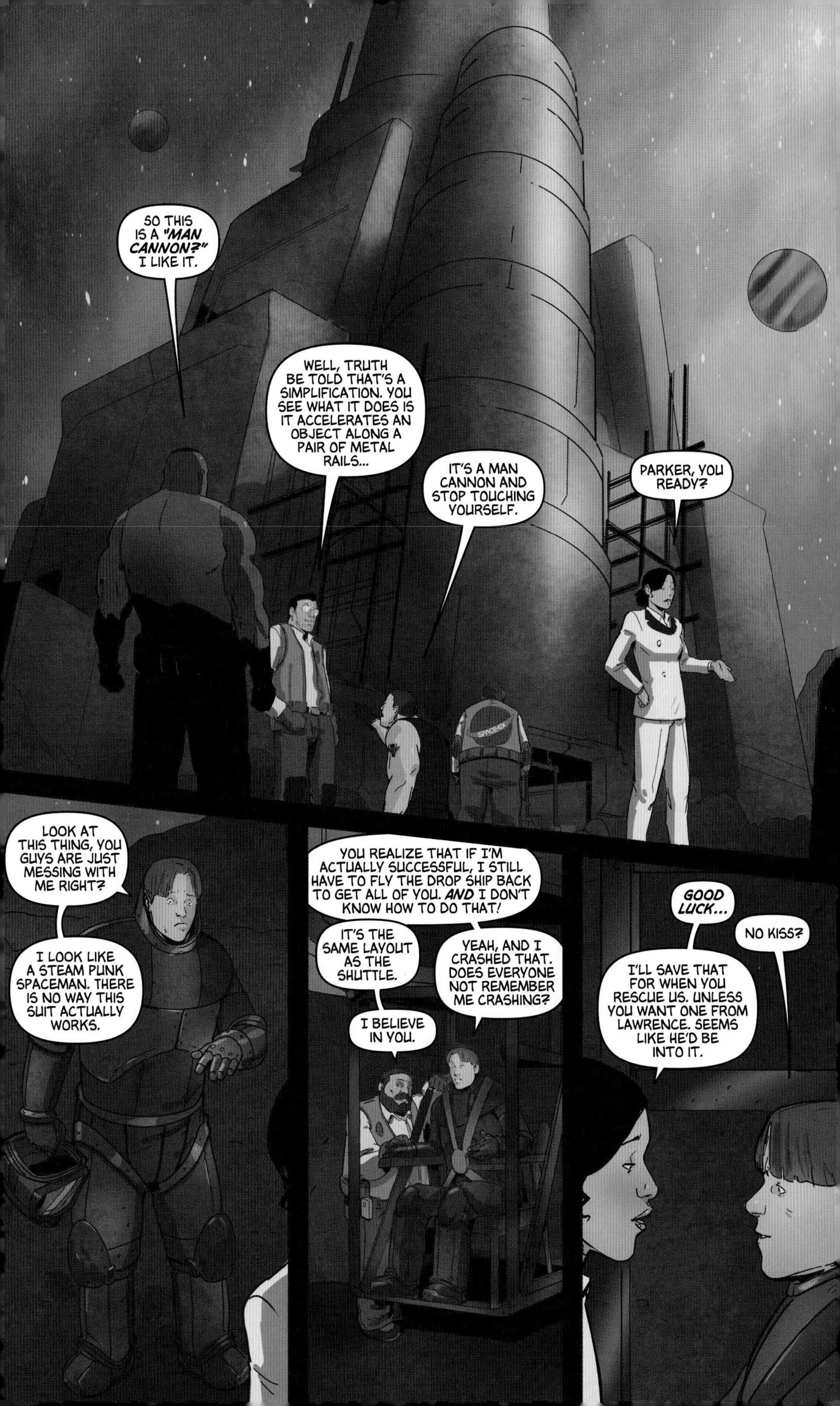
SO THIS IS A "MAN CANNON?" I LIKE IT.
WELL, TRUTH BE TOLD THAT'S A SIMPLIFICATION. YOU SEE WHAT IT DOES IS IT ACCELERATES AN OBJECT ALONG A PAIR OF METAL RAILS...
IT'S A MAN CANNON AND STOP TOUCHING YOURSELF.
PARKER, YOU READY?
SPACE-EX
LOOK AT THIS THING, YOU GUYS ARE JUST MESSING WITH ME RIGHT?
I LOOK LIKE A STEAM PUNK SPACEMAN. THERE IS NO WAY THIS SUIT ACTUALLY WORKS.
YOU REALIZE THAT IF I'M ACTUALLY SUCCESSFUL, I STILL HAVE TO FLY THE DROP SHIP BACK TO GET ALL OF YOU. AND I DON'T KNOW HOW TO DO THAT!
IT'S THE SAME LAYOUT AS THE SHUTTLE.
YEAH, AND I CRASHED THAT. DOES EVERYONE NOT REMEMBER ME CRASHING?
I BELIEVE IN YOU.
GOOD LUCK...
NO KISS?
I'LL SAVE THAT FOR WHEN YOU RESCUE US. UNLESS YOU WANT ONE FROM LAWRENCE. SEEMS LIKE HE'D BE INTO IT.

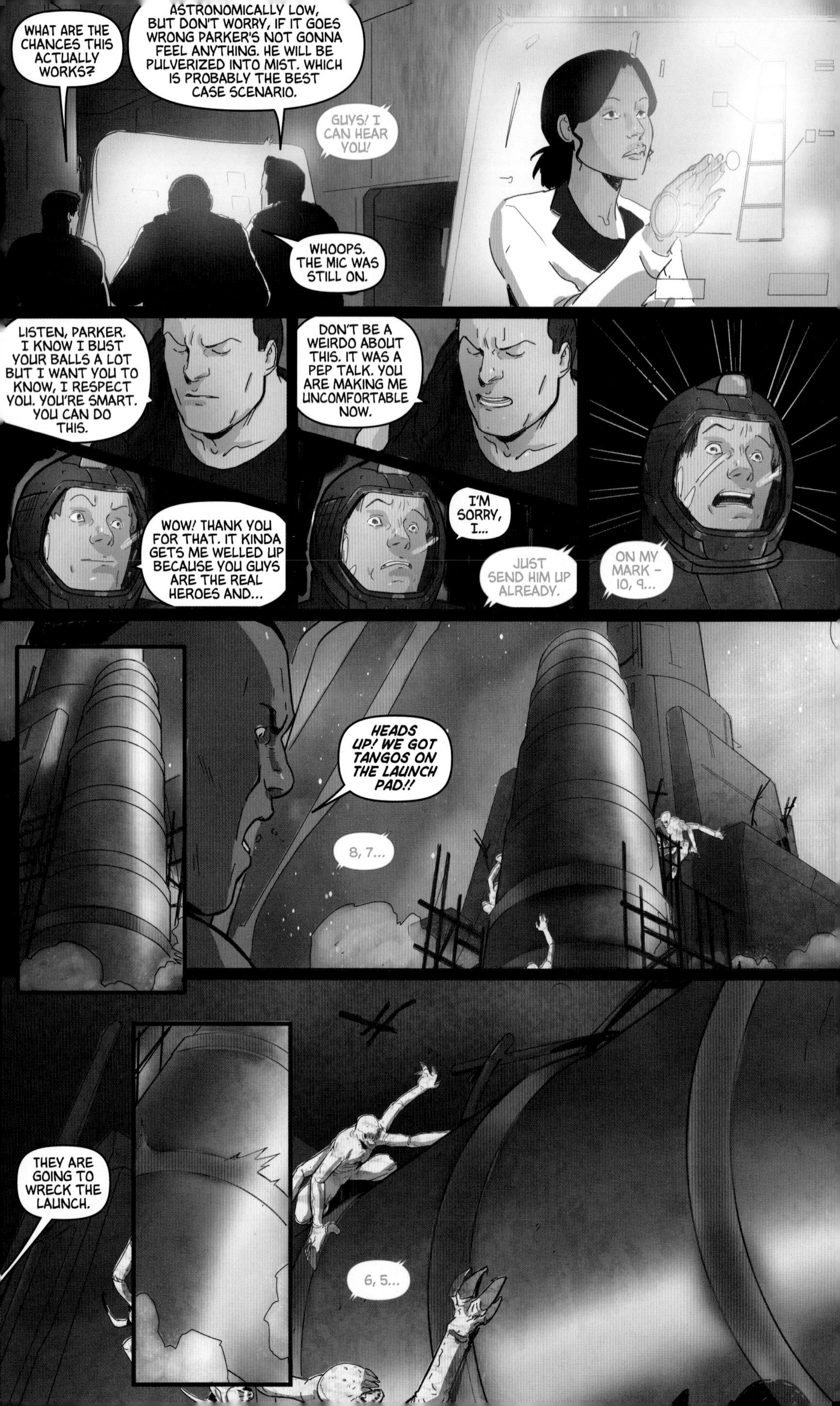
WHAT ARE THE CHANCES THIS ACTUALLY WORKS?
ASTRONOMICALLY LOW, BUT DON'T WORRY, IF IT GOES WRONG PARKER'S NOT GONNA FEEL ANYTHING. HE WILL BE PULVERIZED INTO MIST. WHICH IS PROBABLY THE BEST CASE SCENARIO.
GUYS! I CAN HEAR YOU!
WHOOPS. THE MIC WAS STILL ON.
LISTEN, PARKER. I KNOW I BUST YOUR BALLS A LOT BUT I WANT YOU TO KNOW, I RESPECT YOU. YOU'RE SMART. YOU CAN DO THIS.
WOW! THANK YOU FOR THAT. IT KINDA GETS ME WELLED UP BECAUSE YOU GUYS ARE THE REAL HEROES AND...
DON'T BE A WEIRDO ABOUT THIS. IT WAS A PEP TALK. YOU ARE MAKING ME UNCOMFORTABLE NOW.
I'M SORRY, I...
JUST SEND HIM UP ALREADY.
ON MY MARK - 10, 9...
HEADS UP! WE GOT TANGOS ON THE LAUNCH PAD!!
8, 7...
THEY ARE GOING TO WRECK THE LAUNCH.
6, 5...

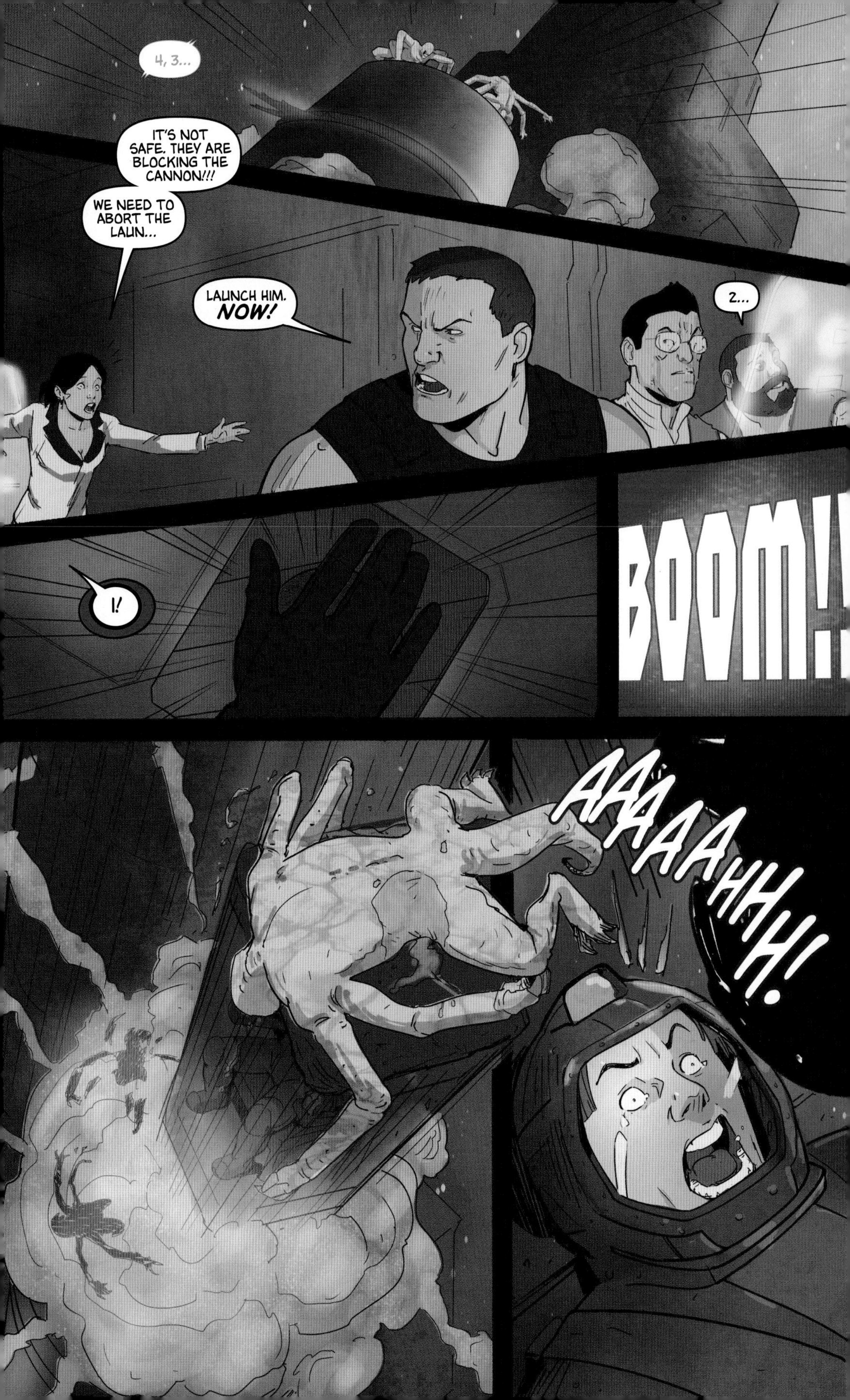
4, 3...
IT'S NOT SAFE. THEY ARE BLOCKING THE CANNON!!!
WE NEED TO ABORT THE LAUN...
LAUNCH HIM. NOW!
2...
1!
BOOM!!
AAAAAAAHHHH!

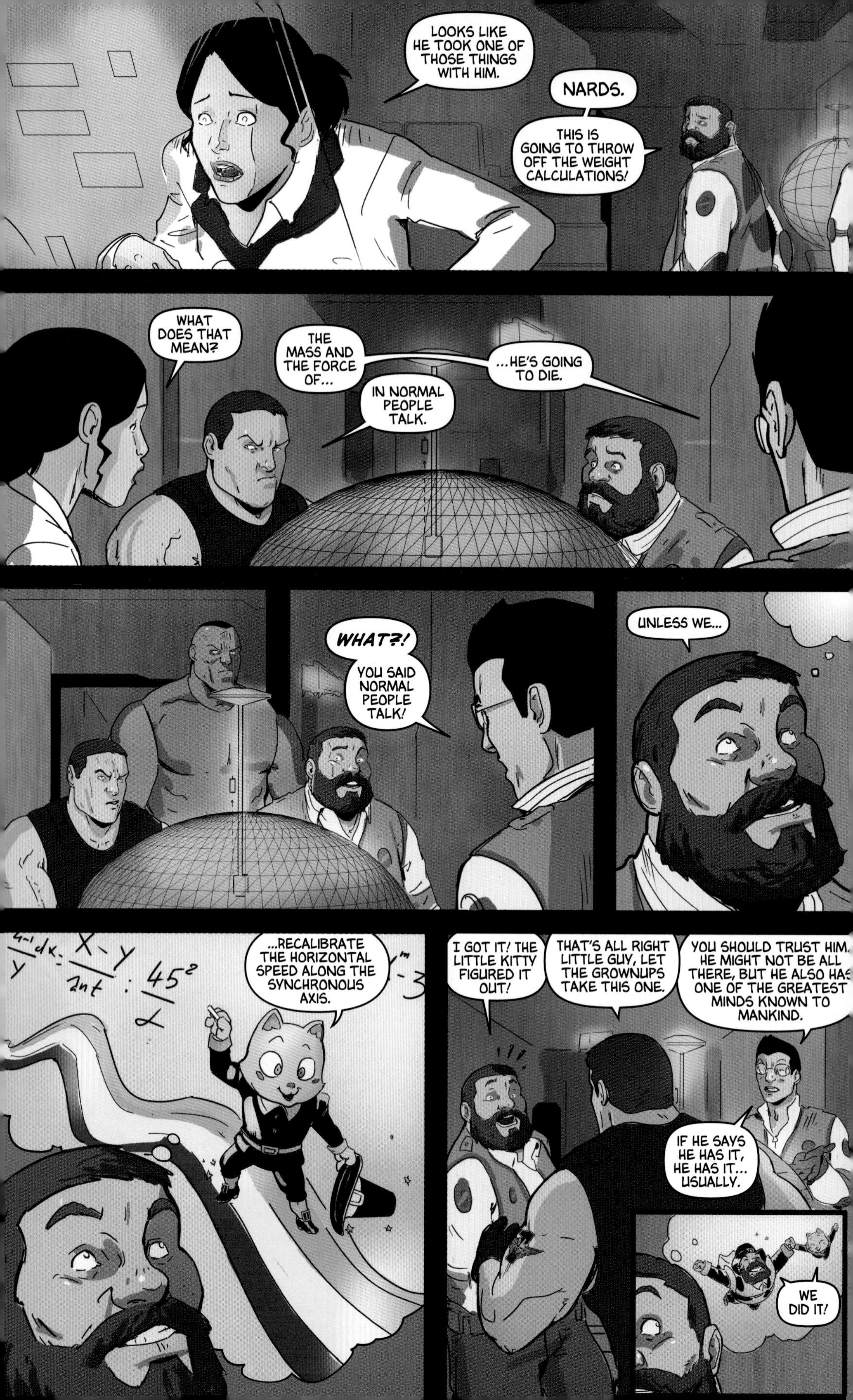
LOOKS LIKE HE TOOK ONE OF THOSE THINGS WITH HIM.
NARDS.
THIS IS GOING TO THROW OFF THE WEIGHT CALCULATIONS!
WHAT DOES THAT MEAN?
THE MASS AND THE FORCE OF...
IN NORMAL PEOPLE TALK.
...HE'S GOING TO DIE.
WHAT?!
YOU SAID NORMAL PEOPLE TALK!
UNLESS WE...
...RECALIBRATE THE HORIZONTAL SPEED ALONG THE SYNCHRONOUS AXIS.
I GOT IT! THE LITTLE KITTY FIGURED IT OUT!
THAT'S ALL RIGHT LITTLE GUY, LET THE GROWNUPS TAKE THIS ONE.
YOU SHOULD TRUST HIM. HE MIGHT NOT BE ALL THERE, BUT HE ALSO HAS ONE OF THE GREATEST MINDS KNOWN TO MANKIND.
IF HE SAYS HE HAS IT, HE HAS IT... USUALLY.
WE DID IT!

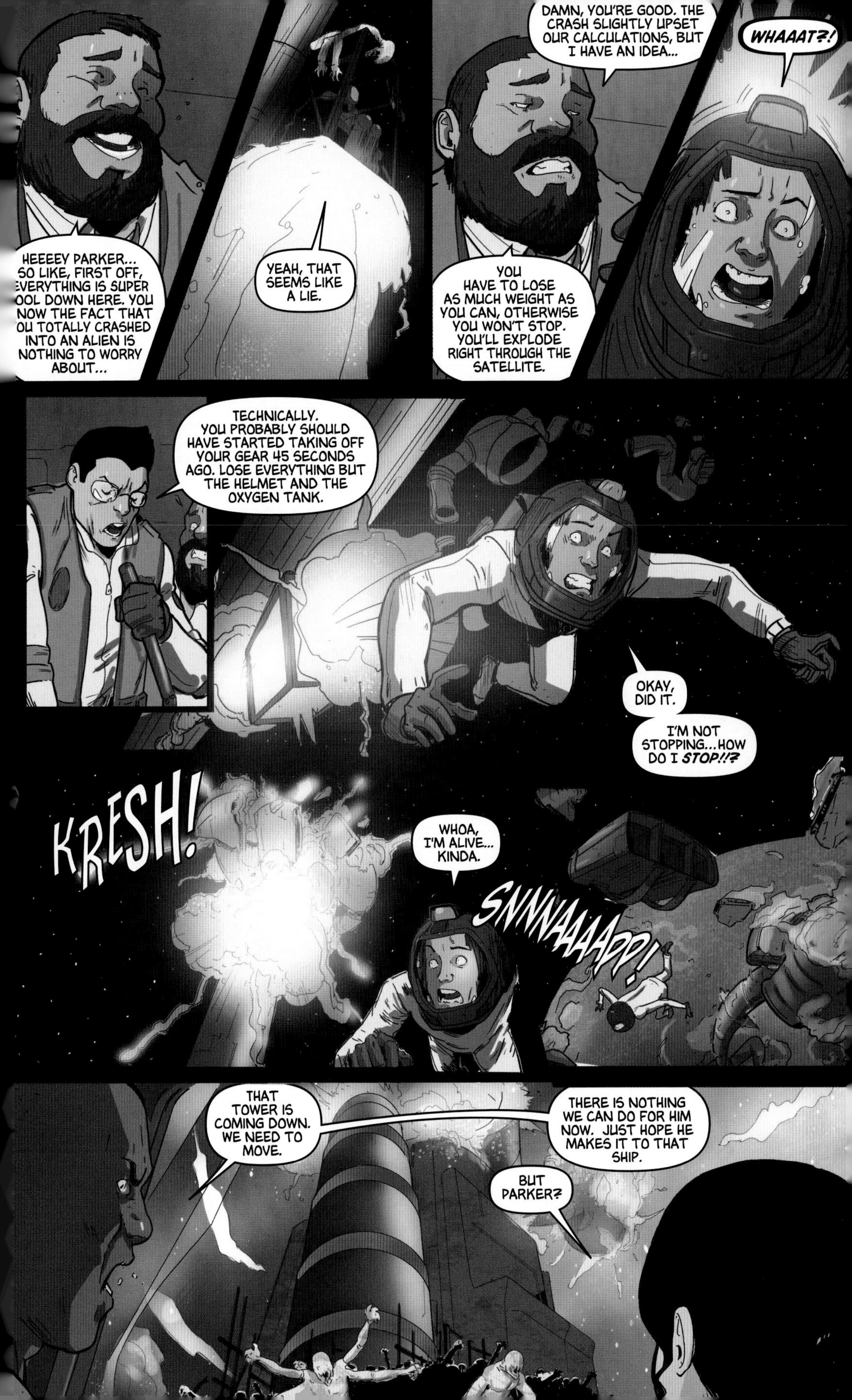
HEEEEY PARKER... SO LIKE, FIRST OFF, EVERYTHING IS SUPER COOL DOWN HERE. YOU KNOW THE FACT THAT YOU TOTALLY CRASHED INTO AN ALIEN IS NOTHING TO WORRY ABOUT...
YEAH, THAT SEEMS LIKE A LIE.
DAMN, YOU'RE GOOD. THE CRASH SLIGHTLY UPSET OUR CALCULATIONS, BUT I HAVE AN IDEA...
YOU HAVE TO LOSE AS MUCH WEIGHT AS YOU CAN, OTHERWISE YOU WON'T STOP. YOU'LL EXPLODE RIGHT THROUGH THE SATELLITE.
WHAAAT?!
TECHNICALLY. YOU PROBABLY SHOULD HAVE STARTED TAKING OFF YOUR GEAR 45 SECONDS AGO. LOSE EVERYTHING BUT THE HELMET AND THE OXYGEN TANK.
OKAY, DID IT.
I'M NOT STOPPING...HOW DO I STOP!!?
KRESH!
WHOA, I'M ALIVE... KINDA.
SNNNAAAAPP!
THAT TOWER IS COMING DOWN. WE NEED TO MOVE.
THERE IS NOTHING WE CAN DO FOR HIM NOW. JUST HOPE HE MAKES IT TO THAT SHIP.
BUT PARKER?

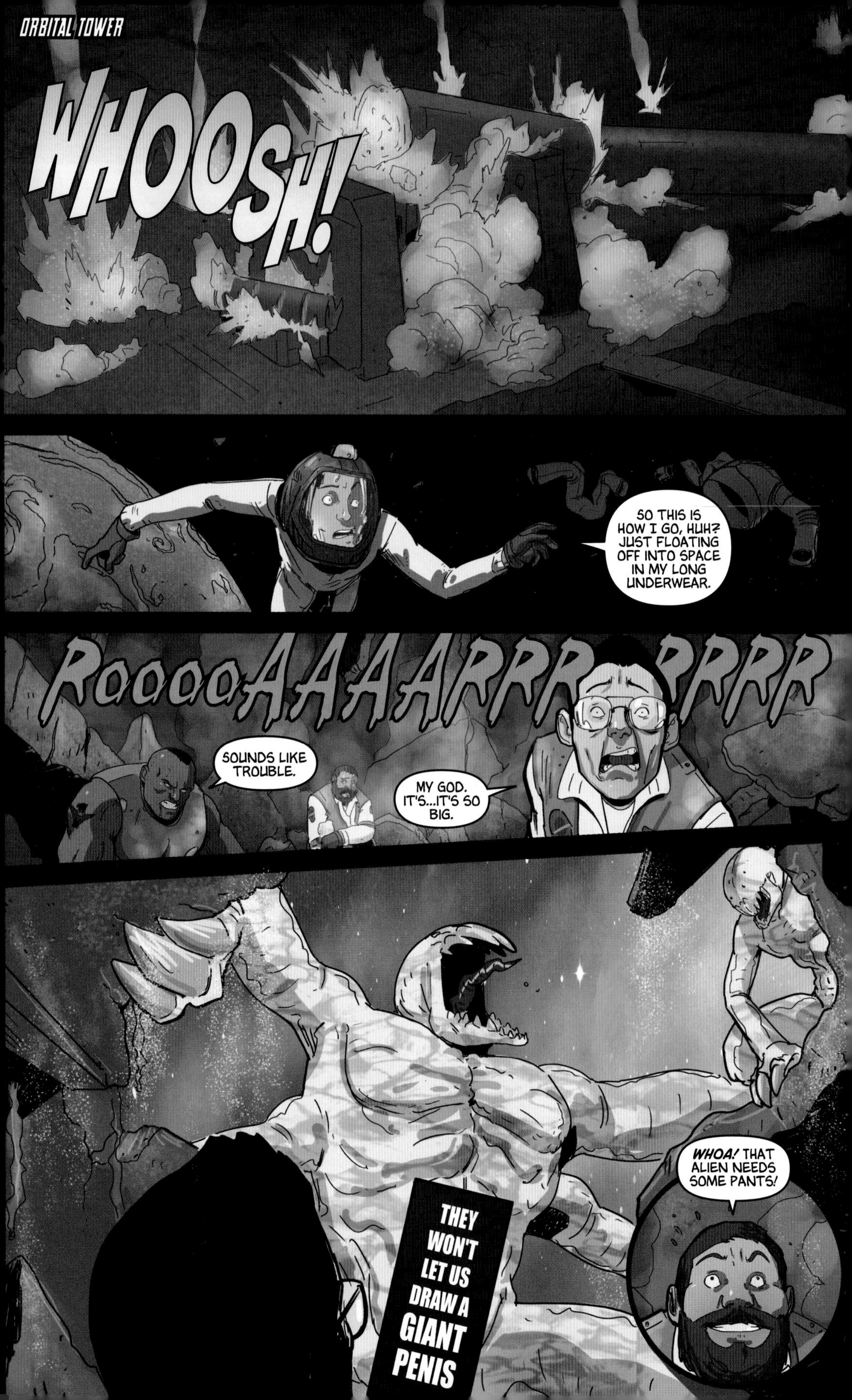
WHOOSH!
SO THIS IS HOW I GO, HUH? JUST FLOATING OFF INTO SPACE IN MY LONG UNDERWEAR.
RaaaaAAAAARRRRRRRR
SOUNDS LIKE TROUBLE.
MY GOD. IT'S...IT'S SO BIG.
WHOA! THAT ALIEN NEEDS SOME PANTS!
THEY WON'T LET US DRAW A GIANT PENIS

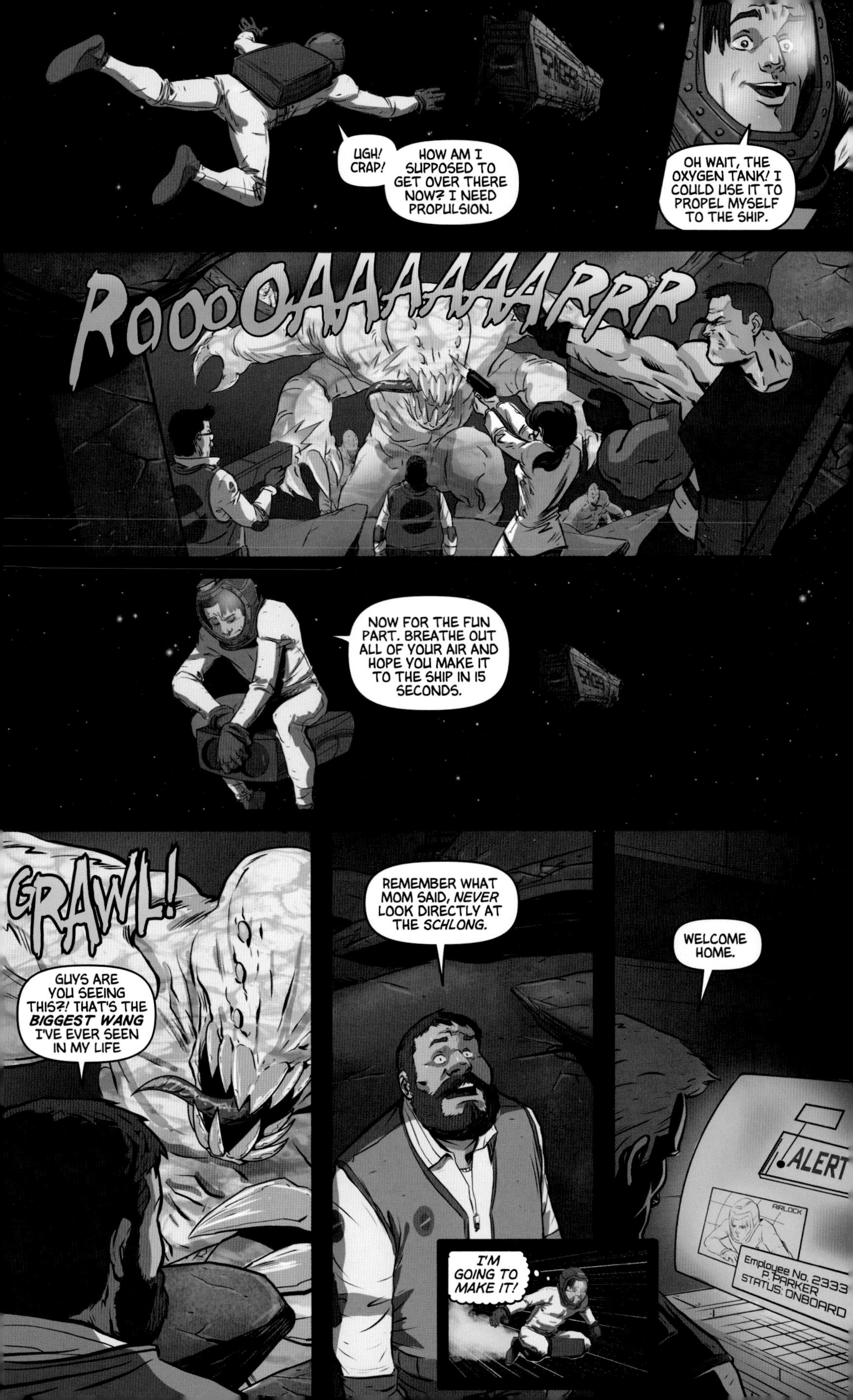
UGH! CRAP!
HOW AM I SUPPOSED TO GET OVER THERE NOW?! I NEED PROPULSION.
OH WAIT, THE OXYGEN TANK! I COULD USE IT TO PROPEL MYSELF TO THE SHIP.
ROOOOAAAAAAARRR
NOW FOR THE FUN PART. BREATHE OUT ALL OF YOUR AIR AND HOPE YOU MAKE IT TO THE SHIP IN 15 SECONDS.
GRAWL!
GUYS ARE YOU SEEING THIS?! THAT'S THE *BIGGEST WANG* I'VE EVER SEEN IN MY LIFE
REMEMBER WHAT MOM SAID, *NEVER* LOOK DIRECTLY AT THE *SCHLONG*.
I'M GOING TO MAKE IT!
WELCOME HOME.
ALERT
AIRLOCK
Employee No. 2333
P. PARKER
STATUS: ONBOARD

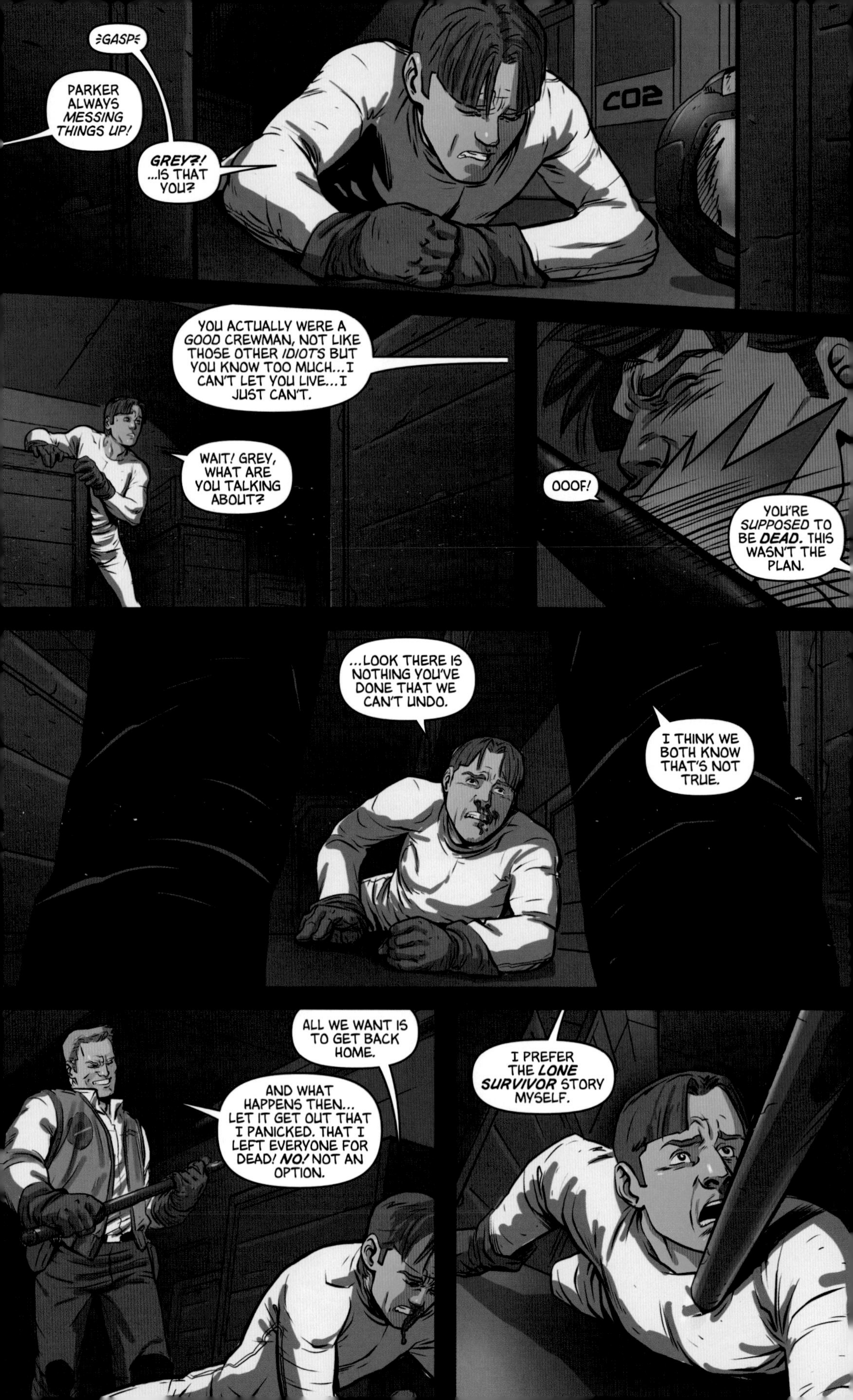

PARKER ALWAYS *MESSING THINGS UP!*
GASP
GREY?! ...IS THAT YOU?
YOU ACTUALLY WERE A *GOOD* CREWMAN, NOT LIKE THOSE OTHER *IDIOTS* BUT YOU KNOW TOO MUCH...I CAN'T LET YOU LIVE...I JUST CAN'T.
WAIT! GREY, WHAT ARE YOU TALKING ABOUT?
OOOF!
YOU'RE *SUPPOSED* TO BE ***DEAD.*** THIS WASN'T THE PLAN.
...LOOK THERE IS NOTHING YOU'VE DONE THAT WE CAN'T UNDO.
I THINK WE BOTH KNOW THAT'S NOT TRUE.
ALL WE WANT IS TO GET BACK HOME.
AND WHAT HAPPENS THEN... LET IT GET OUT THAT I PANICKED. THAT I LEFT EVERYONE FOR DEAD! ***NO!*** NOT AN OPTION.
I PREFER THE ***LONE SURVIVOR*** STORY MYSELF.

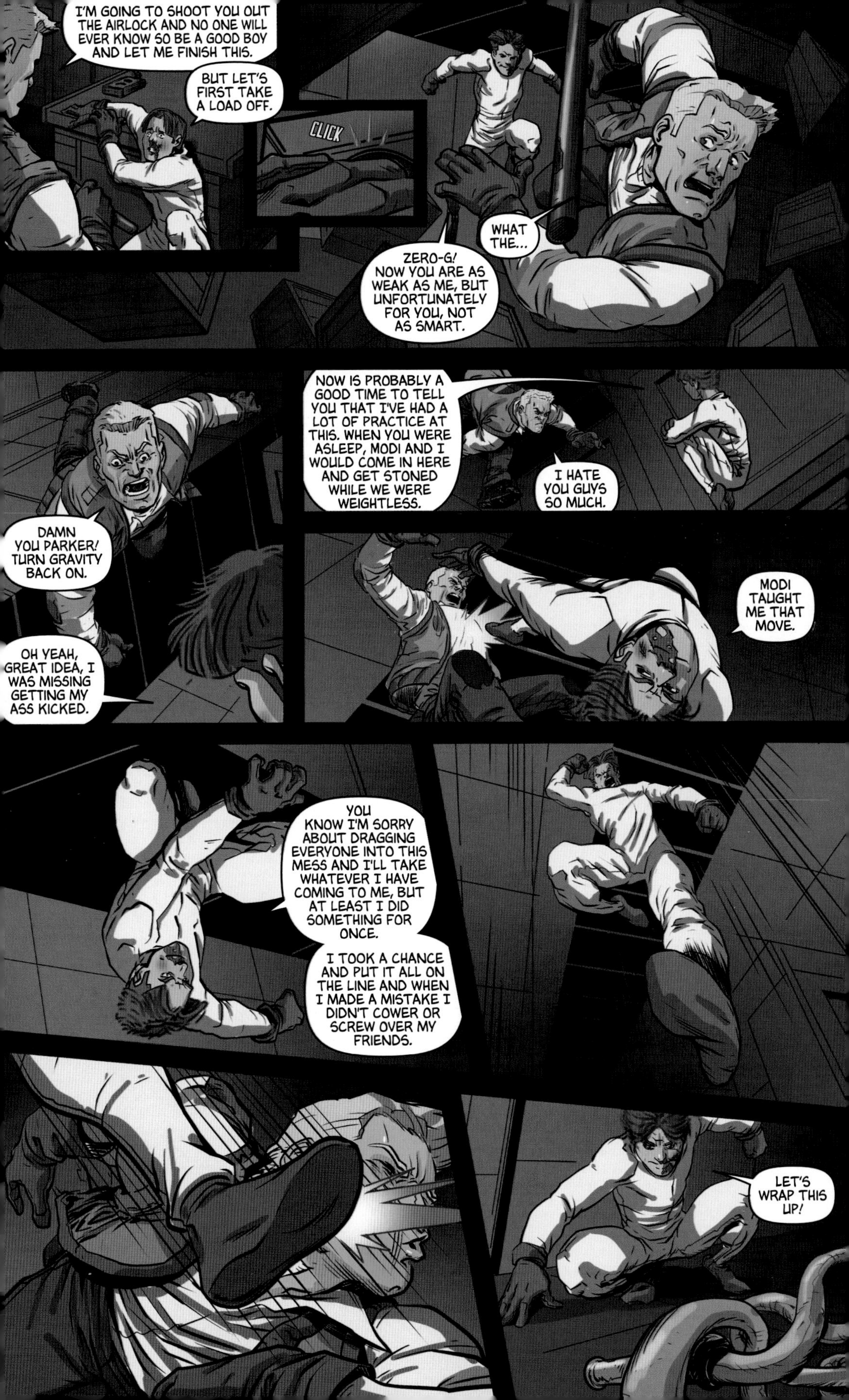
I'M GOING TO SHOOT YOU OUT THE AIRLOCK AND NO ONE WILL EVER KNOW SO BE A GOOD BOY AND LET ME FINISH THIS.
BUT LET'S FIRST TAKE A LOAD OFF.
CLICK
WHAT THE...
ZERO-G! NOW YOU ARE AS WEAK AS ME, BUT UNFORTUNATELY FOR YOU, NOT AS SMART.
DAMN YOU PARKER! TURN GRAVITY BACK ON.
OH YEAH, GREAT IDEA, I WAS MISSING GETTING MY ASS KICKED.
NOW IS PROBABLY A GOOD TIME TO TELL YOU THAT I'VE HAD A LOT OF PRACTICE AT THIS. WHEN YOU WERE ASLEEP, MODI AND I WOULD COME IN HERE AND GET STONED WHILE WE WERE WEIGHTLESS.
I HATE YOU GUYS SO MUCH.
MODI TAUGHT ME THAT MOVE.
YOU KNOW I'M SORRY ABOUT DRAGGING EVERYONE INTO THIS MESS AND I'LL TAKE WHATEVER I HAVE COMING TO ME, BUT AT LEAST I DID SOMETHING FOR ONCE.
I TOOK A CHANCE AND PUT IT ALL ON THE LINE AND WHEN I MADE A MISTAKE I DIDN'T COWER OR SCREW OVER MY FRIENDS.
LET'S WRAP THIS UP!

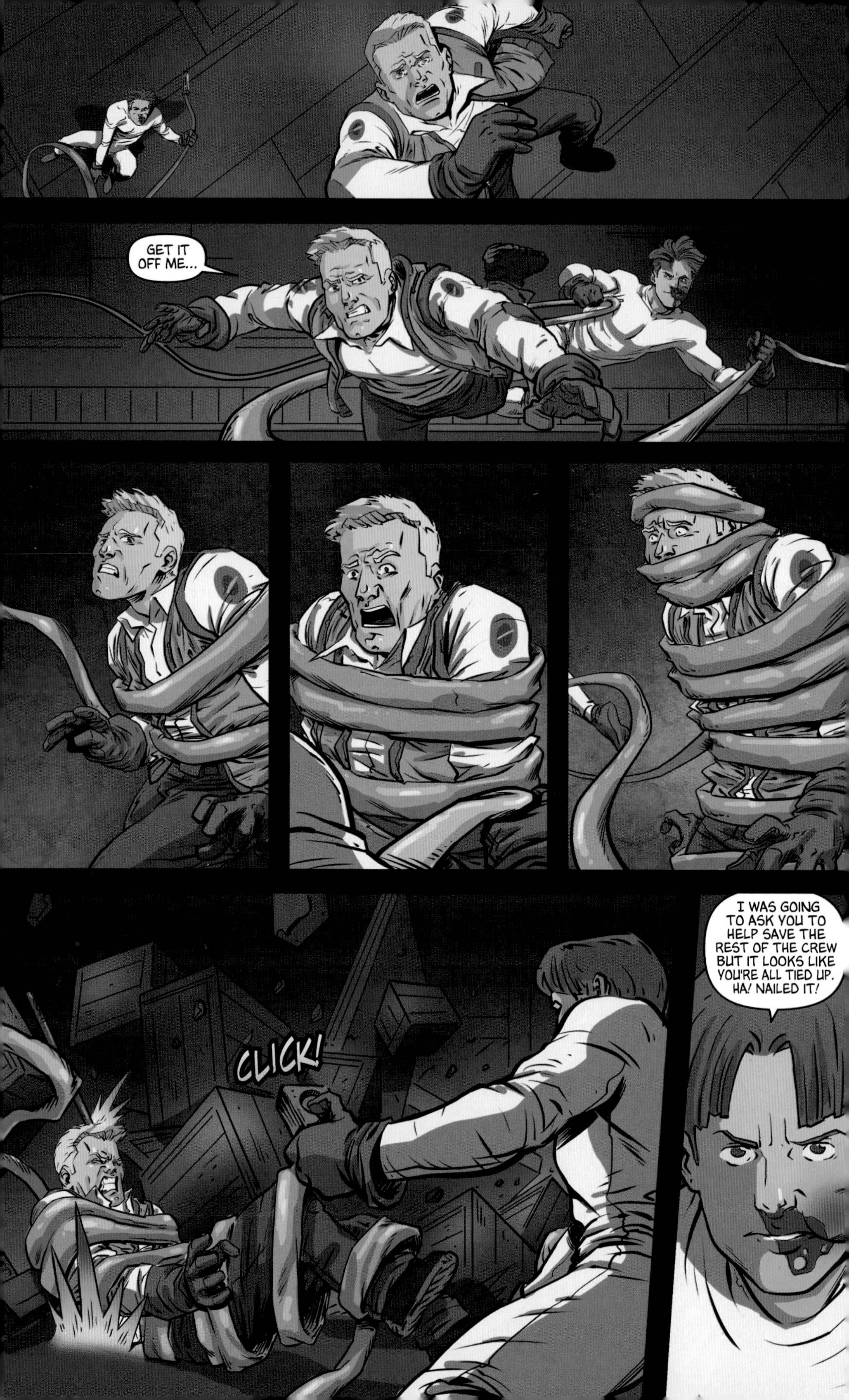
GET IT OFF ME...
CLICK!
I WAS GOING TO ASK YOU TO HELP SAVE THE REST OF THE CREW BUT IT LOOKS LIKE YOU'RE ALL TIED UP. HA! NAILED IT!

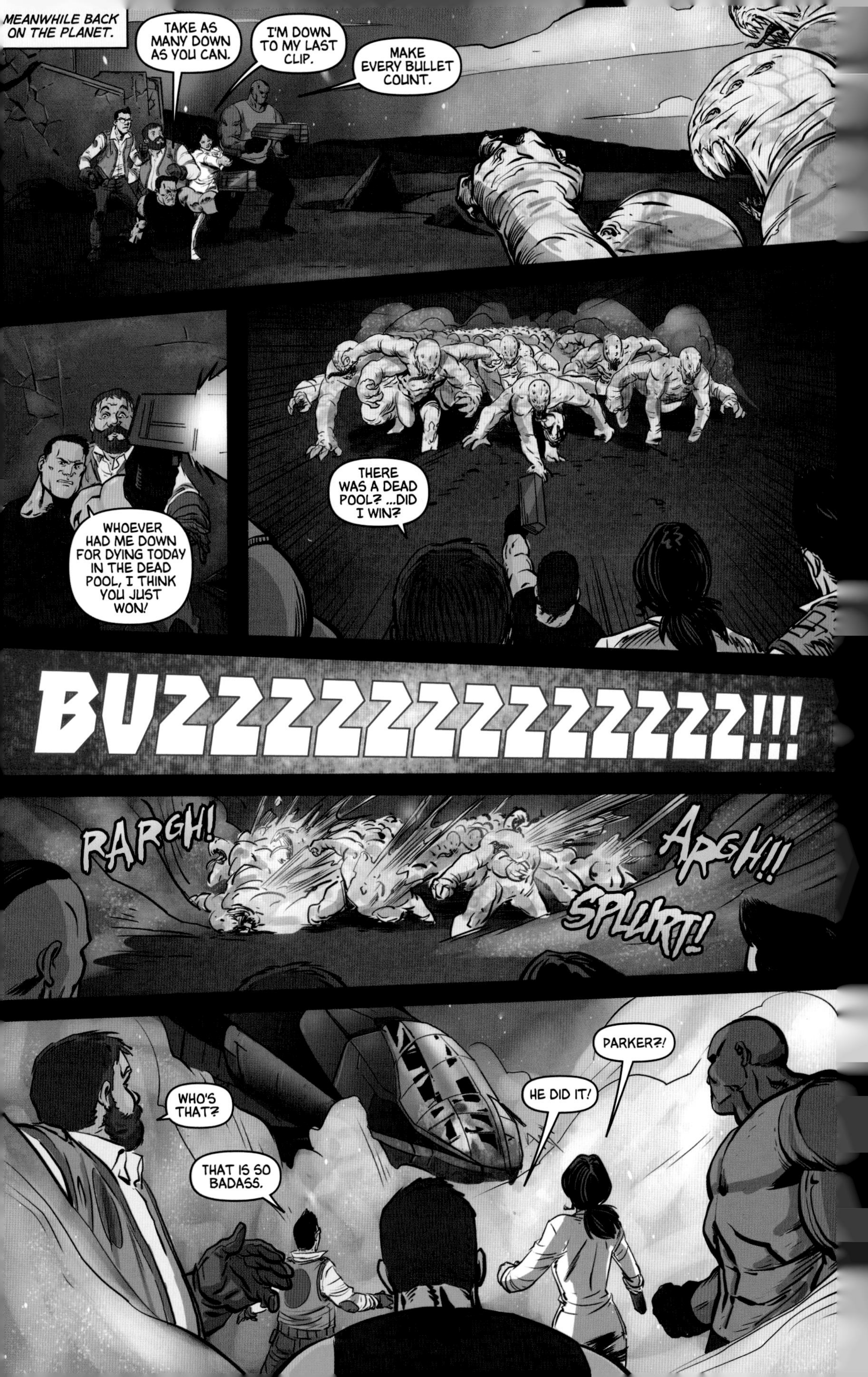

MEANWHILE BACK ON THE PLANET.
TAKE AS MANY DOWN AS YOU CAN.
I'M DOWN TO MY LAST CLIP.
MAKE EVERY BULLET COUNT.
WHOEVER HAD ME DOWN FOR DYING TODAY IN THE DEAD POOL, I THINK YOU JUST WON!
THERE WAS A DEAD POOL? ...DID I WIN?
BUZZZZZZZZZZZZZ!!!
RARGH!
ARGH!!
SPLURT!
WHO'S THAT?
THAT IS SO BADASS.
HE DID IT!
PARKER?!

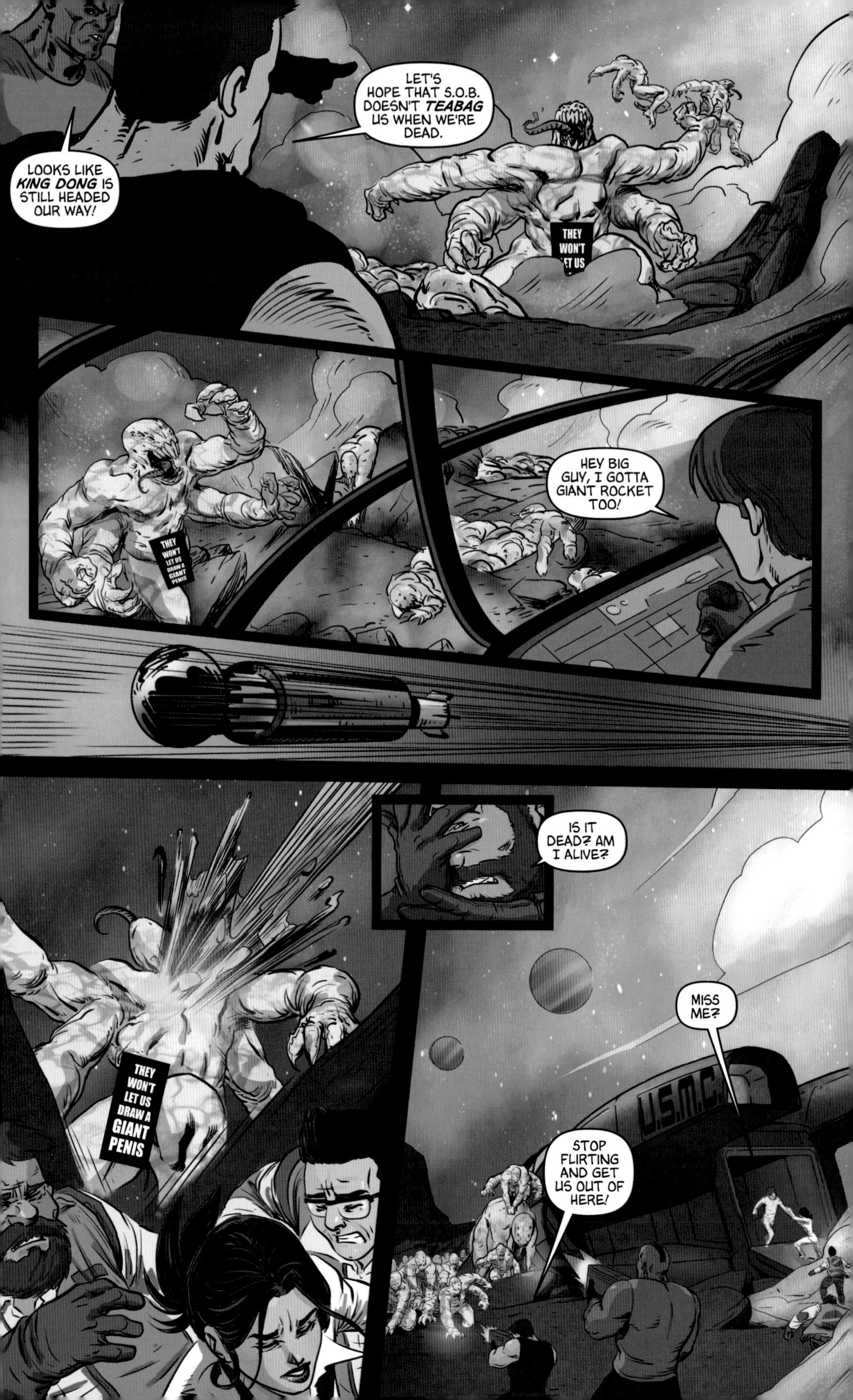
LOOKS LIKE **KING DONG** IS STILL HEADED OUR WAY!
LET'S HOPE THAT S.O.B. DOESN'T ***TEABAG*** US WHEN WE'RE DEAD.
THEY WON'T
THEY WON'T LET US DRAW A GIANT PENIS
HEY BIG GUY, I GOTTA GIANT ROCKET TOO!
THEY WON'T LET US DRAW A GIANT PENIS
IS IT DEAD? AM I ALIVE?
MISS ME?
U.S.M.C.
STOP FLIRTING AND GET US OUT OF HERE!

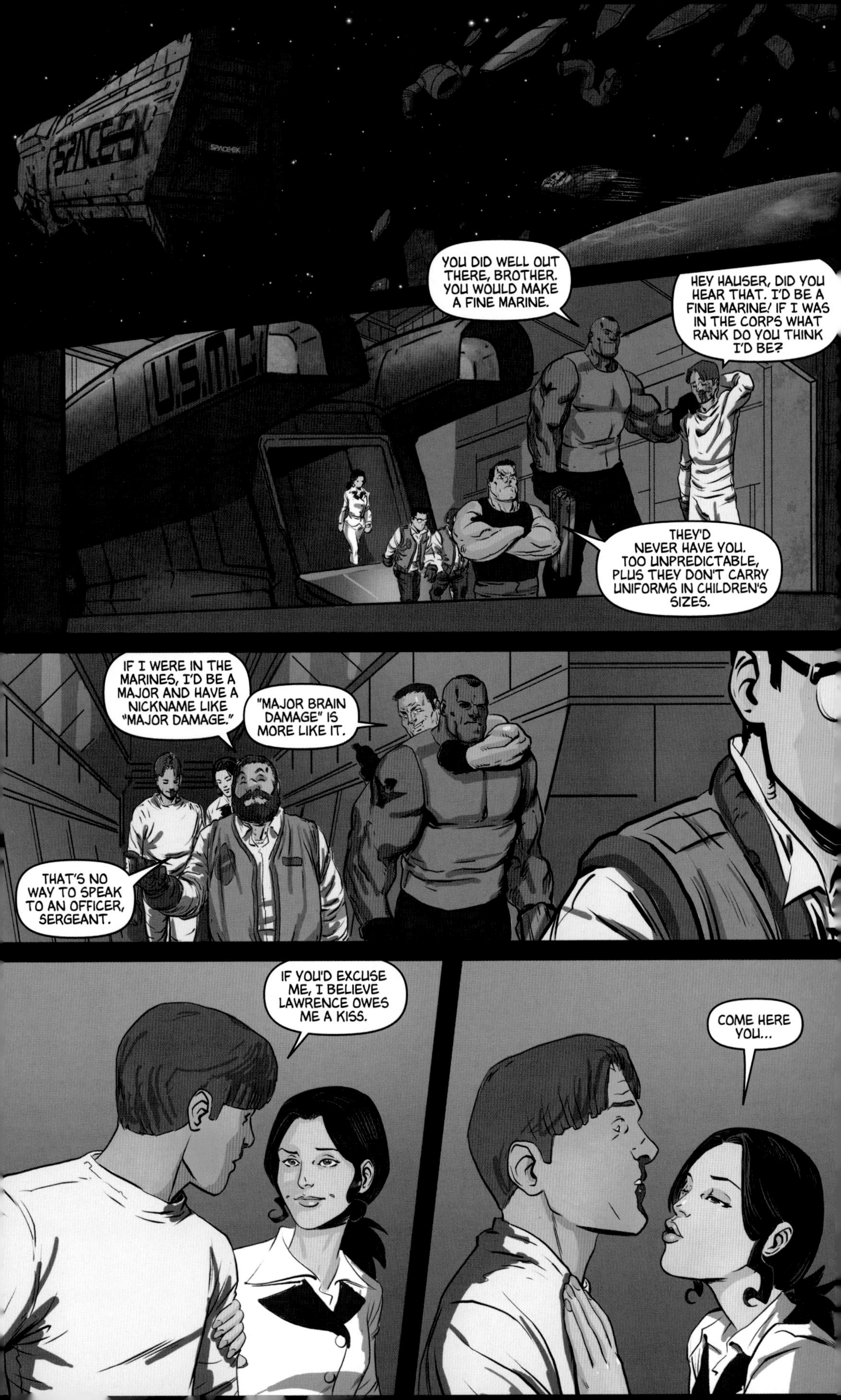
SPACEX
SPACEX
U.S.M.C.
YOU DID WELL OUT THERE, BROTHER. YOU WOULD MAKE A FINE MARINE.
HEY HAUSER, DID YOU HEAR THAT. I'D BE A FINE MARINE! IF I WAS IN THE CORPS WHAT RANK DO YOU THINK I'D BE?
THEY'D NEVER HAVE YOU. TOO UNPREDICTABLE, PLUS THEY DON'T CARRY UNIFORMS IN CHILDREN'S SIZES.
IF I WERE IN THE MARINES, I'D BE A MAJOR AND HAVE A NICKNAME LIKE "MAJOR DAMAGE."
"MAJOR BRAIN DAMAGE" IS MORE LIKE IT.
THAT'S NO WAY TO SPEAK TO AN OFFICER, SERGEANT.
IF YOU'D EXCUSE ME, I BELIEVE LAWRENCE OWES ME A KISS.
COME HERE YOU...

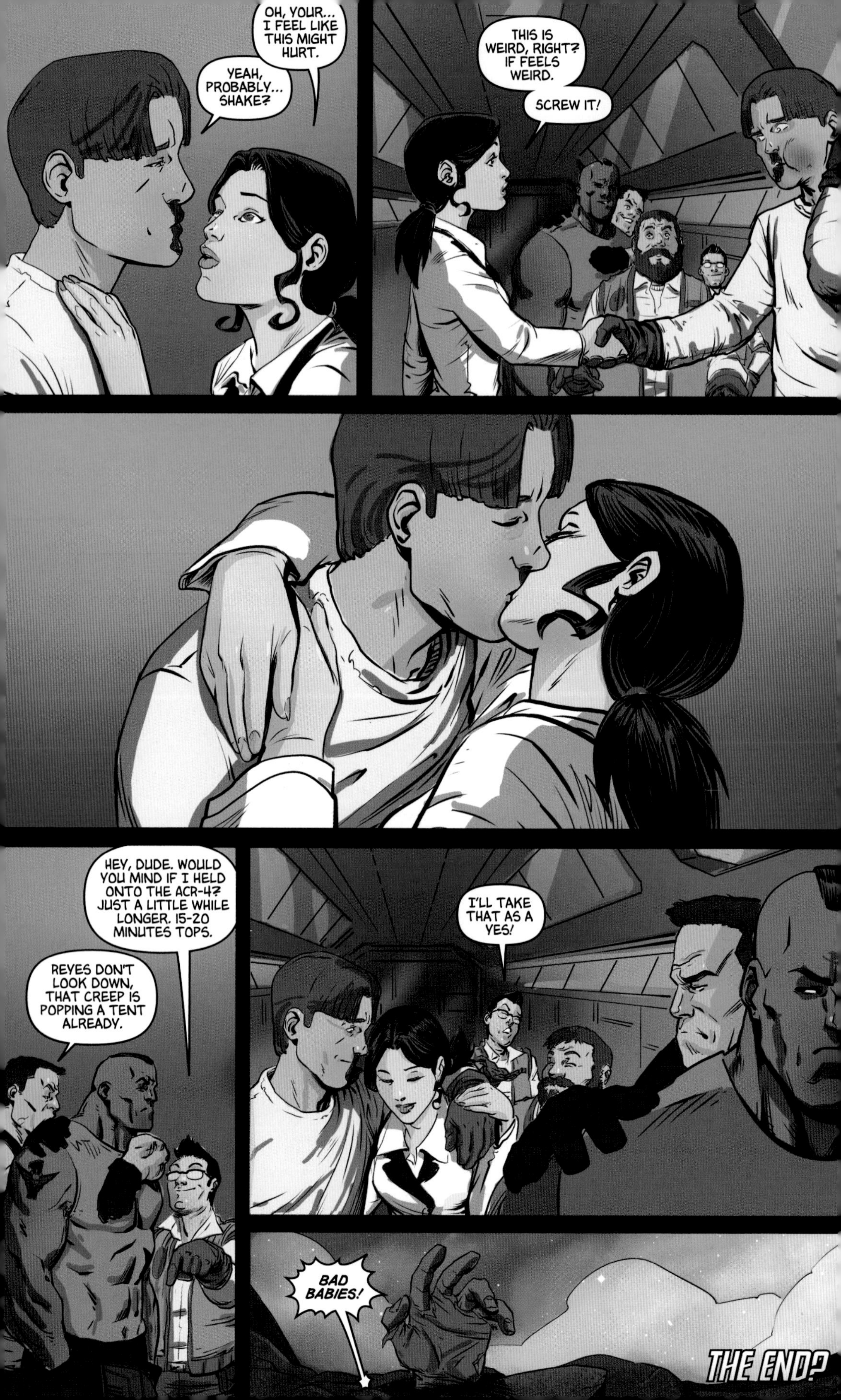

OH, YOUR... I FEEL LIKE THIS MIGHT HURT.
YEAH, PROBABLY... SHAKE?
THIS IS WEIRD, RIGHT? IF FEELS WEIRD.
SCREW IT!
HEY, DUDE. WOULD YOU MIND IF I HELD ONTO THE ACR-4? JUST A LITTLE WHILE LONGER. 15-20 MINUTES TOPS.
REYES DON'T LOOK DOWN, THAT CREEP IS POPPING A TENT ALREADY.
I'LL TAKE THAT AS A YES!
BAD BABIES!
THE END?

SPACE-EX

"We know how to handle your package."

NTSF:SD:SUV::

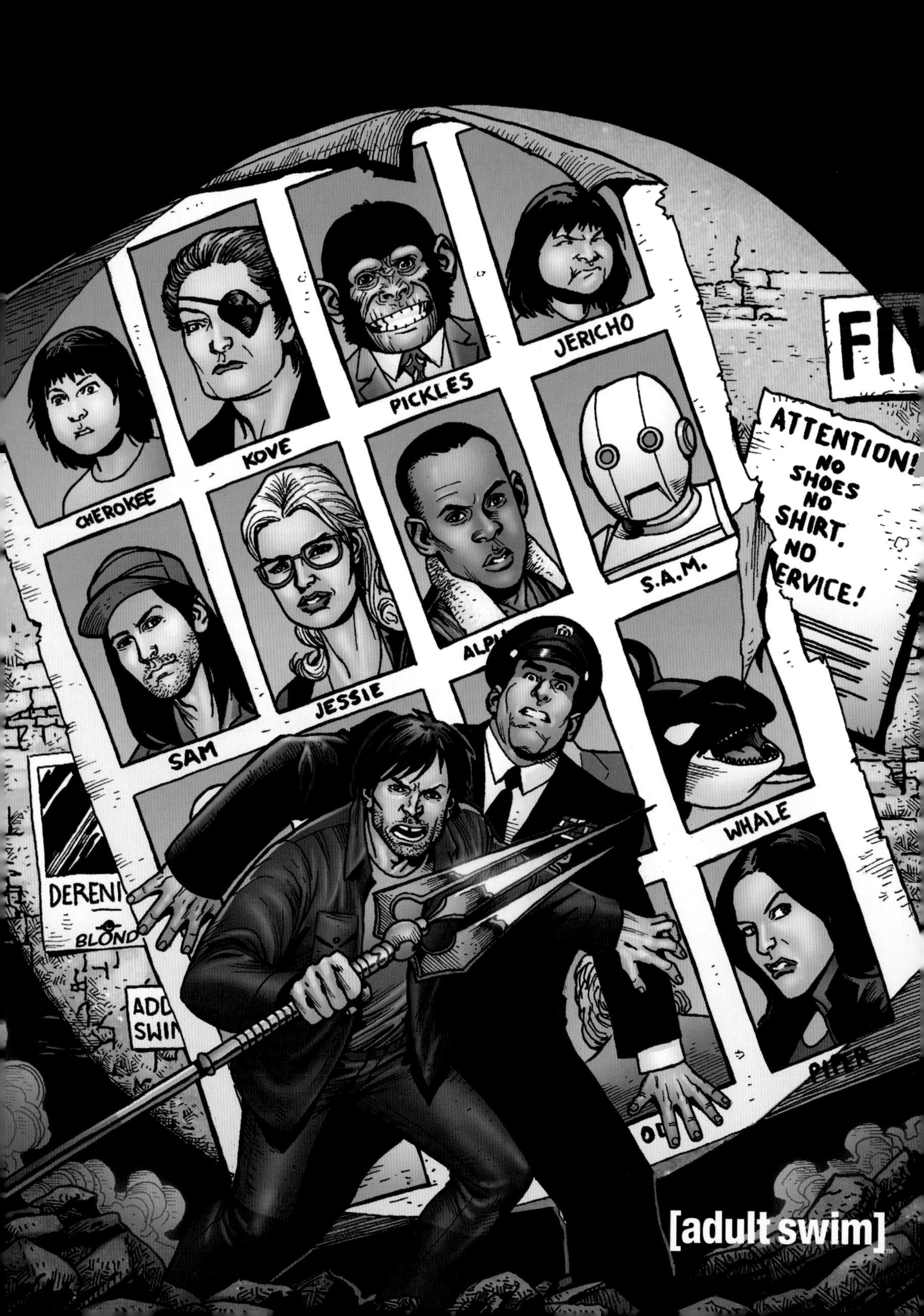
CHEROKEE
KOVE
PICKLES
JERICHO
SAM
JESSIE
S.A.M.
WHALE
ATTENTION!
NO SHOES
NO SHIRT,
NO
ERVICE!
DERENI
BLOND
[adult swim]

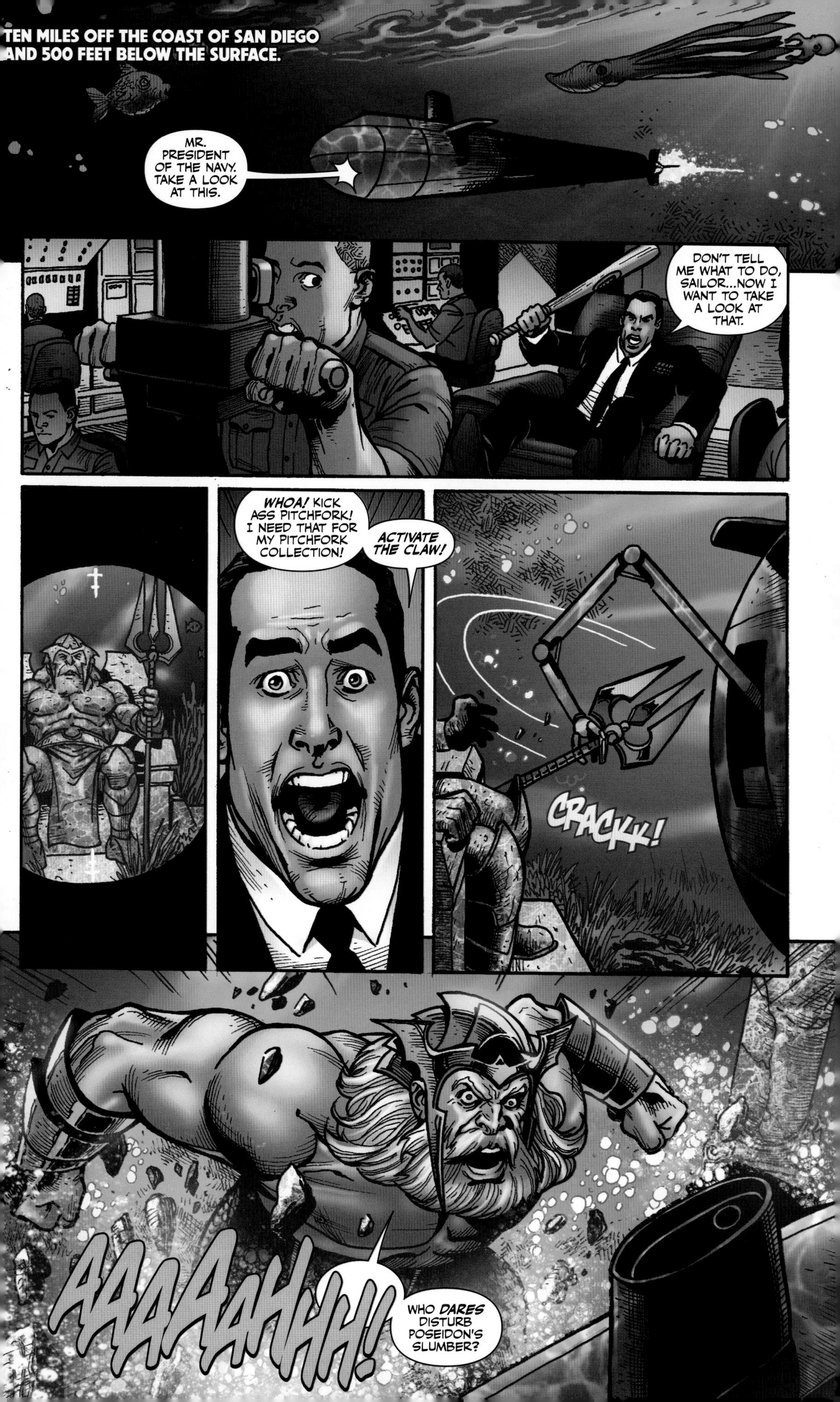
TEN MILES OFF THE COAST OF SAN DIEGO AND 500 FEET BELOW THE SURFACE.
MR. PRESIDENT OF THE NAVY. TAKE A LOOK AT THIS.
DON'T TELL ME WHAT TO DO, SAILOR...NOW I WANT TO TAKE A LOOK AT THAT.
WHOA! KICK ASS PITCHFORK! I NEED THAT FOR MY PITCHFORK COLLECTION!
ACTIVATE THE CLAW!
CRACKK!
AAAAAHHH!
WHO DARES DISTURB POSEIDON'S SLUMBER?

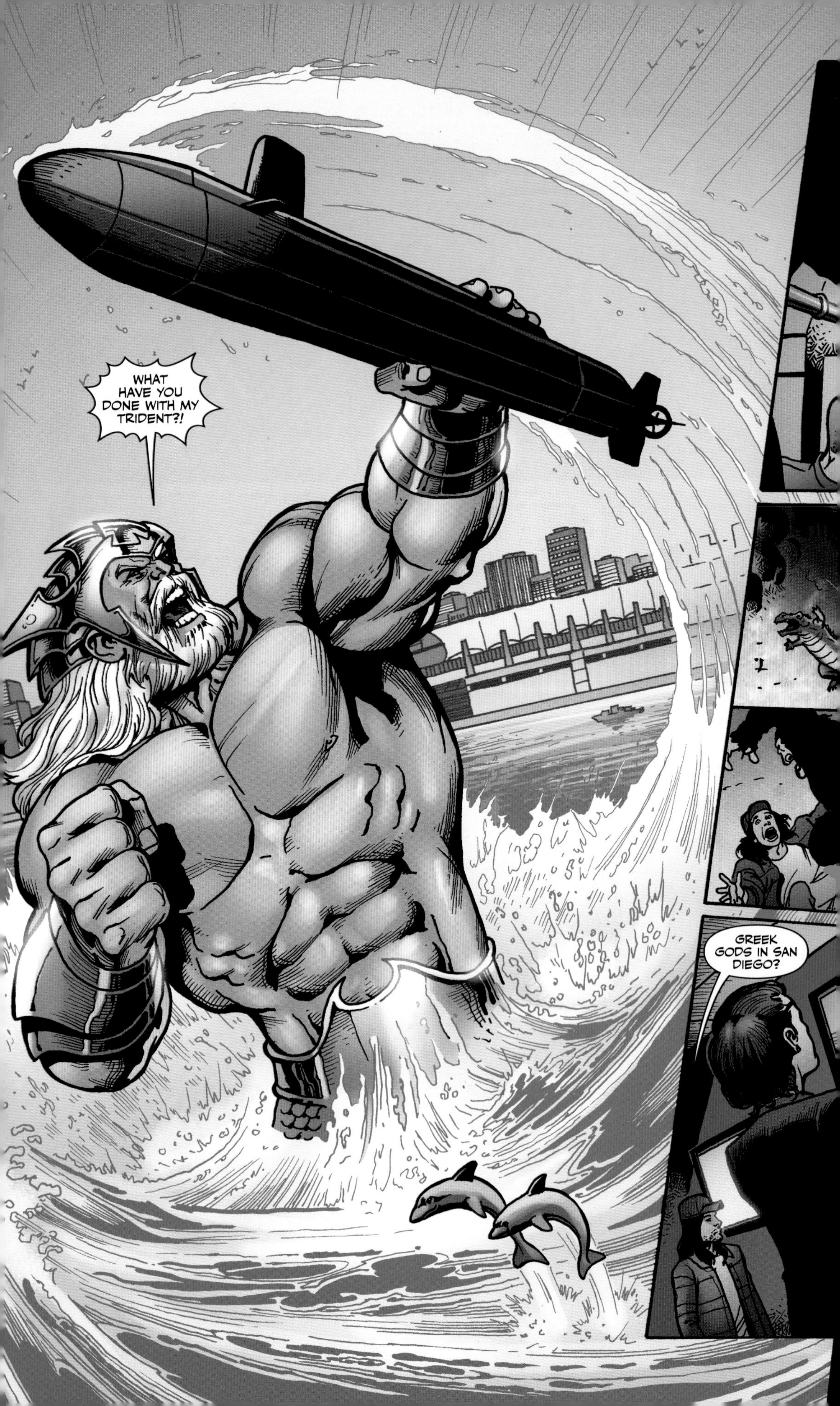
WHAT HAVE YOU DONE WITH MY TRIDENT?!
GREEK GODS IN SAN DIEGO?

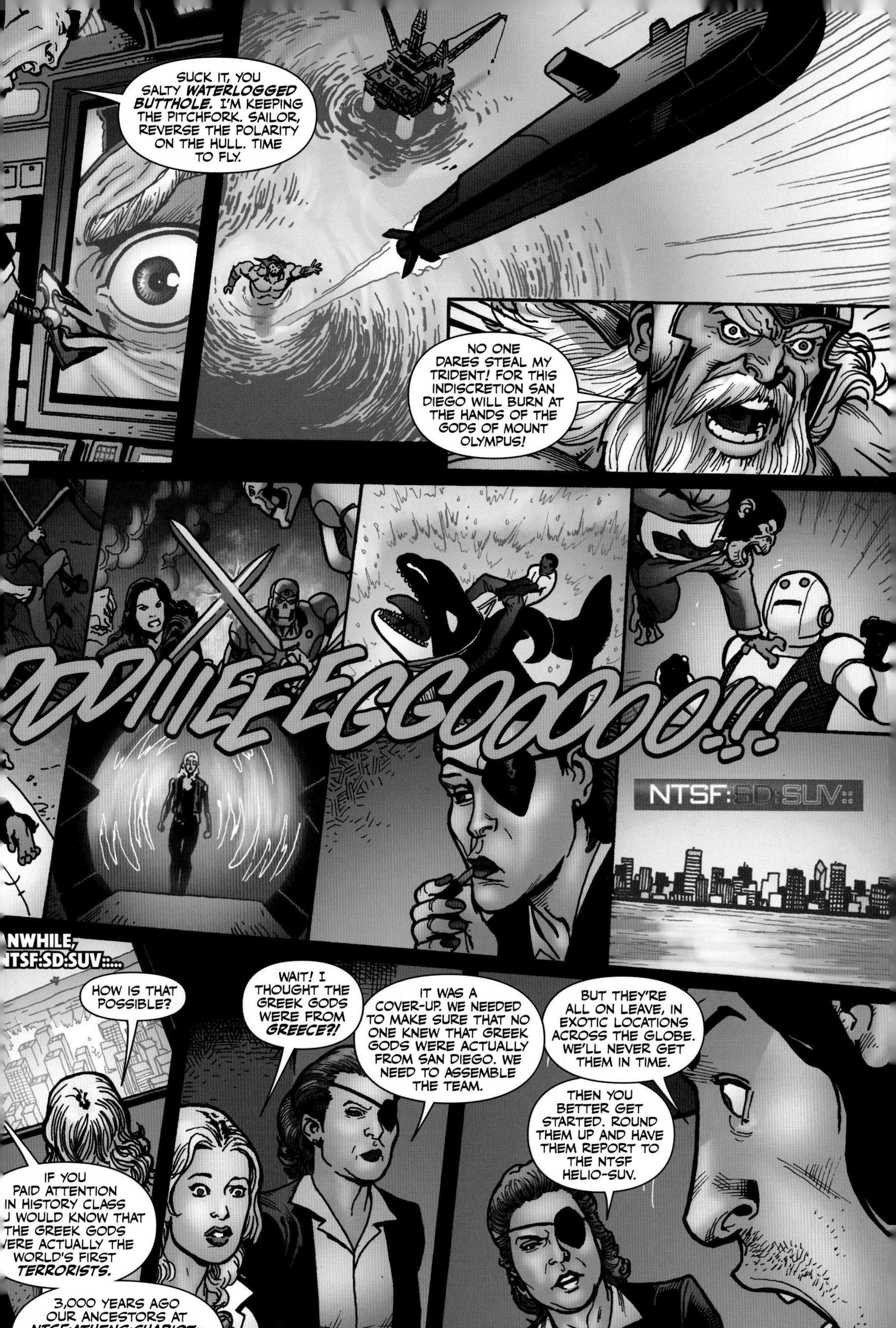

SUCK IT, YOU SALTY *WATERLOGGED BUTTHOLE.* I'M KEEPING THE PITCHFORK. SAILOR, REVERSE THE POLARITY ON THE HULL. TIME TO FLY.
NO ONE DARES STEAL MY TRIDENT! FOR THIS INDISCRETION SAN DIEGO WILL BURN AT THE HANDS OF THE GODS OF MOUNT OLYMPUS!
DDIIIEEEGGOOOOOO!!!
NTSF:SD:SUV::
NWHILE, NTSF:SD:SUV::...
HOW IS THAT POSSIBLE?
IF YOU PAID ATTENTION IN HISTORY CLASS U WOULD KNOW THAT THE GREEK GODS VERE ACTUALLY THE WORLD'S FIRST *TERRORISTS.*
3,000 YEARS AGO OUR ANCESTORS AT *NTSF:ATHENS:CHARIOT::* DEFEATED THEM, TURNED THEM TO STONE, AND BURIED
WAIT! I THOUGHT THE GREEK GODS WERE FROM *GREECE?!*
IT WAS A COVER-UP. WE NEEDED TO MAKE SURE THAT NO ONE KNEW THAT GREEK GODS WERE ACTUALLY FROM SAN DIEGO. WE NEED TO ASSEMBLE THE TEAM.
BUT THEY'RE ALL ON LEAVE, IN EXOTIC LOCATIONS ACROSS THE GLOBE. WE'LL NEVER GET THEM IN TIME.
THEN YOU BETTER GET STARTED. ROUND THEM UP AND HAVE THEM REPORT TO THE NTSF HELIO-SUV.

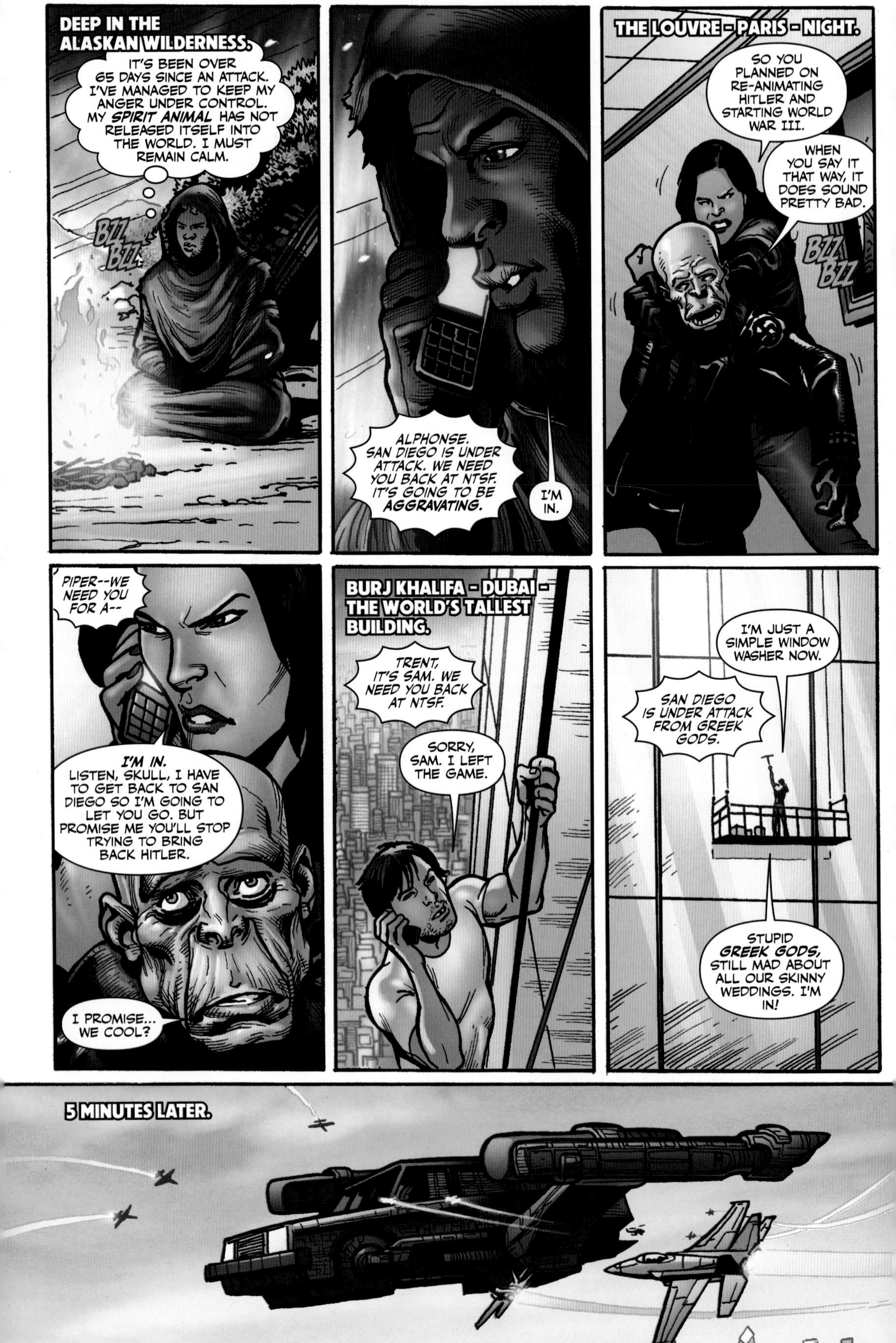
DEEP IN THE ALASKAN WILDERNESS.
IT'S BEEN OVER 65 DAYS SINCE AN ATTACK. I'VE MANAGED TO KEEP MY ANGER UNDER CONTROL. MY SPIRIT ANIMAL HAS NOT RELEASED ITSELF INTO THE WORLD. I MUST REMAIN CALM.
BZZ BZZ
ALPHONSE. SAN DIEGO IS UNDER ATTACK. WE NEED YOU BACK AT NTSF. IT'S GOING TO BE AGGRAVATING.
I'M IN.
THE LOUVRE - PARIS - NIGHT.
SO YOU PLANNED ON RE-ANIMATING HITLER AND STARTING WORLD WAR III.
WHEN YOU SAY IT THAT WAY, IT DOES SOUND PRETTY BAD.
BZZ BZZ
PIPER--WE NEED YOU FOR A--
I'M IN. LISTEN, SKULL, I HAVE TO GET BACK TO SAN DIEGO SO I'M GOING TO LET YOU GO. BUT PROMISE ME YOU'LL STOP TRYING TO BRING BACK HITLER.
I PROMISE... WE COOL?
BURJ KHALIFA - DUBAI - THE WORLD'S TALLEST BUILDING.
TRENT, IT'S SAM. WE NEED YOU BACK AT NTSF.
SORRY, SAM. I LEFT THE GAME.
I'M JUST A SIMPLE WINDOW WASHER NOW.
SAN DIEGO IS UNDER ATTACK FROM GREEK GODS.
STUPID GREEK GODS, STILL MAD ABOUT ALL OUR SKINNY WEDDINGS. I'M IN!
5 MINUTES LATER.

--MEDUSA HAS TAKEN CONTROL OF WONDER WORLD, *PROMETHEUS* HAS DESTROYED SAN DIEGO STADIUM, CYCLOPS SET THE GASLAMP DISTRICT ABLAZE, *ATHENA* UNLEASHED HER RAGE ON LA JOLLA AND *HADES* HAS HIJACKED THE SAN DIEGO TROLLEY LINE INTO *HELL*.

MEANWHILE *POSEIDON* CONTINUES TO UNLEASH HOURLY TSUNAMIS ON THE COAST OF SAN DIEGO...

OH... MY...

...GODS!

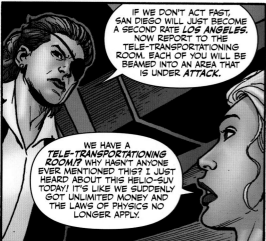

IF WE DON'T ACT FAST, SAN DIEGO WILL JUST BECOME A SECOND RATE *LOS ANGELES.* NOW REPORT TO THE TELE-TRANSPORTATIONING ROOM. EACH OF YOU WILL BE BEAMED INTO AN AREA THAT IS UNDER *ATTACK.*

WE HAVE A *TELE-TRANSPORTATIONING ROOM!?* WHY HASN'T ANYONE EVER MENTIONED THIS? I JUST HEARD ABOUT THIS HELIO-SUV TODAY! IT'S LIKE WE SUDDENLY GOT UNLIMITED MONEY AND THE LAWS OF PHYSICS NO LONGER APPLY.

DEAL WITH IT.

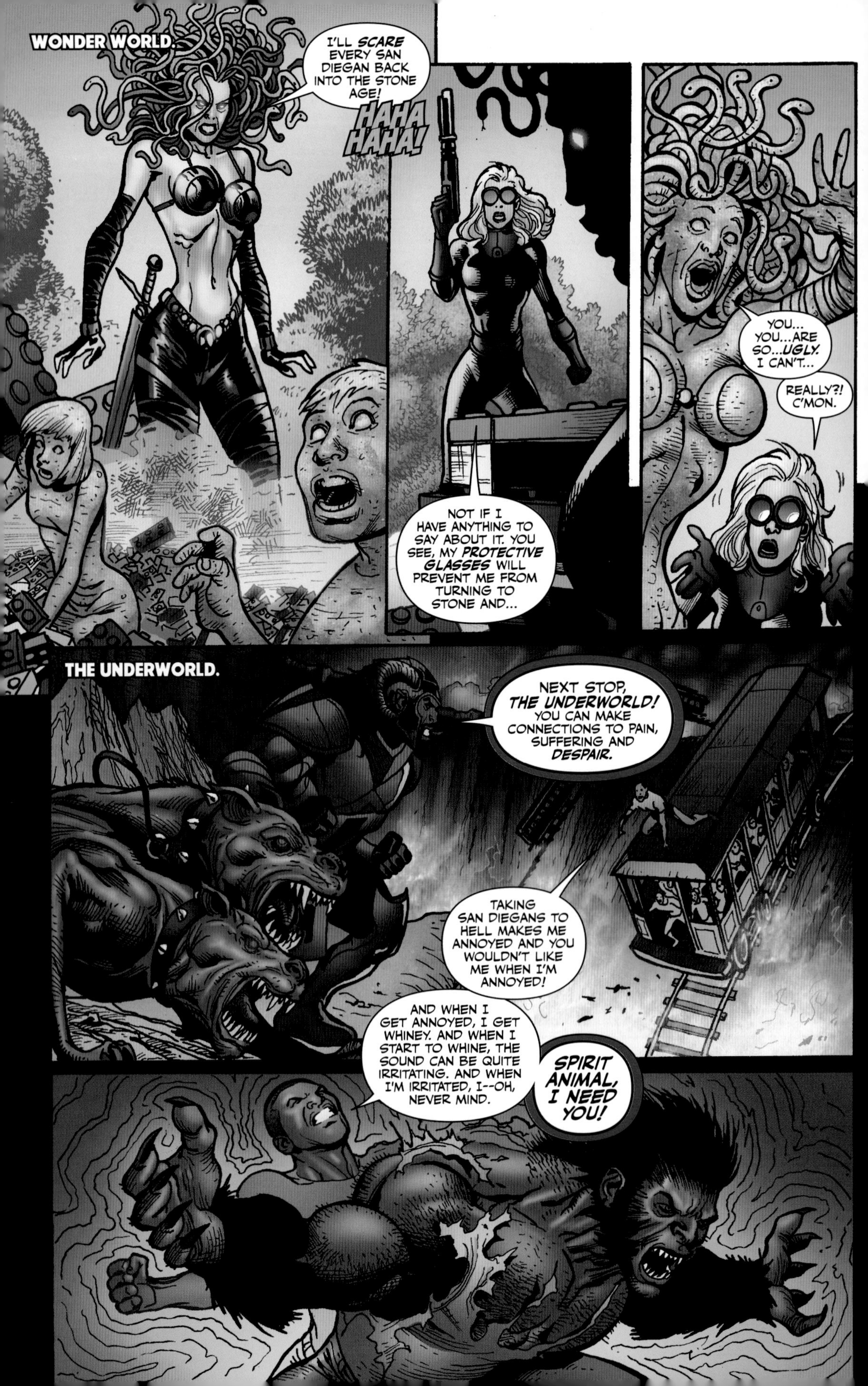
WONDER WORLD.
I'LL SCARE EVERY SAN DIEGAN BACK INTO THE STONE AGE!
HAHA HAHA!
NOT IF I HAVE ANYTHING TO SAY ABOUT IT. YOU SEE, MY PROTECTIVE GLASSES WILL PREVENT ME FROM TURNING TO STONE AND...
YOU... YOU...ARE SO...UGLY. I CAN'T...
REALLY?! C'MON.
THE UNDERWORLD.
NEXT STOP, THE UNDERWORLD! YOU CAN MAKE CONNECTIONS TO PAIN, SUFFERING AND DESPAIR.
TAKING SAN DIEGANS TO HELL MAKES ME ANNOYED AND YOU WOULDN'T LIKE ME WHEN I'M ANNOYED!
AND WHEN I GET ANNOYED, I GET WHINEY. AND WHEN I START TO WHINE, THE SOUND CAN BE QUITE IRRITATING. AND WHEN I'M IRRITATED, I--OH, NEVER MIND.
SPIRIT ANIMAL, I NEED YOU!

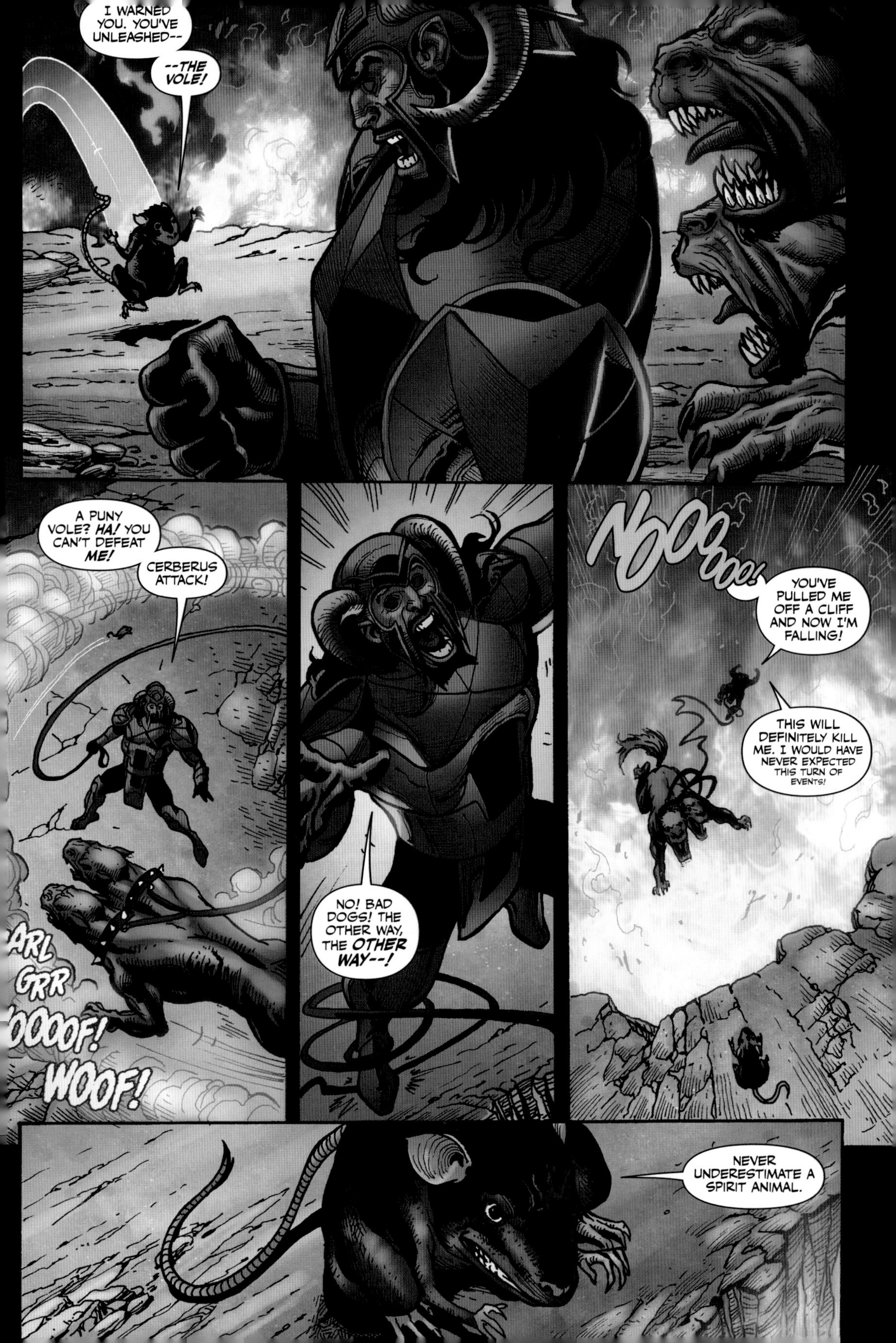
I WARNED YOU. YOU'VE UNLEASHED--
--THE VOLE!
A PUNY VOLE? HA! YOU CAN'T DEFEAT ME!
CERBERUS ATTACK!
ARL
GRR
OOOOF!
WOOF!
NO! BAD DOGS! THE OTHER WAY, THE OTHER WAY--!
NOOOOOOO!
YOU'VE PULLED ME OFF A CLIFF AND NOW I'M FALLING!
THIS WILL DEFINITELY KILL ME. I WOULD HAVE NEVER EXPECTED THIS TURN OF EVENTS!
NEVER UNDERESTIMATE A SPIRIT ANIMAL.

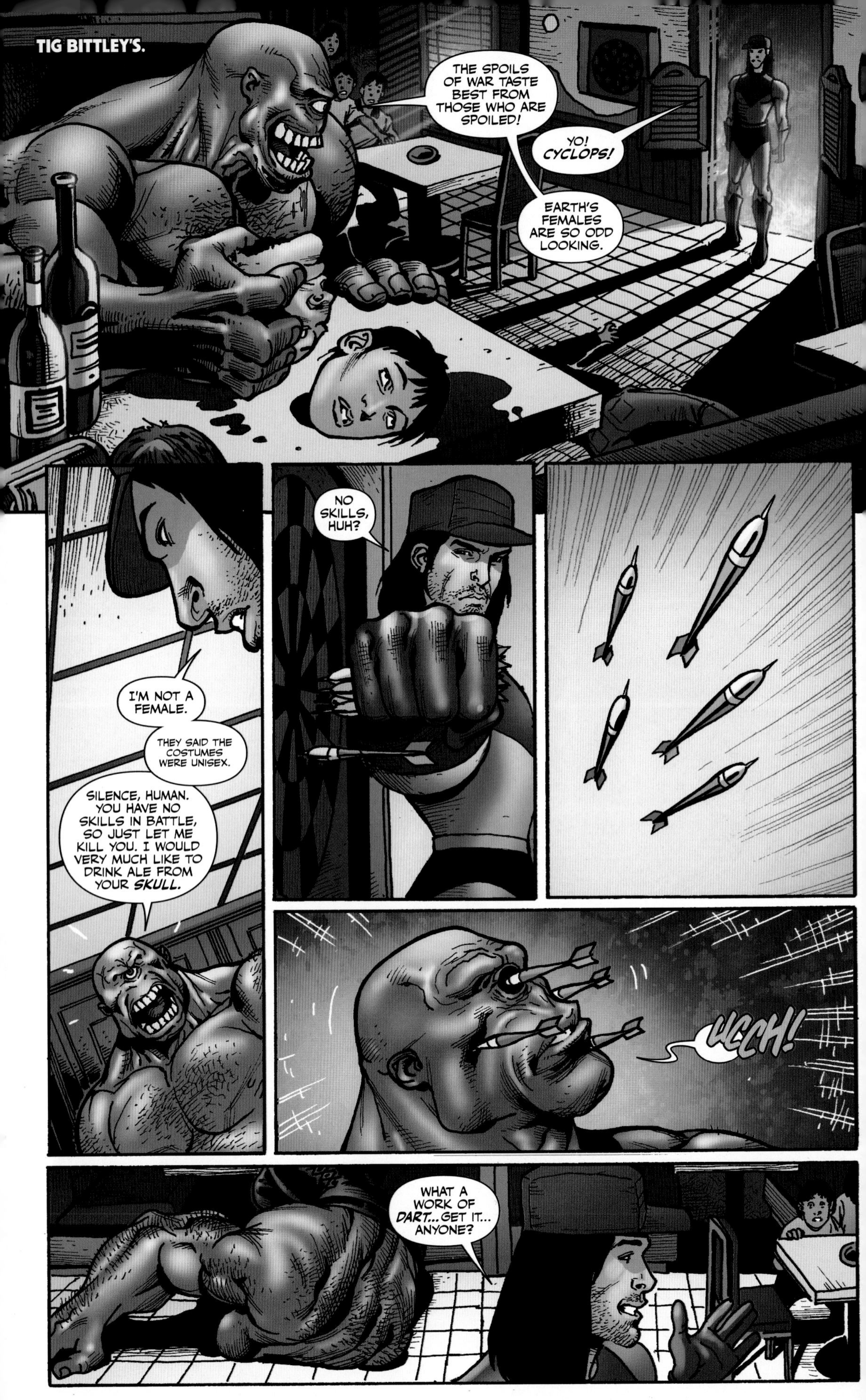
TIG BITTLEY'S.
THE SPOILS OF WAR TASTE BEST FROM THOSE WHO ARE SPOILED!
YO! CYCLOPS!
EARTH'S FEMALES ARE SO ODD LOOKING.
I'M NOT A FEMALE.
THEY SAID THE COSTUMES WERE UNISEX.
SILENCE, HUMAN. YOU HAVE NO SKILLS IN BATTLE, SO JUST LET ME KILL YOU. I WOULD VERY MUCH LIKE TO DRINK ALE FROM YOUR SKULL.
NO SKILLS, HUH?
UCCH!
WHAT A WORK OF DART...GET IT... ANYONE?

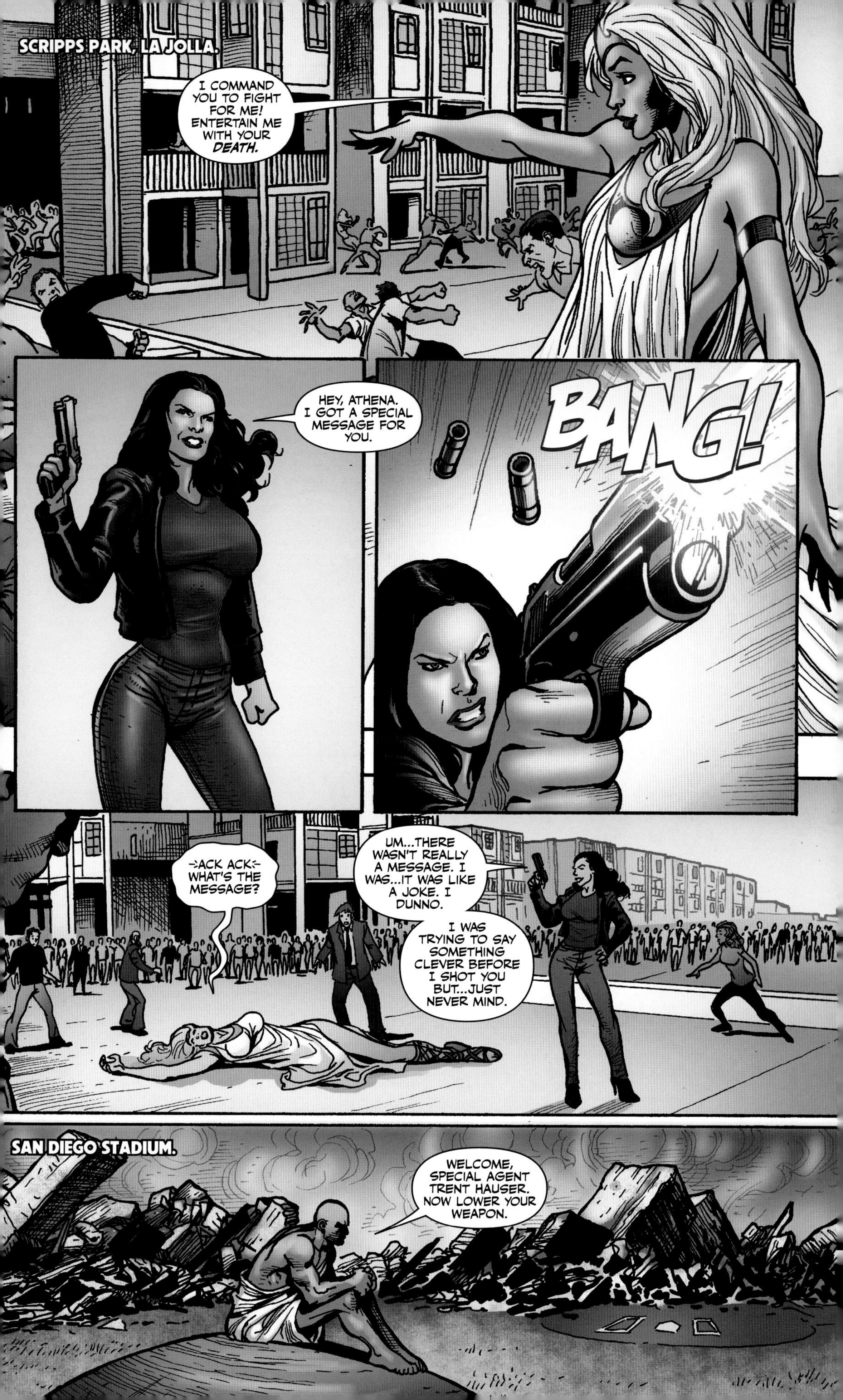
SCRIPPS PARK, LA JOLLA.
I COMMAND YOU TO FIGHT FOR ME! ENTERTAIN ME WITH YOUR DEATH.
HEY, ATHENA. I GOT A SPECIAL MESSAGE FOR YOU.
BANG!
-ACK ACK- WHAT'S THE MESSAGE?
UM...THERE WASN'T REALLY A MESSAGE. I WAS...IT WAS LIKE A JOKE. I DUNNO.
I WAS TRYING TO SAY SOMETHING CLEVER BEFORE I SHOT YOU BUT...JUST NEVER MIND.
SAN DIEGO STADIUM.
WELCOME, SPECIAL AGENT TRENT HAUSER. NOW LOWER YOUR WEAPON.

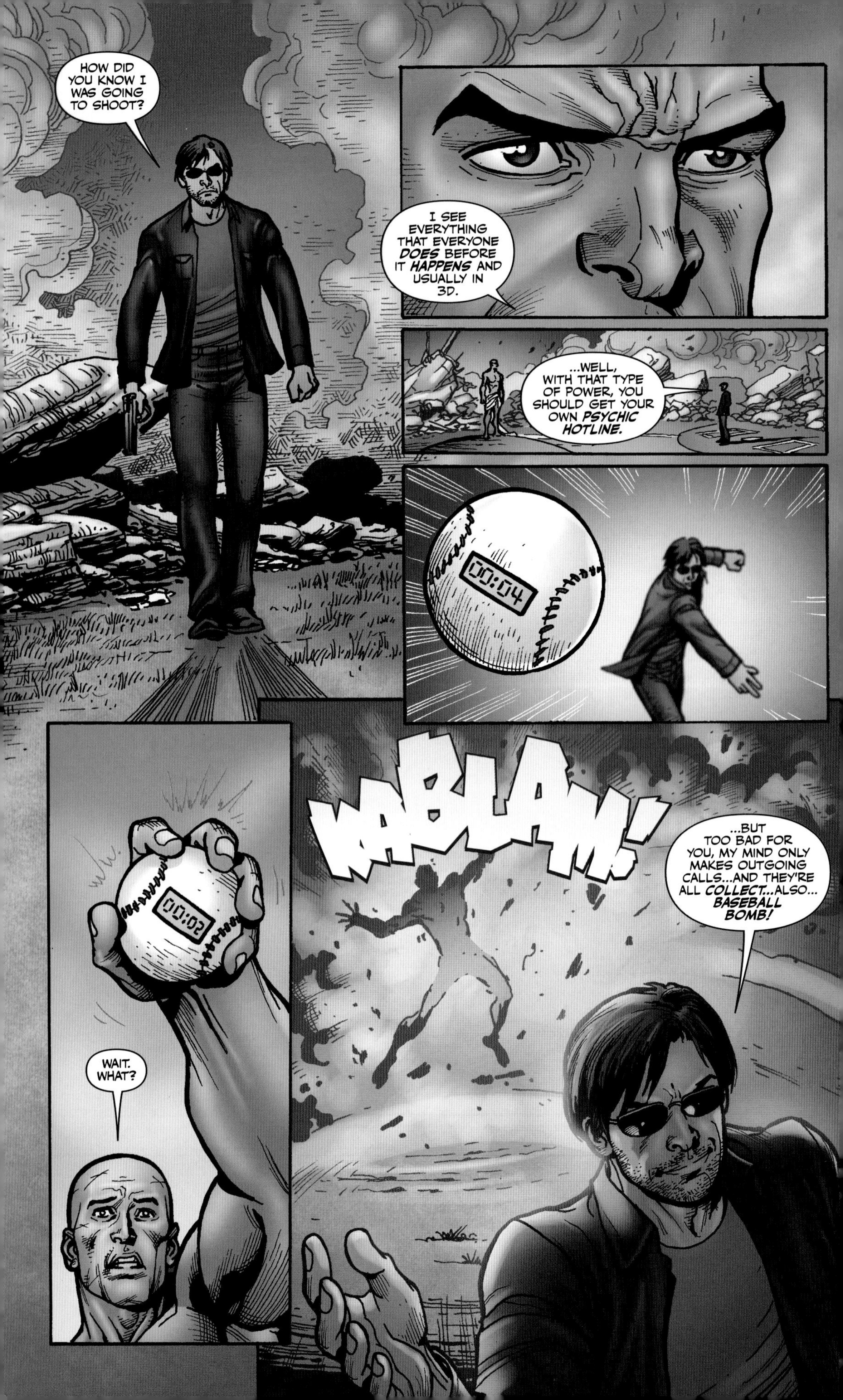
HOW DID YOU KNOW I WAS GOING TO SHOOT?
I SEE EVERYTHING THAT EVERYONE *DOES* BEFORE IT *HAPPENS* AND USUALLY IN 3D.
...WELL, WITH THAT TYPE OF POWER, YOU SHOULD GET YOUR OWN *PSYCHIC HOTLINE.*
00:04
00:02
WAIT. WHAT?
KABLAM!
...BUT TOO BAD FOR YOU, MY MIND ONLY MAKES OUTGOING CALLS...AND THEY'RE ALL *COLLECT*...ALSO... *BASEBALL BOMB!*

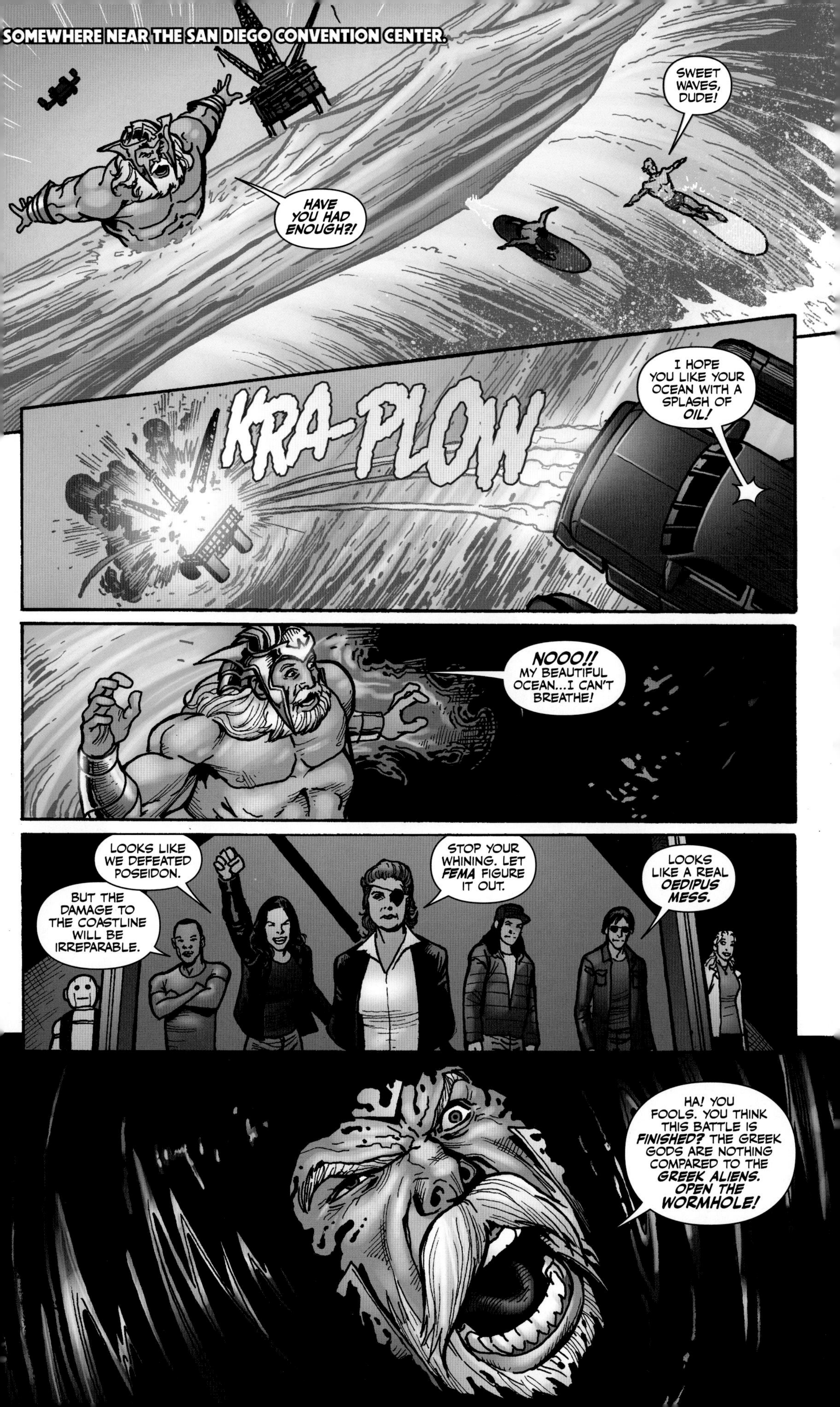
SOMEWHERE NEAR THE SAN DIEGO CONVENTION CENTER.
SWEET WAVES, DUDE!
HAVE YOU HAD ENOUGH?!
KRA-PLOW
I HOPE YOU LIKE YOUR OCEAN WITH A SPLASH OF OIL!
NOOO!! MY BEAUTIFUL OCEAN...I CAN'T BREATHE!
LOOKS LIKE WE DEFEATED POSEIDON.
BUT THE DAMAGE TO THE COASTLINE WILL BE IRREPARABLE.
STOP YOUR WHINING. LET FEMA FIGURE IT OUT.
LOOKS LIKE A REAL OEDIPUS MESS.
HA! YOU FOOLS. YOU THINK THIS BATTLE IS FINISHED? THE GREEK GODS ARE NOTHING COMPARED TO THE GREEK ALIENS. OPEN THE WORMHOLE!

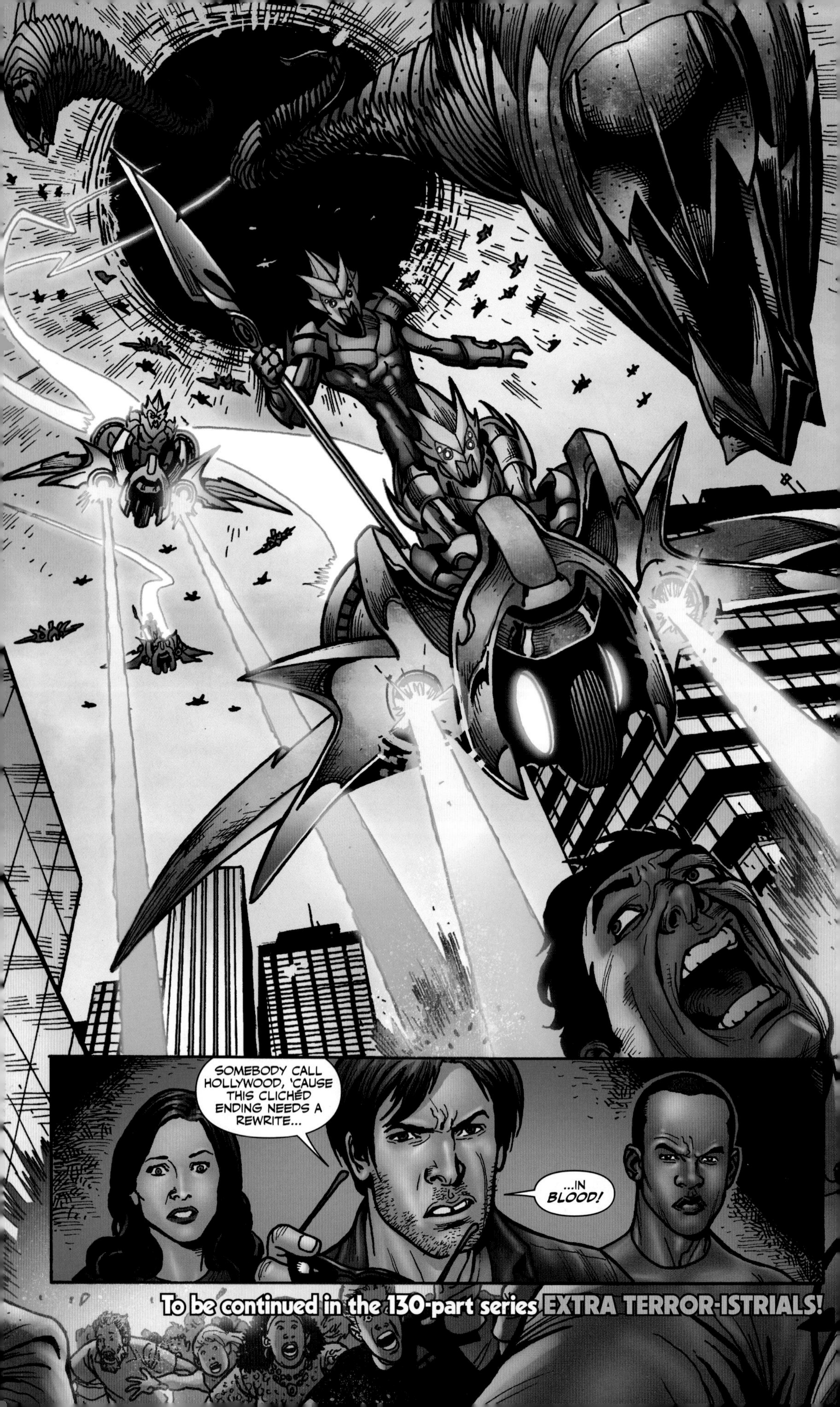
SOMEBODY CALL HOLLYWOOD, 'CAUSE THIS CLICHÉD ENDING NEEDS A REWRITE...
...IN BLOOD!
To be continued in the 130-part series EXTRA TERROR-ISTRIALS!